FALSE KNEES

KNEES

An Illustrated Guide to Animal Behavior

Joshua Barkman

Andrews McMeel
PUBLISHING®

FOR ALL THE ANIMALS
HUDDLING AWAY FROM
THE ELEMENTS.

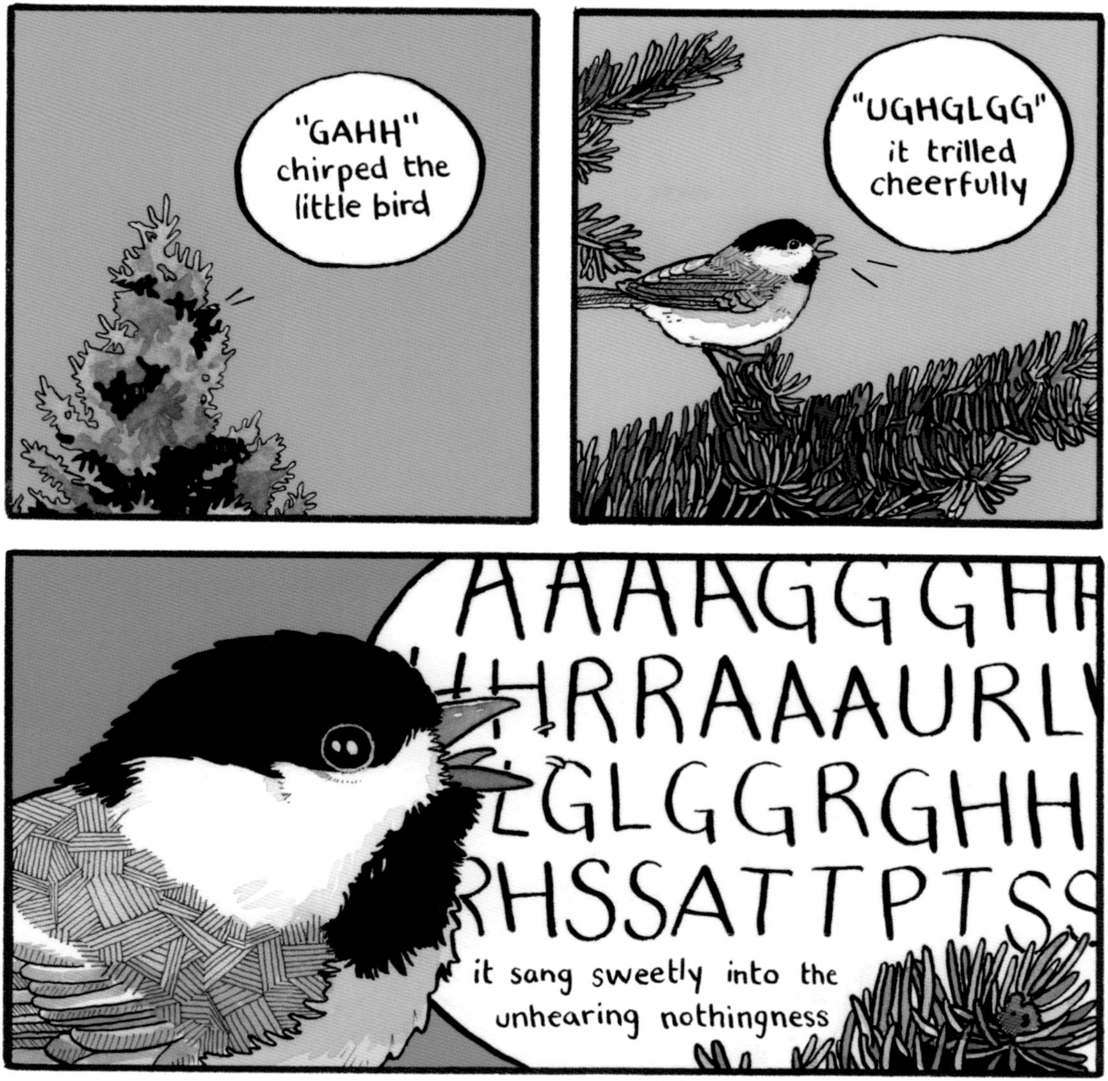
"GAHH" chirped the little bird
"UGHGLGG" it trilled cheerfully
AAAAGGGH
HRRAAAURL
GLGGRGHH
HSSATTPTS
it sang sweetly into the unhearing nothingness

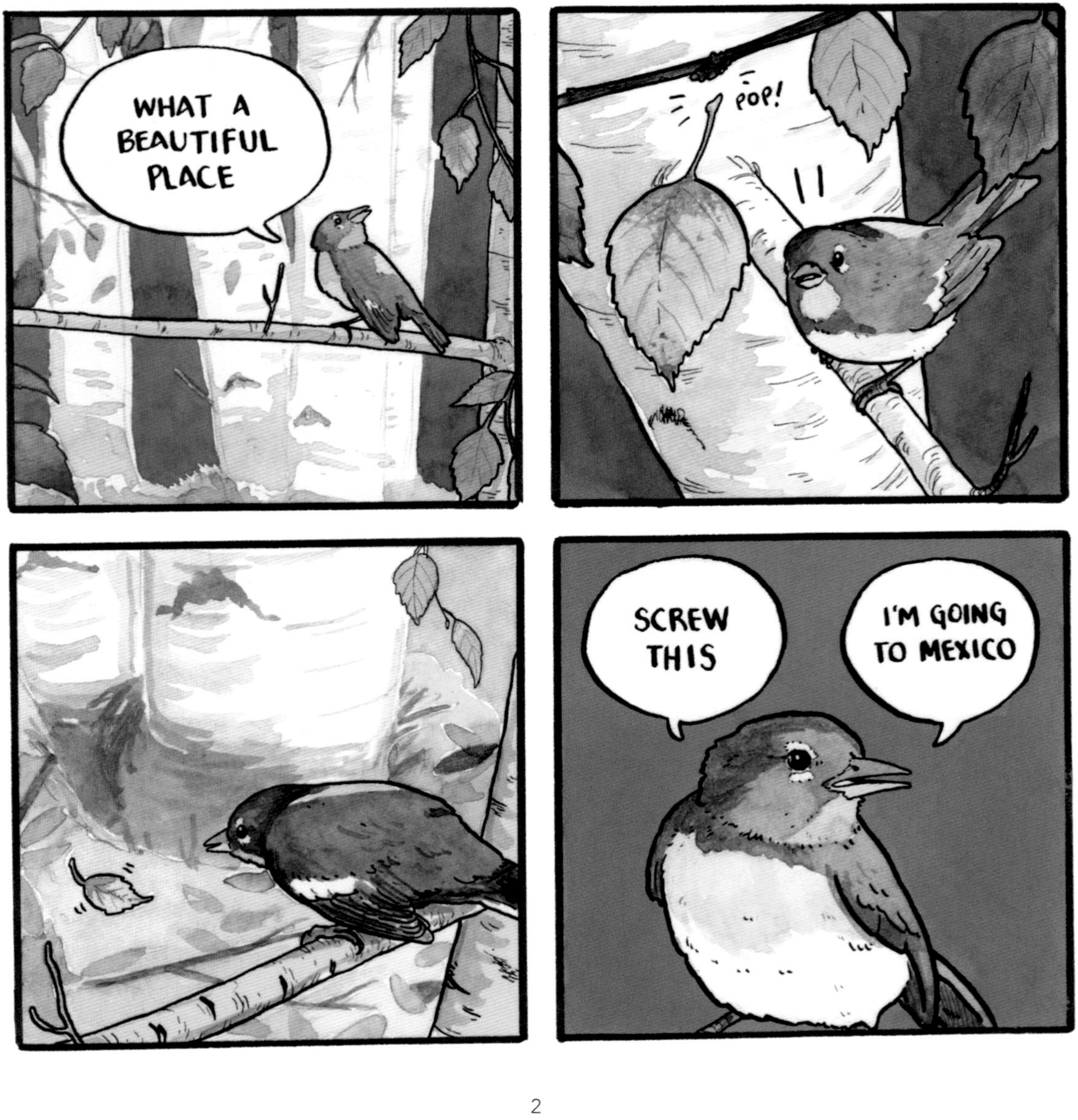
WHAT A BEAUTIFUL PLACE
POP!
SCREW THIS
I'M GOING TO MEXICO

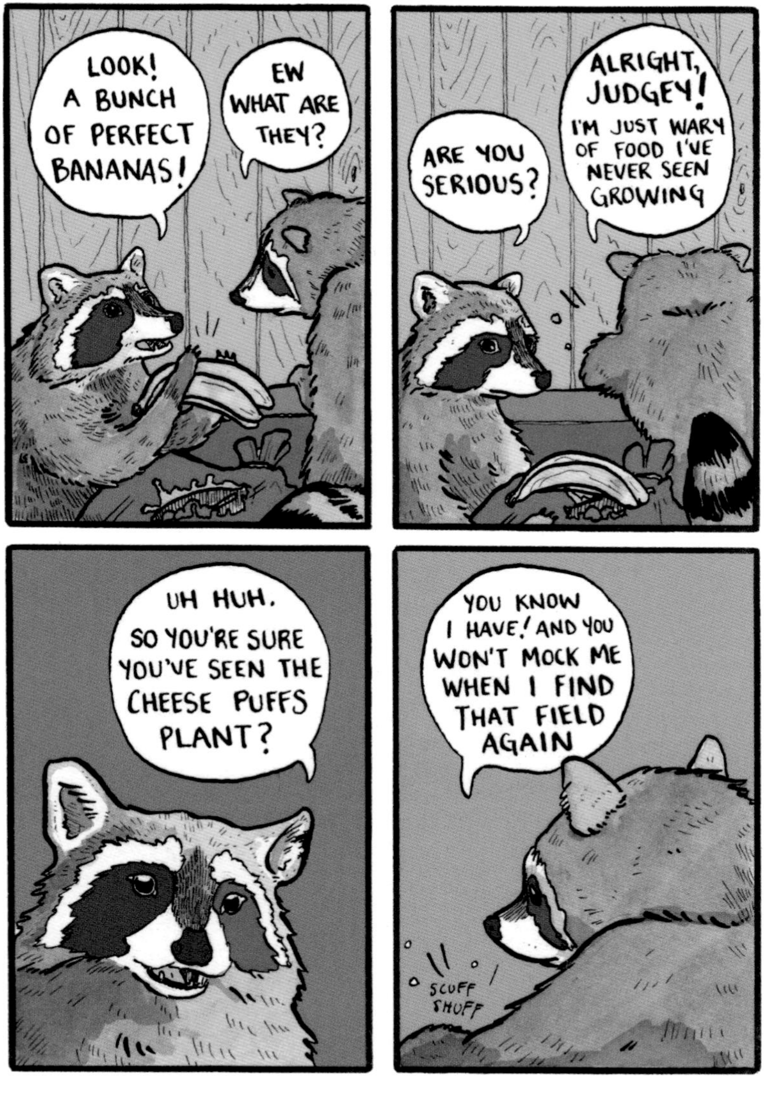
LOOK! A BUNCH OF PERFECT BANANAS!
EW WHAT ARE THEY?
ARE YOU SERIOUS?
ALRIGHT, JUDGEY! I'M JUST WARY OF FOOD I'VE NEVER SEEN GROWING
UH HUH. SO YOU'RE SURE YOU'VE SEEN THE CHEESE PUFFS PLANT?
YOU KNOW I HAVE! AND YOU WON'T MOCK ME WHEN I FIND THAT FIELD AGAIN
SCUFF SHUFF

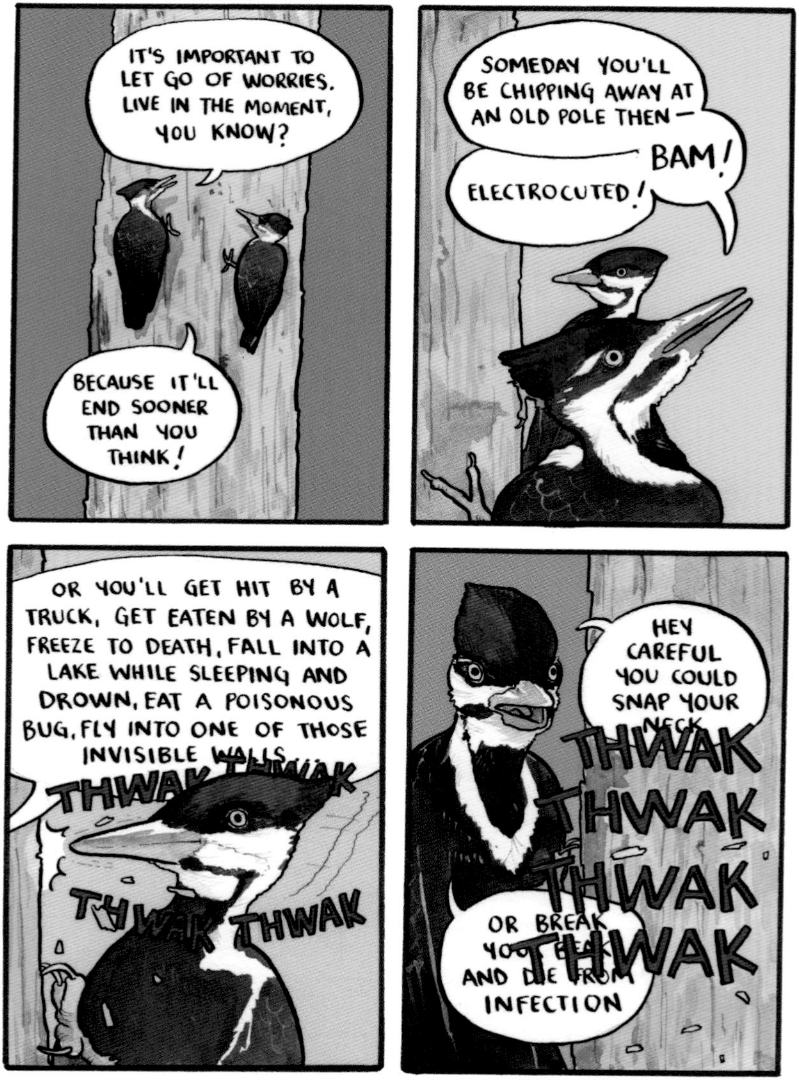
IT'S IMPORTANT TO LET GO OF WORRIES. LIVE IN THE MOMENT, YOU KNOW?
BECAUSE IT'LL END SOONER THAN YOU THINK!
SOMEDAY YOU'LL BE CHIPPING AWAY AT AN OLD POLE THEN—
ELECTROCUTED!
BAM!
OR YOU'LL GET HIT BY A TRUCK, GET EATEN BY A WOLF, FREEZE TO DEATH, FALL INTO A LAKE WHILE SLEEPING AND DROWN, EAT A POISONOUS BUG, FLY INTO ONE OF THOSE INVISIBLE WALLS...
THWAK THWAK
THWAK THWAK
HEY CAREFUL YOU COULD SNAP YOUR NECK
THWAK
THWAK
THWAK
THWAK
OR BREAK YOUR BEAK AND DIE FROM INFECTION

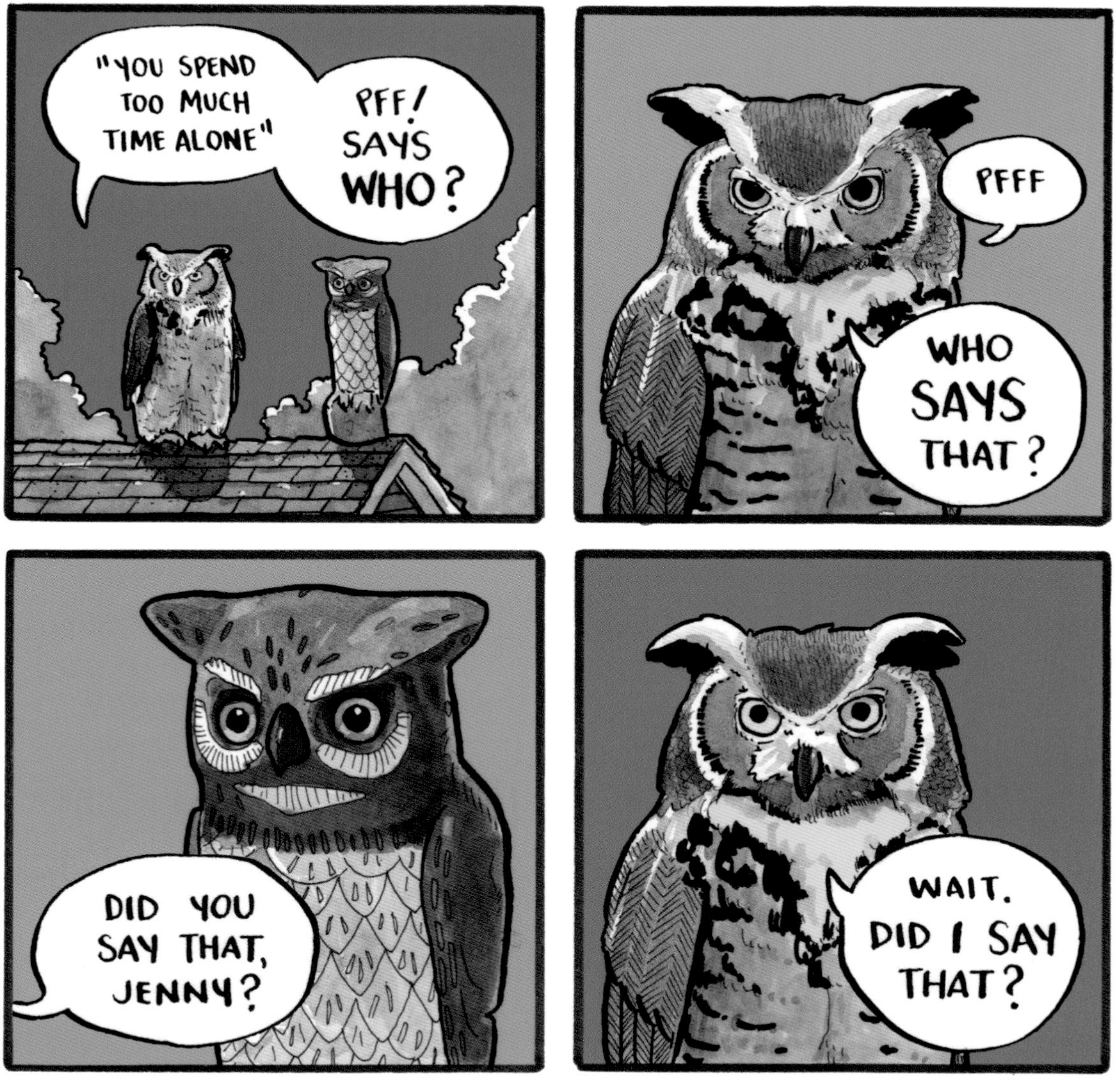
"YOU SPEND TOO MUCH TIME ALONE"
PFF! SAYS WHO?
PFFF
WHO SAYS THAT?
DID YOU SAY THAT, JENNY?
WAIT. DID I SAY THAT?

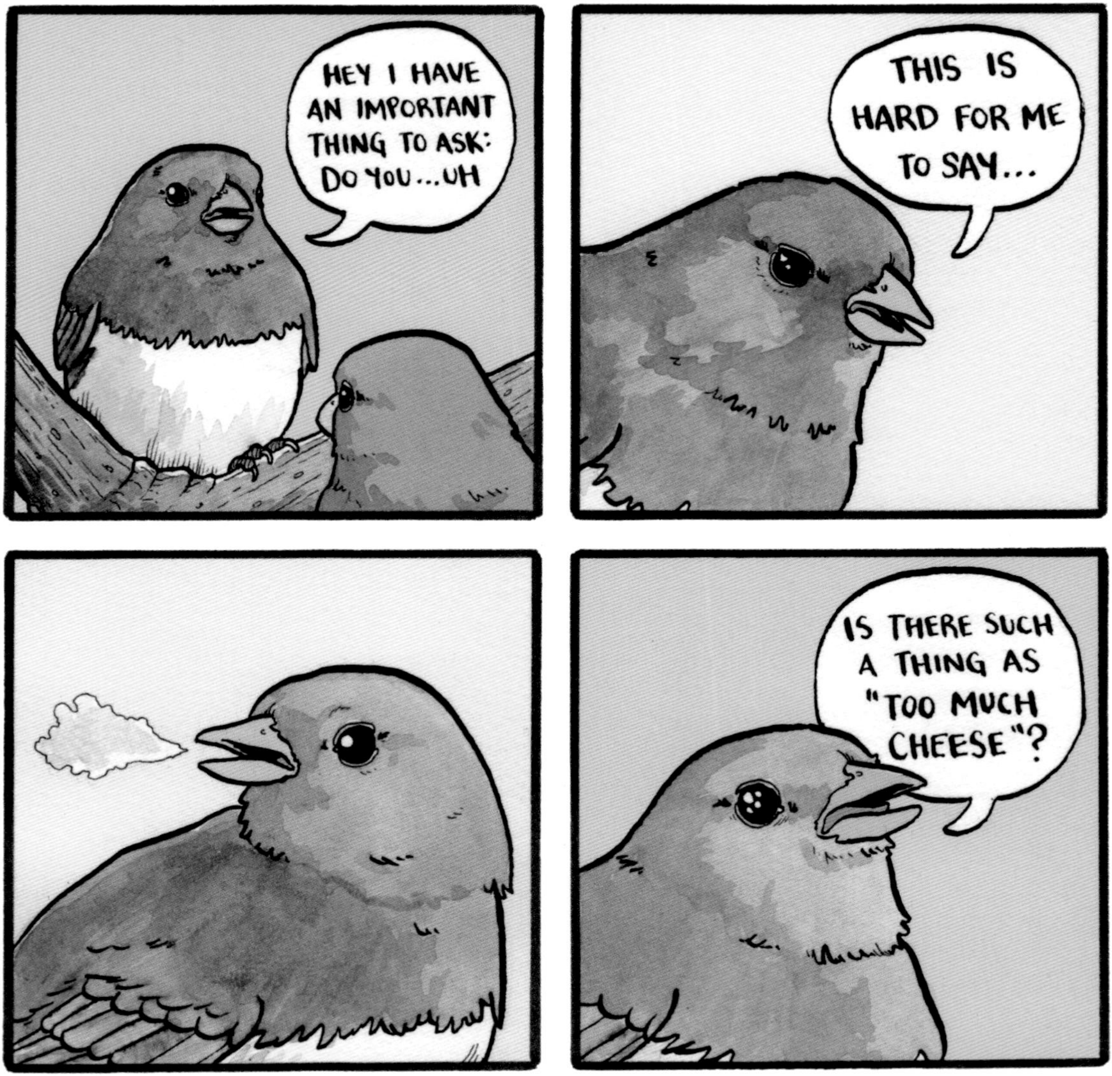
HEY I HAVE AN IMPORTANT THING TO ASK: DO YOU...UH
THIS IS HARD FOR ME TO SAY...
IS THERE SUCH A THING AS "TOO MUCH CHEESE"?

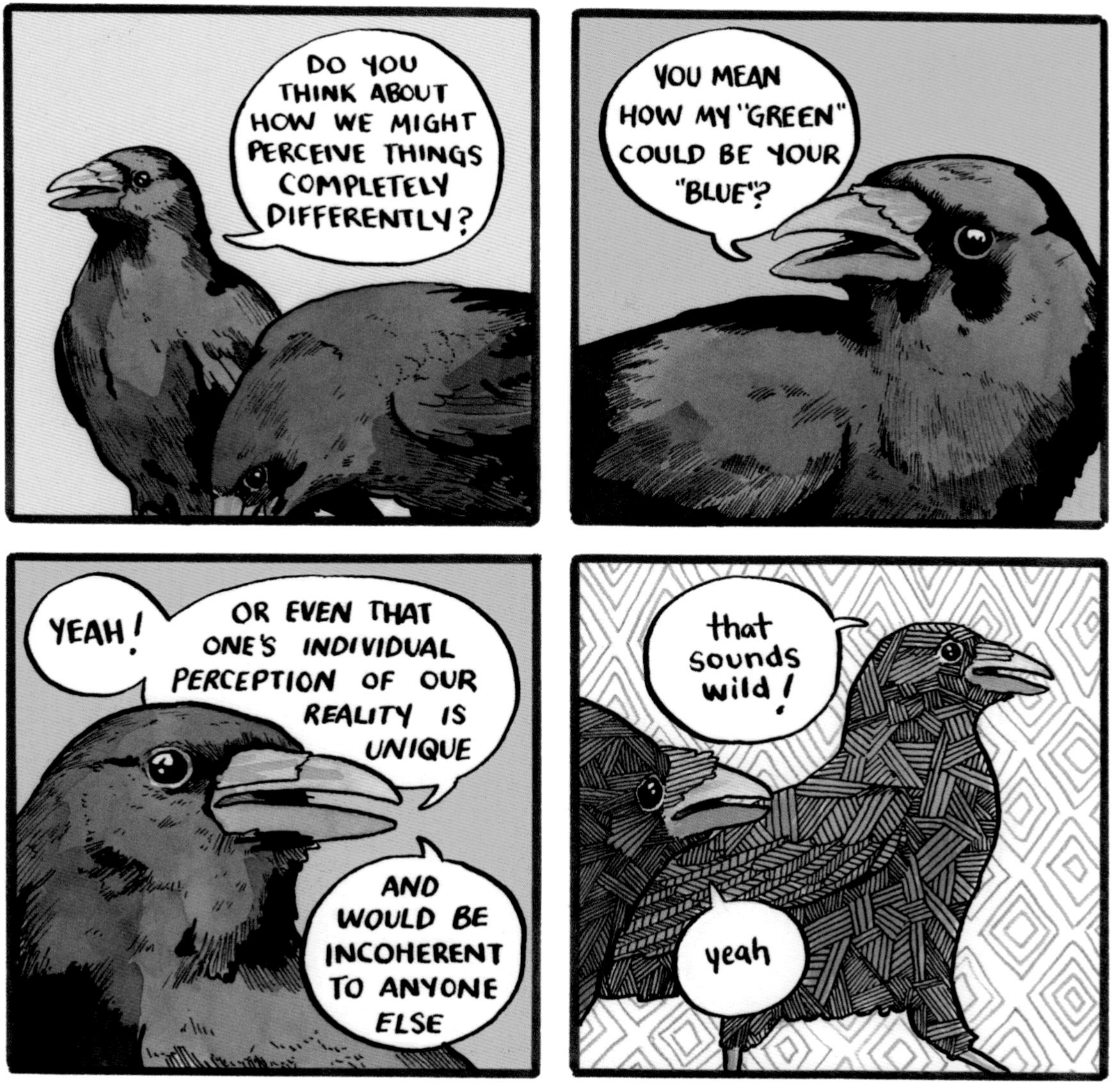
DO YOU THINK ABOUT HOW WE MIGHT PERCEIVE THINGS COMPLETELY DIFFERENTLY?
YOU MEAN HOW MY "GREEN" COULD BE YOUR "BLUE"?
YEAH!
OR EVEN THAT ONE'S INDIVIDUAL PERCEPTION OF OUR REALITY IS UNIQUE
AND WOULD BE INCOHERENT TO ANYONE ELSE
that sounds wild!
yeah

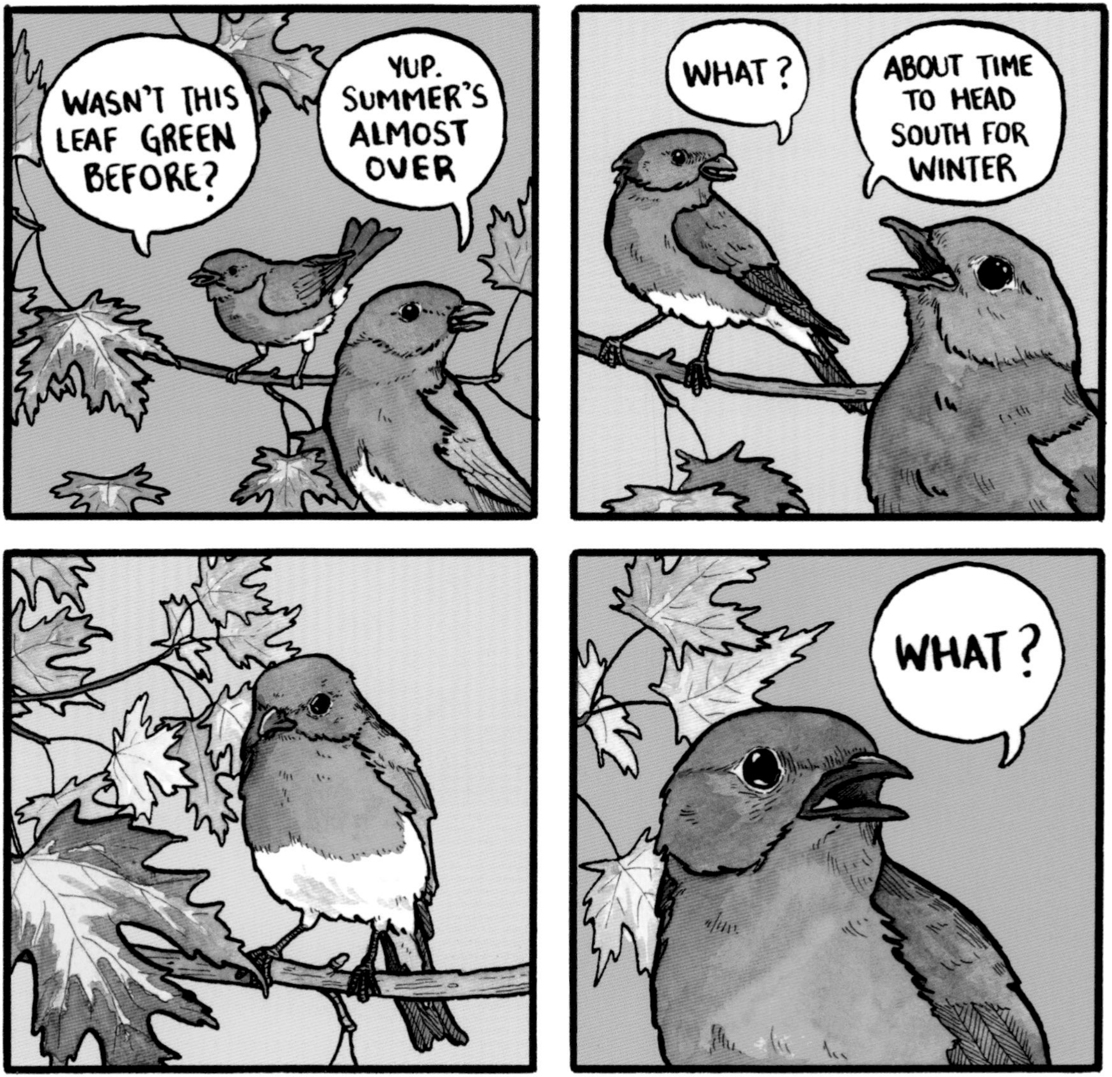

WASN'T THIS LEAF GREEN BEFORE?
YUP. SUMMER'S ALMOST OVER
WHAT?
ABOUT TIME TO HEAD SOUTH FOR WINTER
WHAT?

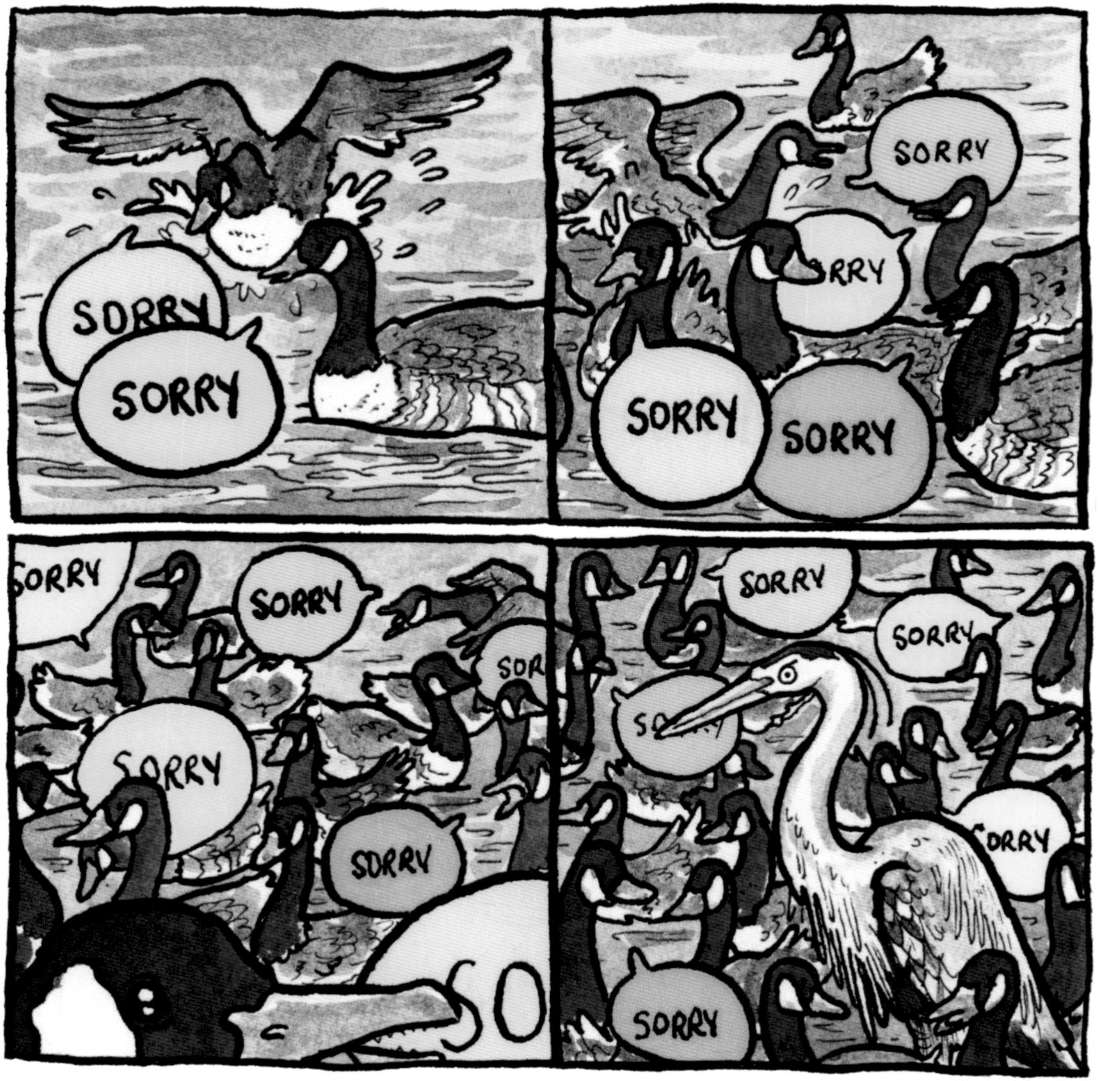

SORRY
SORRY
SORRY
SORRY
SORRY
SORRY
SORRY
SORRY
SORRY
SORRY

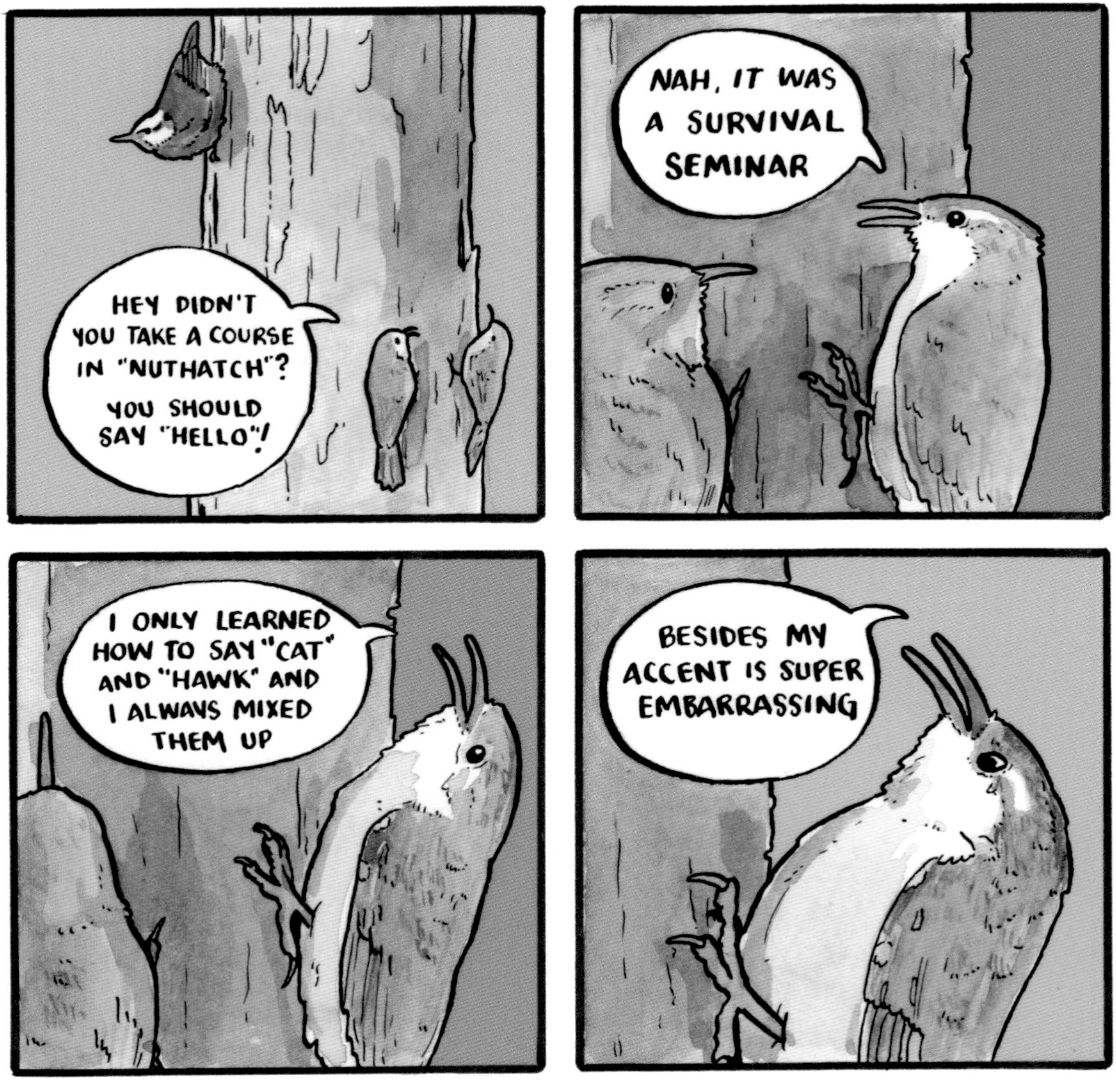
HEY DIDN'T YOU TAKE A COURSE IN "NUTHATCH"? YOU SHOULD SAY "HELLO"!
NAH, IT WAS A SURVIVAL SEMINAR
I ONLY LEARNED HOW TO SAY "CAT" AND "HAWK" AND I ALWAYS MIXED THEM UP
BESIDES MY ACCENT IS SUPER EMBARRASSING

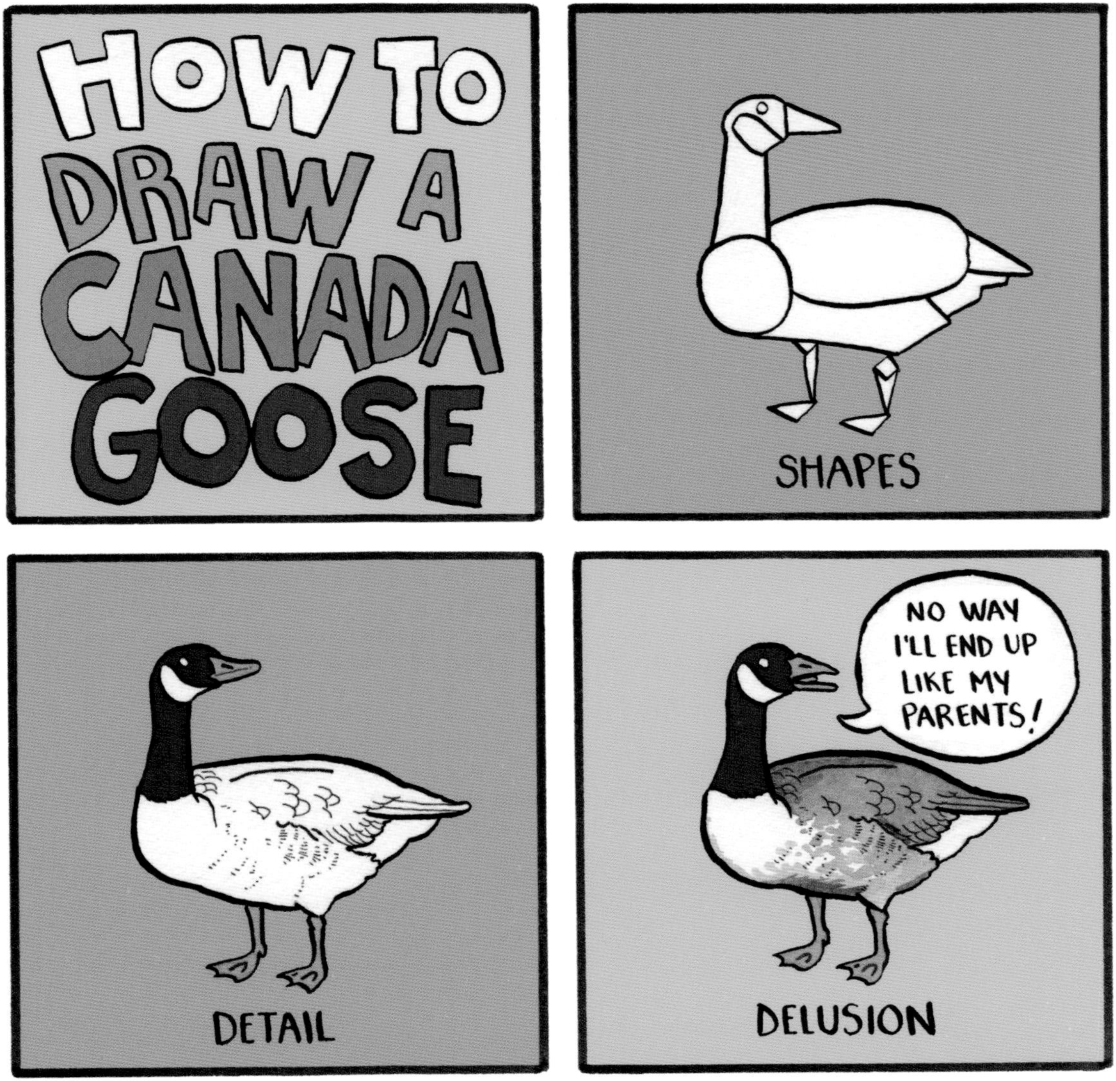
HOW TO DRAW A CANADA GOOSE
SHAPES
DETAIL
NO WAY I'LL END UP LIKE MY PARENTS!
DELUSION

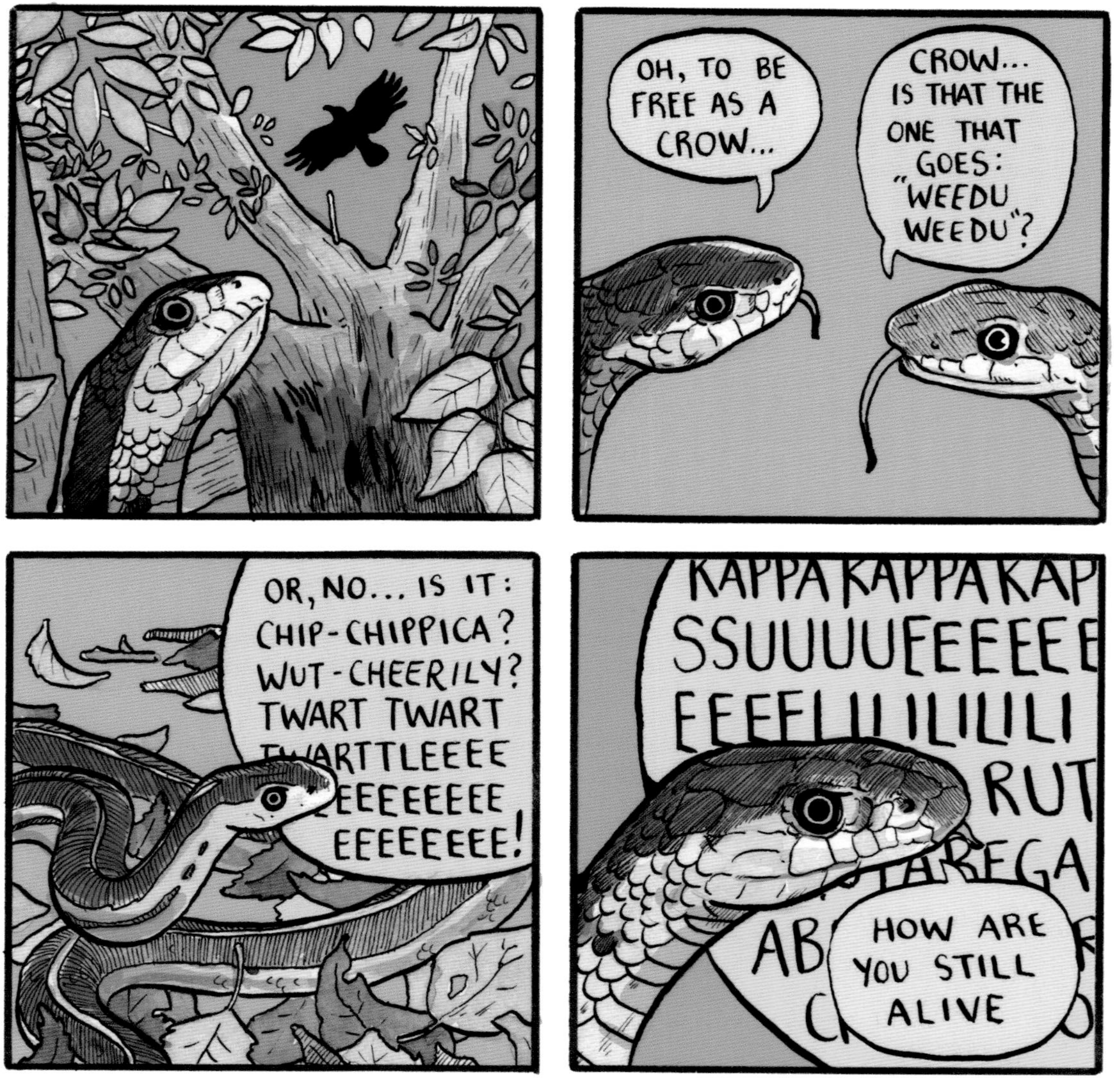
OH, TO BE FREE AS A CROW...
CROW... IS THAT THE ONE THAT GOES: "WEEDU WEEDU"?
OR, NO... IS IT: CHIP-CHIPPICA? WUT-CHEERILY? TWART TWART
ARTTLEEEE
EEEEEEEE
EEEEEEEE!
KAPPA KAPPA KAP
SSUUUUEEEEEE
EEEELIIILILILI
RUT
REGA
HOW ARE YOU STILL ALIVE

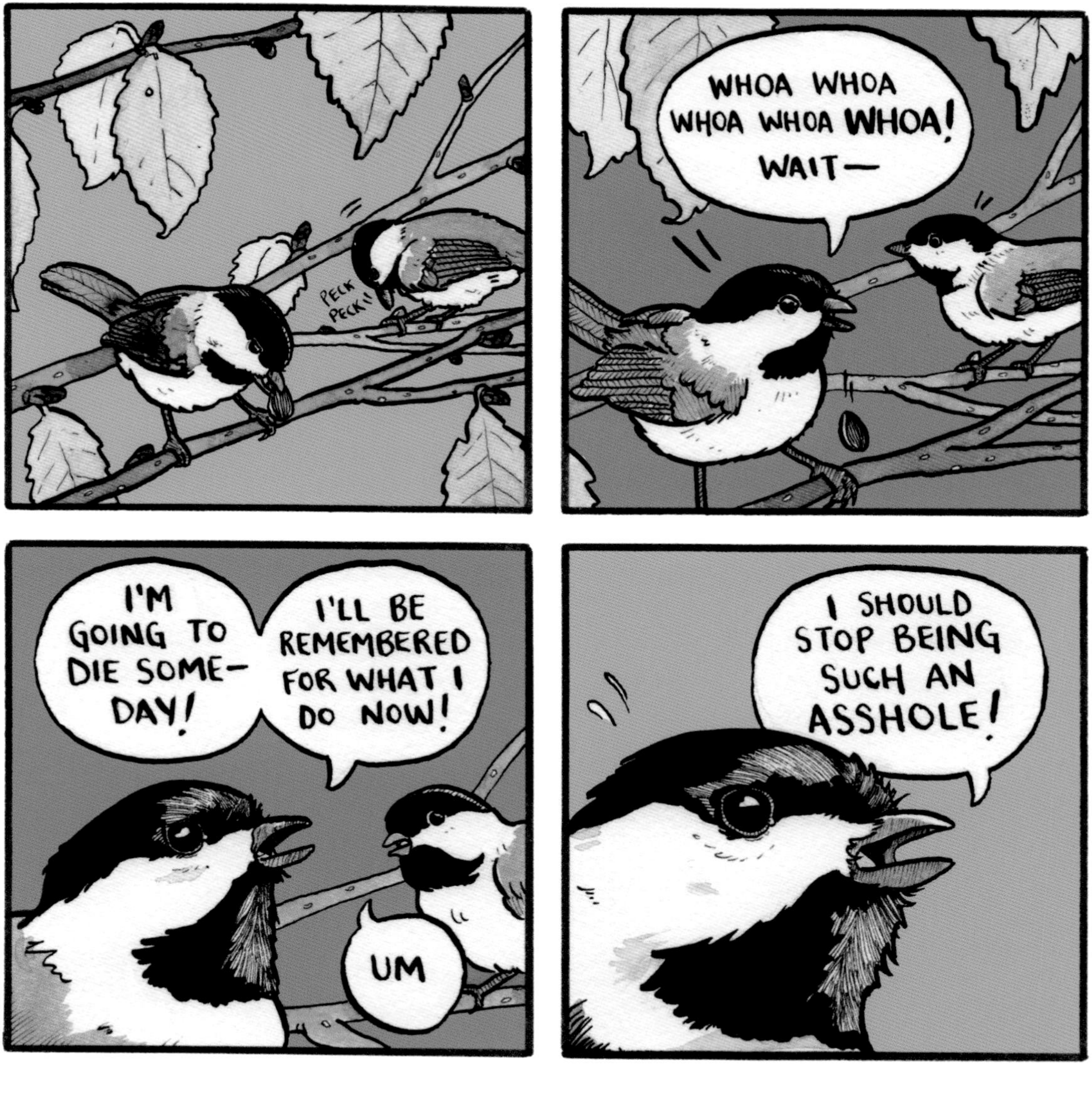
PECK PECK!!
WHOA WHOA WHOA WHOA WHOA! WAIT—
I'M GOING TO DIE SOMEDAY!
I'LL BE REMEMBERED FOR WHAT I DO NOW!
UM
I SHOULD STOP BEING SUCH AN ASSHOLE!

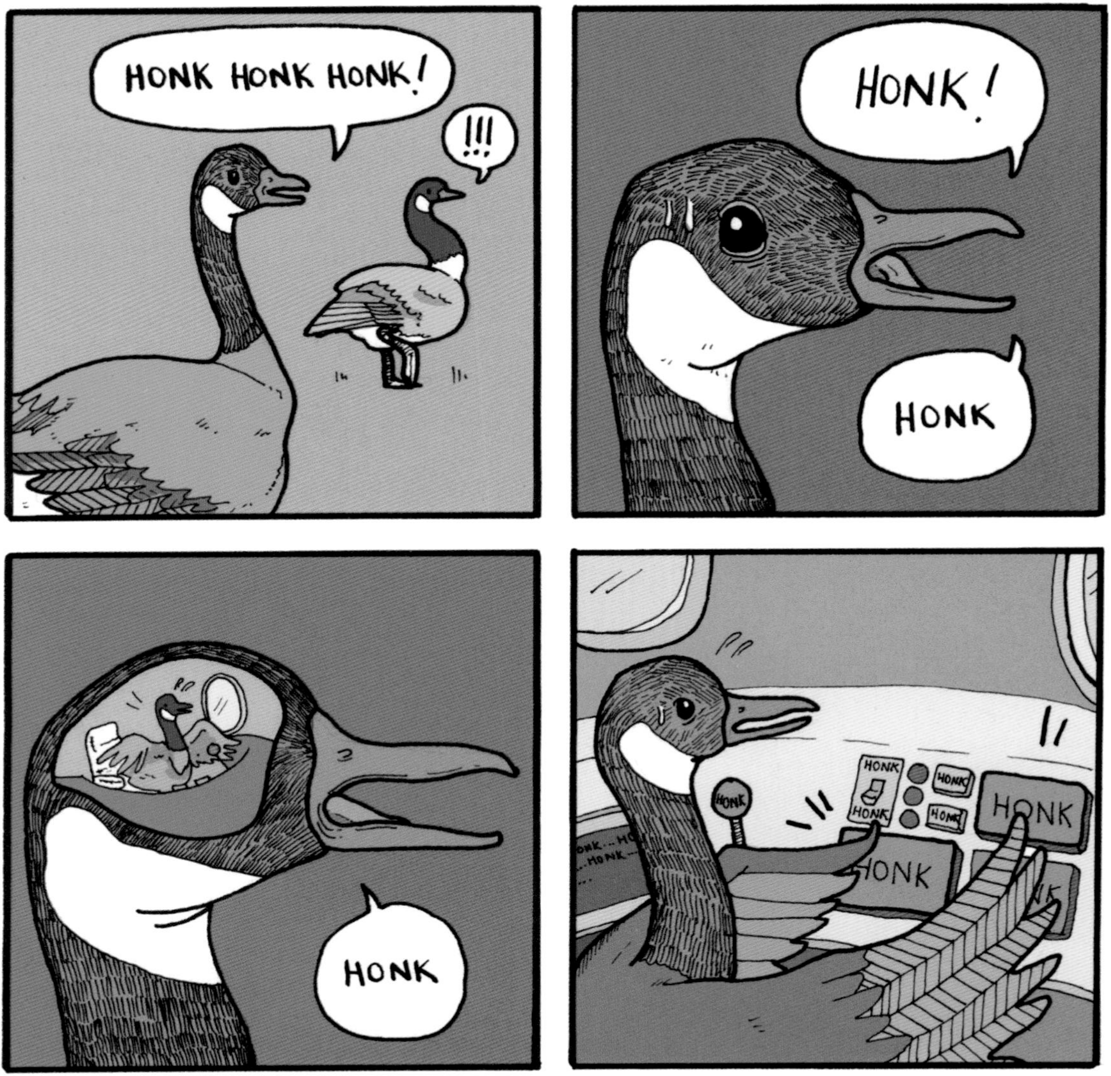
HONK HONK HONK!
!!!
HONK!
HONK
HONK
HONK
HONK
HONK
HONK
HONK
HONK
HONK

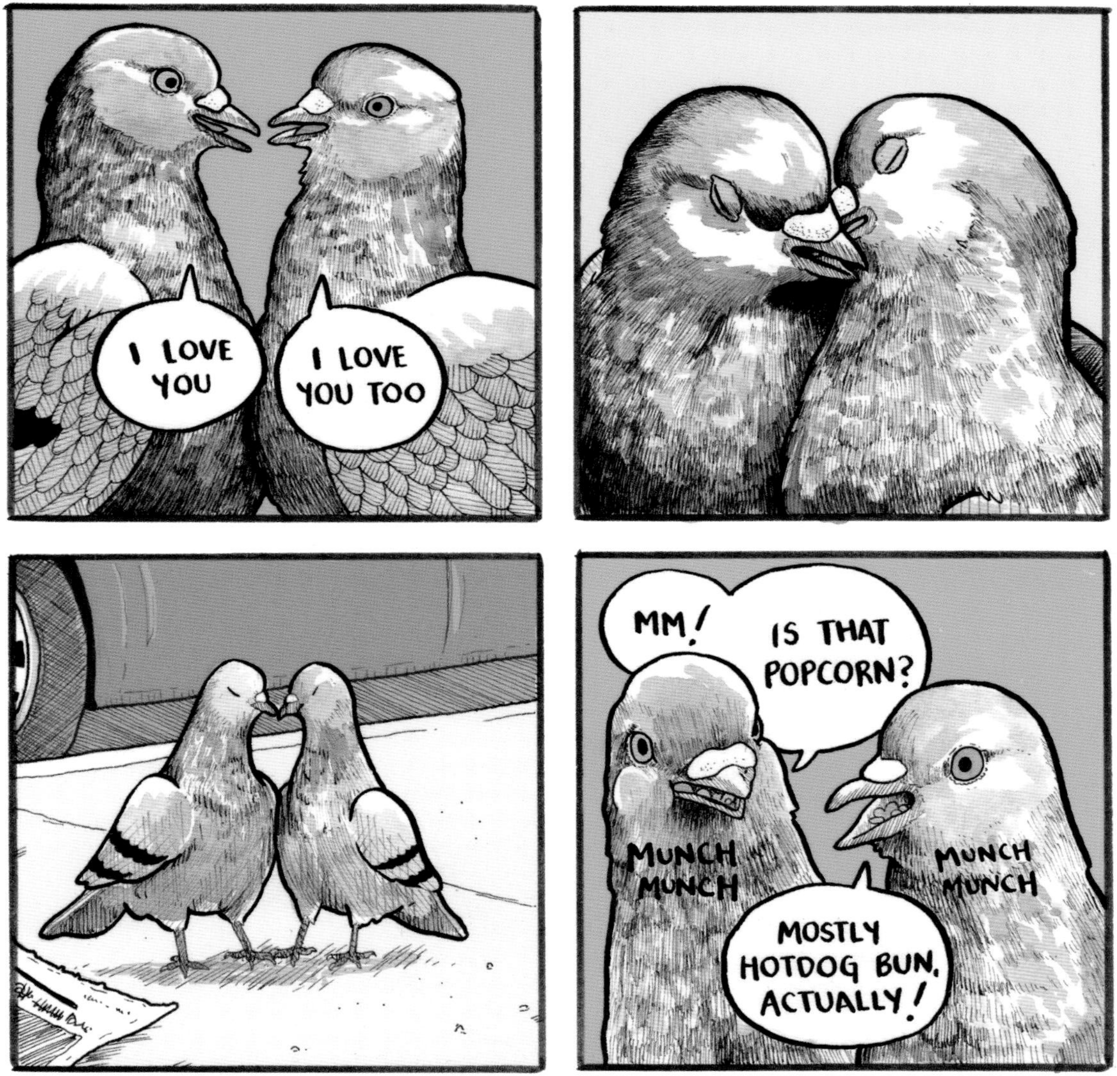
I LOVE YOU
I LOVE YOU TOO
MM!
IS THAT POPCORN?
MUNCH MUNCH
MUNCH MUNCH
MOSTLY HOTDOG BUN, ACTUALLY!

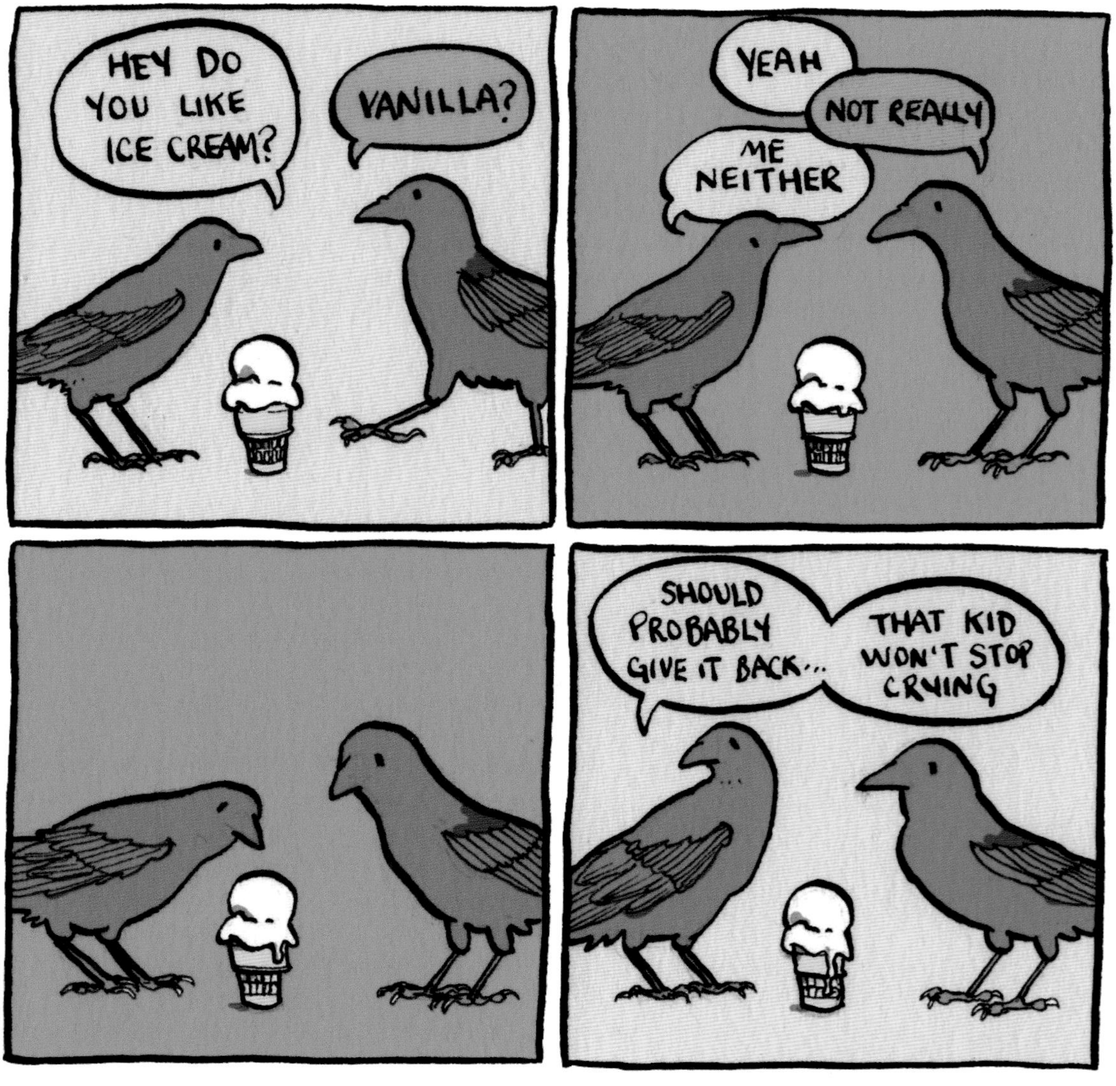
HEY DO YOU LIKE ICE CREAM?
VANILLA?
YEAH
NOT REALLY
ME NEITHER
SHOULD PROBABLY GIVE IT BACK...
THAT KID WON'T STOP CRYING

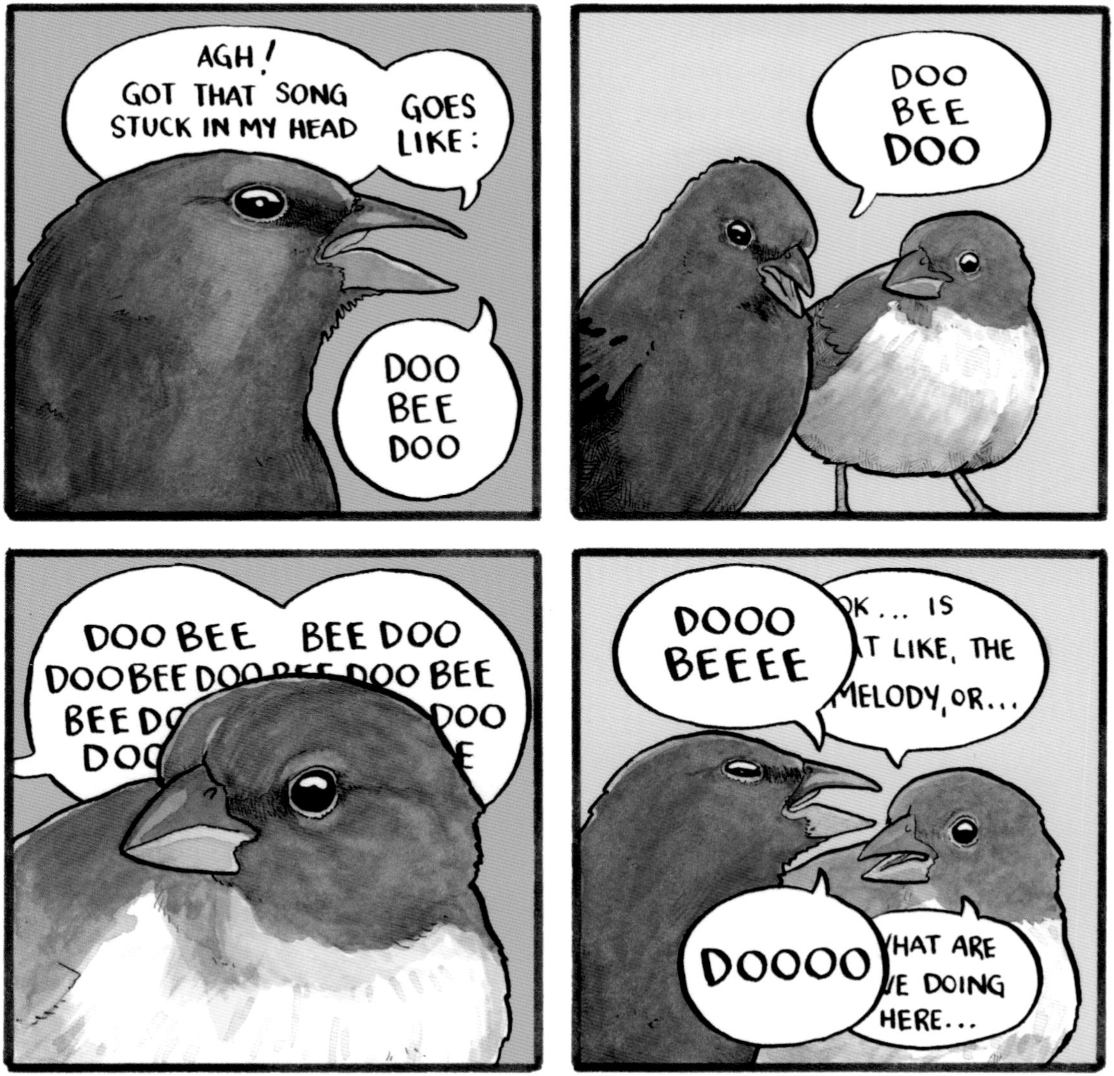
AGH! GOT THAT SONG STUCK IN MY HEAD
GOES LIKE:
DOO BEE DOO
DOO BEE DOO
DOO BEE BEE DOO
DOOBEEDOO
DOO BEE
BEE DO
DOO
DOO
DOOO BEEEE
OK... IS
T LIKE, THE
MELODY, OR...
DOOOO
HAT ARE
E DOING
HERE...

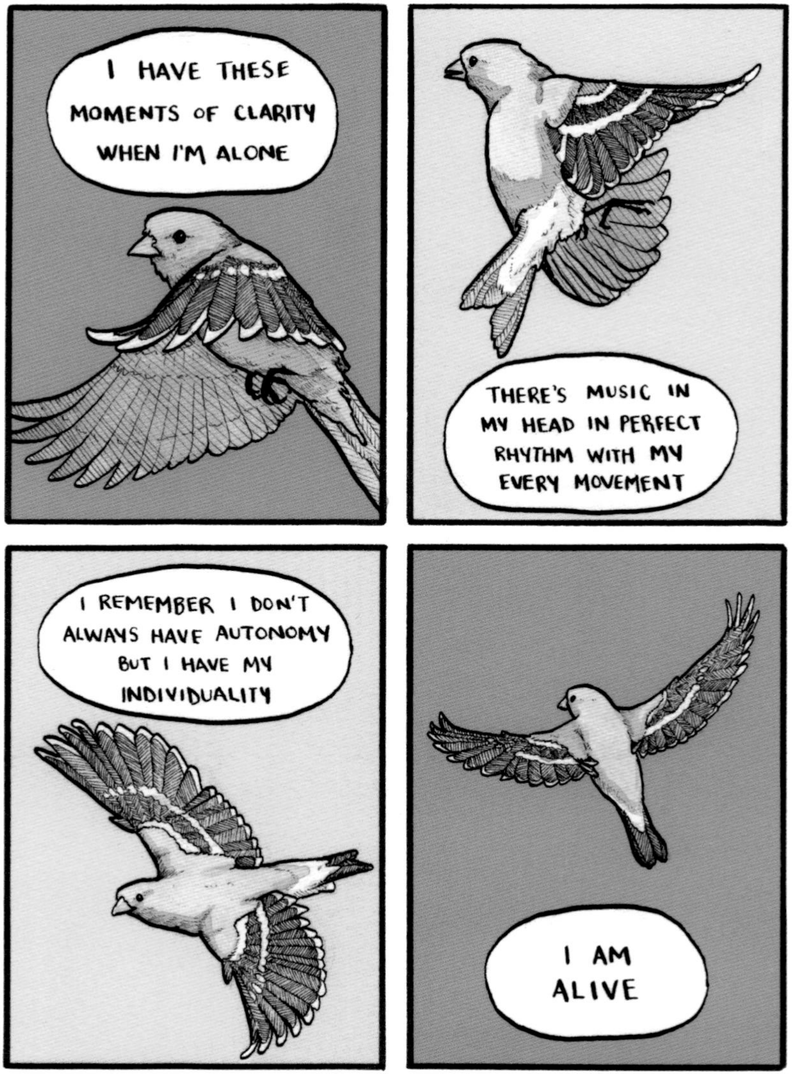
I HAVE THESE MOMENTS OF CLARITY WHEN I'M ALONE
THERE'S MUSIC IN MY HEAD IN PERFECT RHYTHM WITH MY EVERY MOVEMENT
I REMEMBER I DON'T ALWAYS HAVE AUTONOMY BUT I HAVE MY INDIVIDUALITY
I AM ALIVE

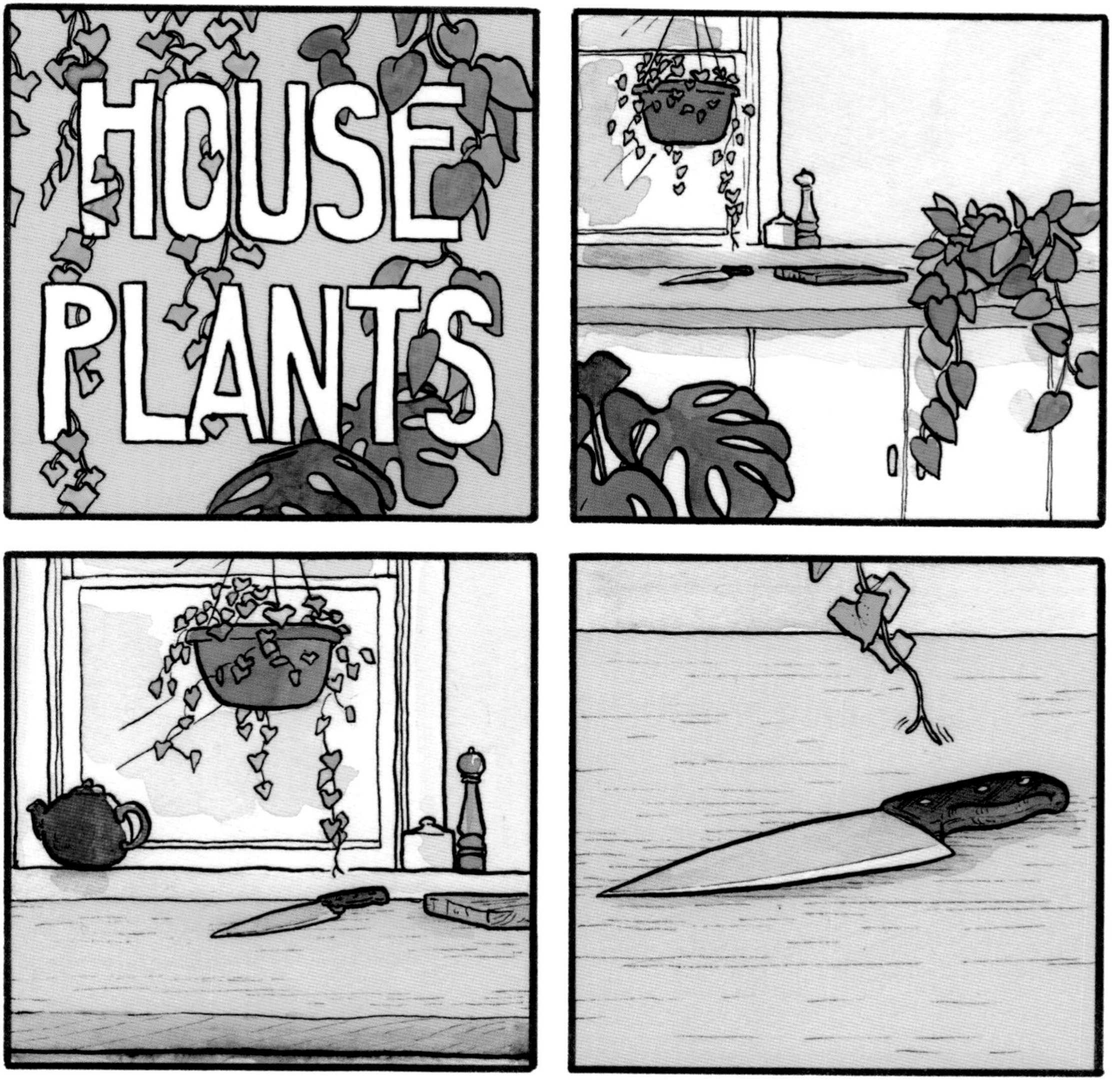
HOUSE PLANTS

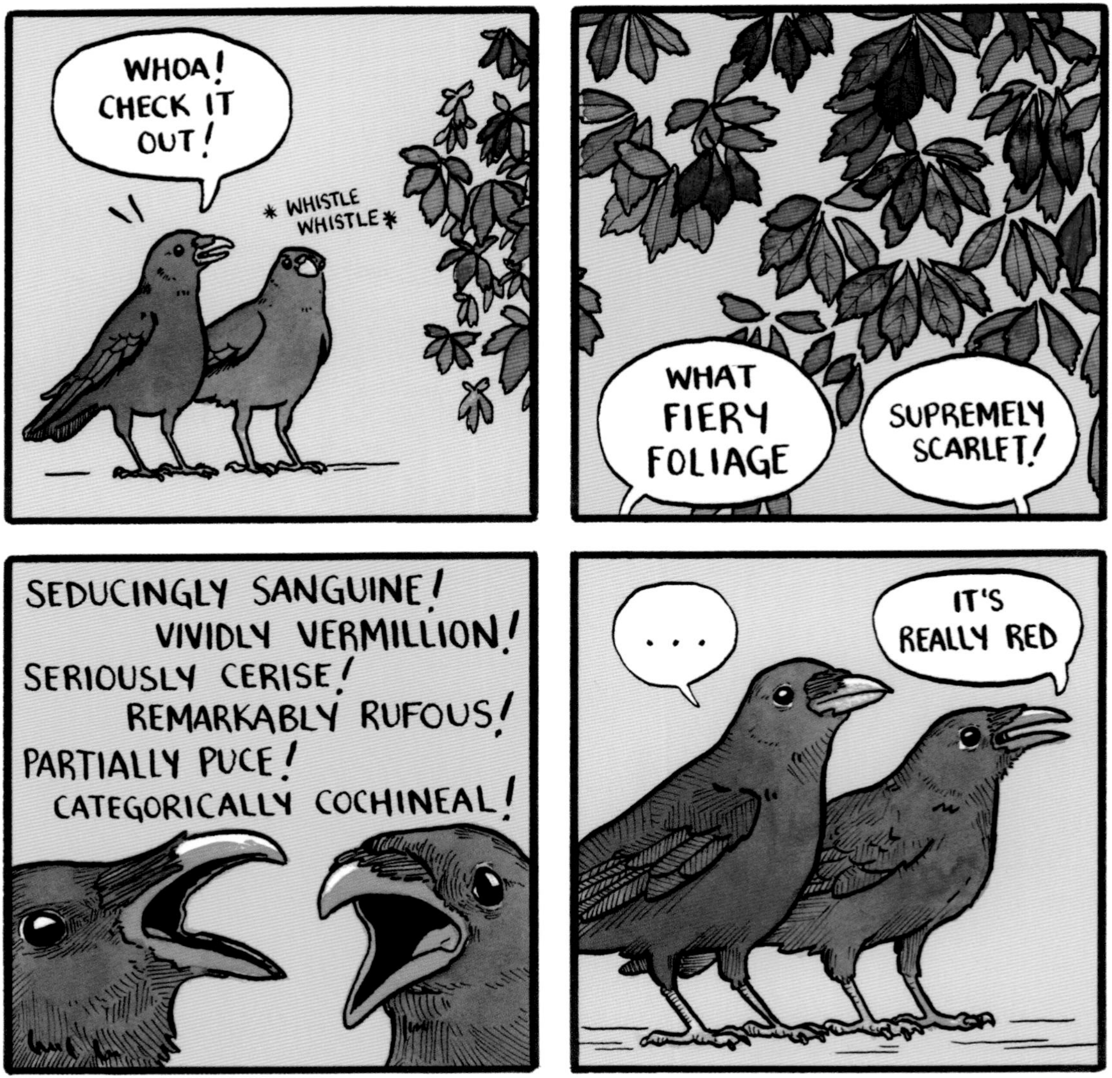

WHOA! CHECK IT OUT!
* WHISTLE WHISTLE *
WHAT FIERY FOLIAGE
SUPREMELY SCARLET!
SEDUCINGLY SANGUINE!
VIVIDLY VERMILLION!
SERIOUSLY CERISE!
REMARKABLY RUFOUS!
PARTIALLY PUCE!
CATEGORICALLY COCHINEAL!
. . .
IT'S REALLY RED

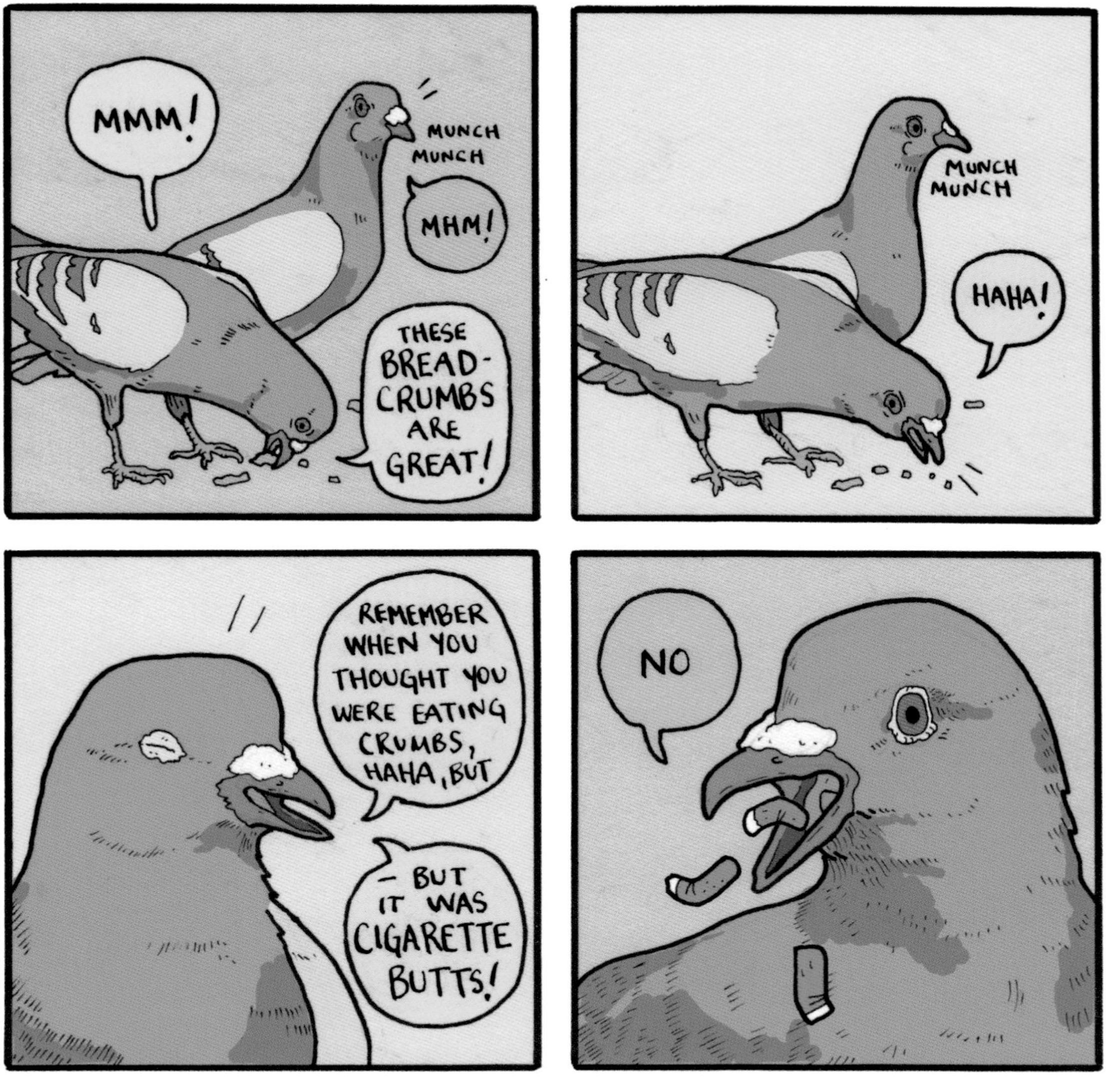
MMM!
MUNCH MUNCH
MHM!
THESE BREAD-CRUMBS ARE GREAT!
MUNCH MUNCH
HAHA!
REMEMBER WHEN YOU THOUGHT YOU WERE EATING CRUMBS, HAHA, BUT
- BUT IT WAS CIGARETTE BUTTS!
NO

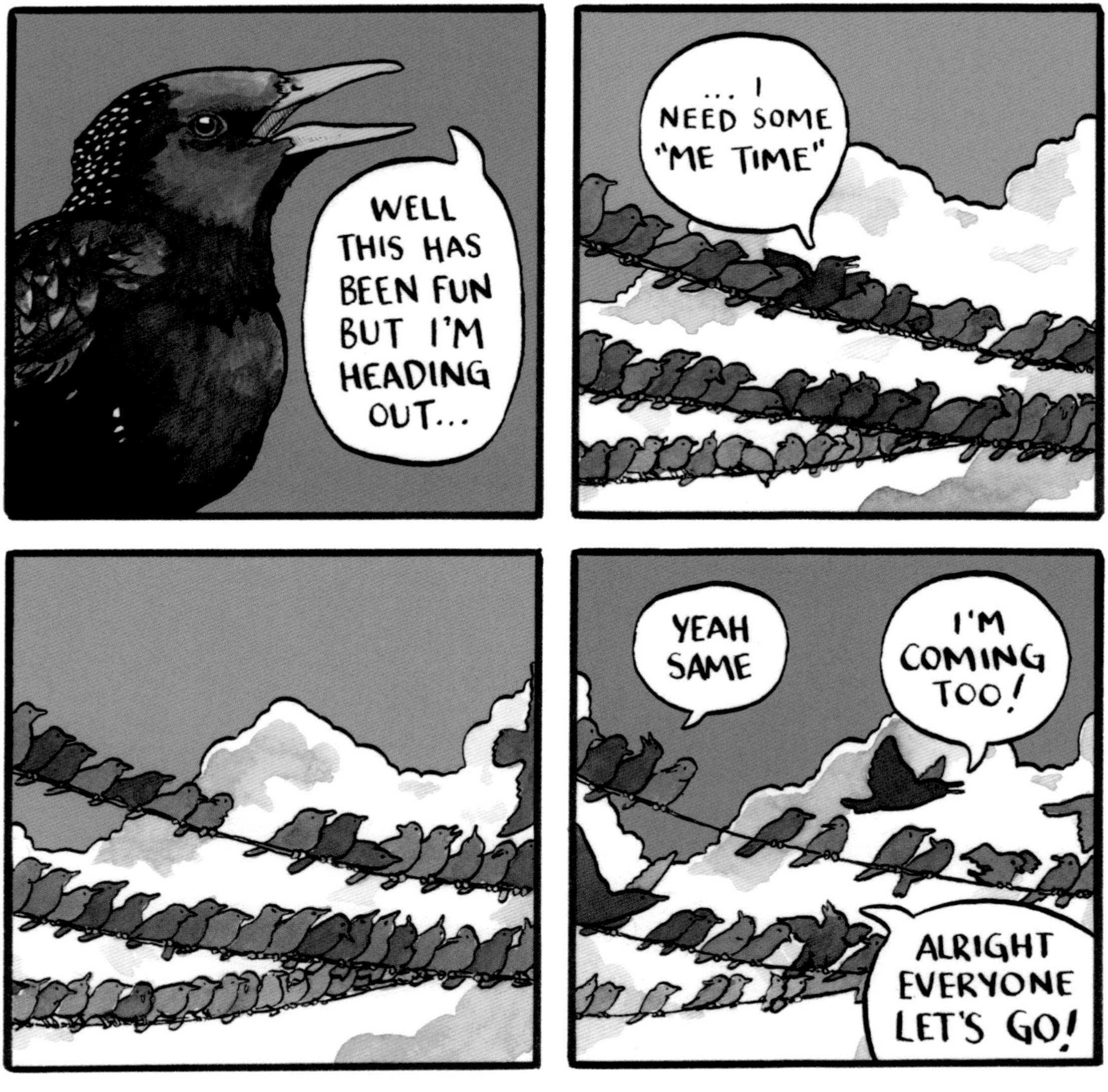
WELL THIS HAS BEEN FUN BUT I'M HEADING OUT...
... I NEED SOME "ME TIME"
YEAH SAME
I'M COMING TOO!
ALRIGHT EVERYONE LET'S GO!

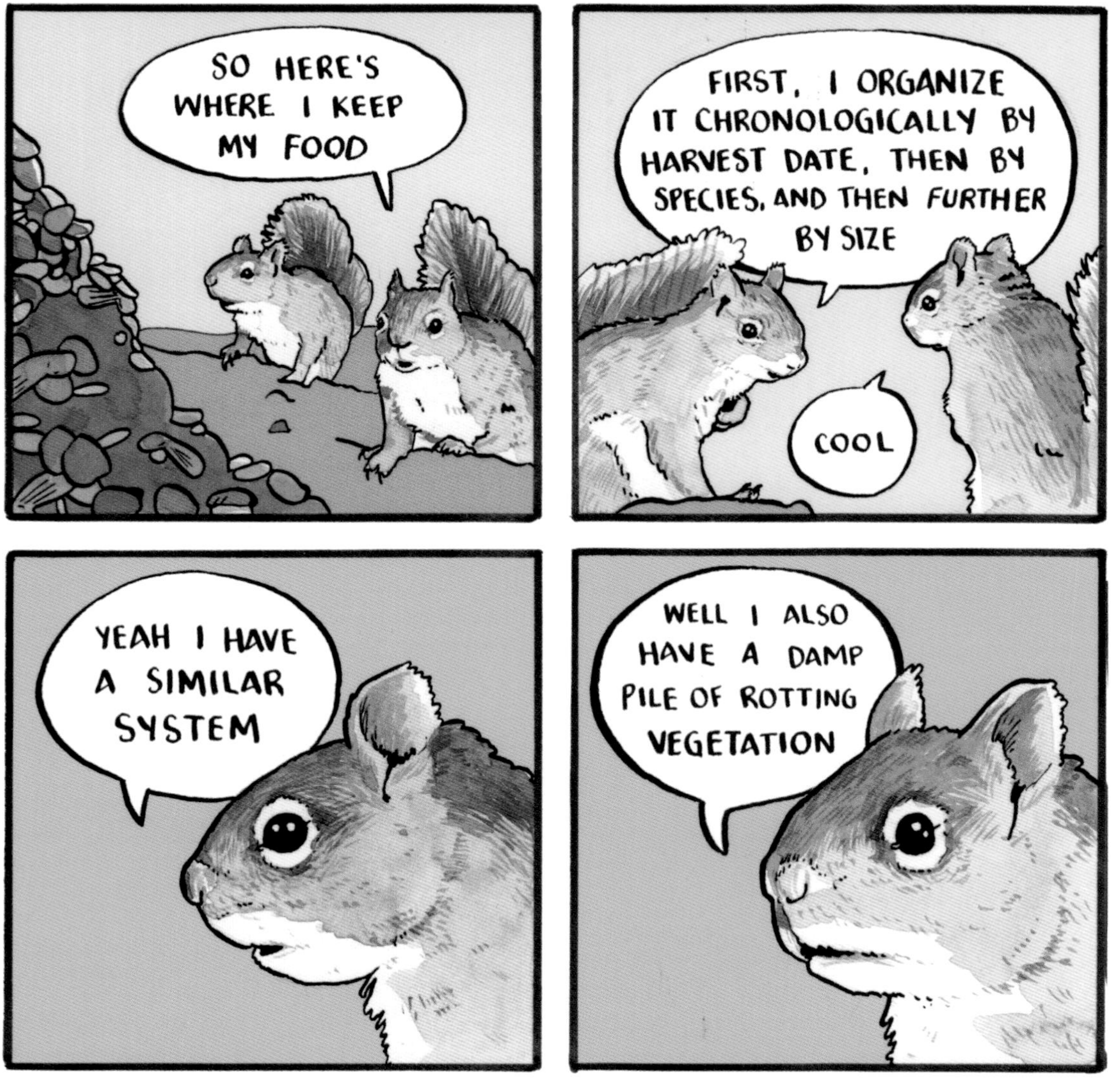
SO HERE'S WHERE I KEEP MY FOOD
FIRST, I ORGANIZE IT CHRONOLOGICALLY BY HARVEST DATE, THEN BY SPECIES, AND THEN FURTHER BY SIZE
COOL
YEAH I HAVE A SIMILAR SYSTEM
WELL I ALSO HAVE A DAMP PILE OF ROTTING VEGETATION

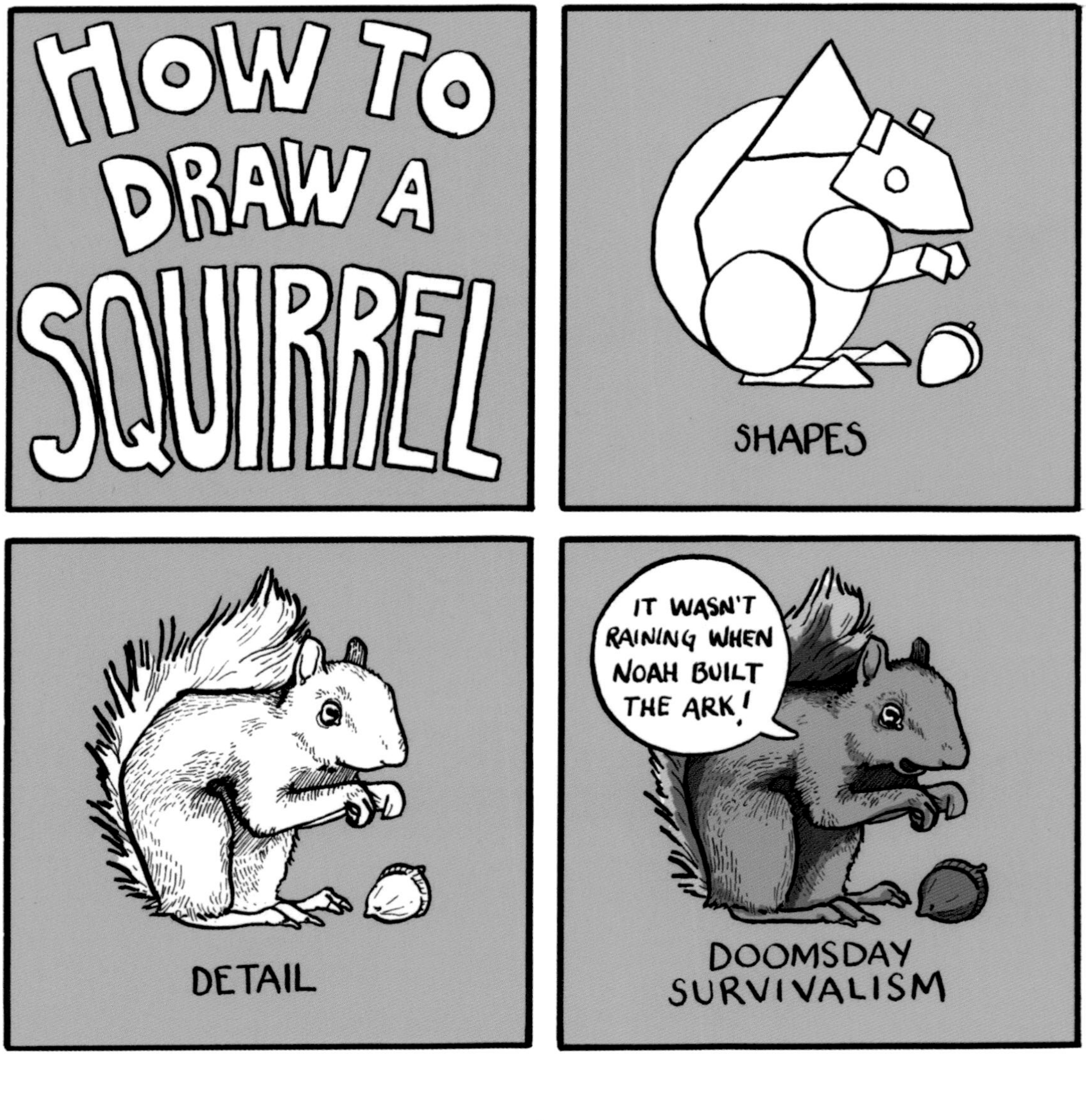
HOW TO DRAW A SQUIRREL
SHAPES
DETAIL
IT WASN'T RAINING WHEN NOAH BUILT THE ARK!
DOOMSDAY SURVIVALISM

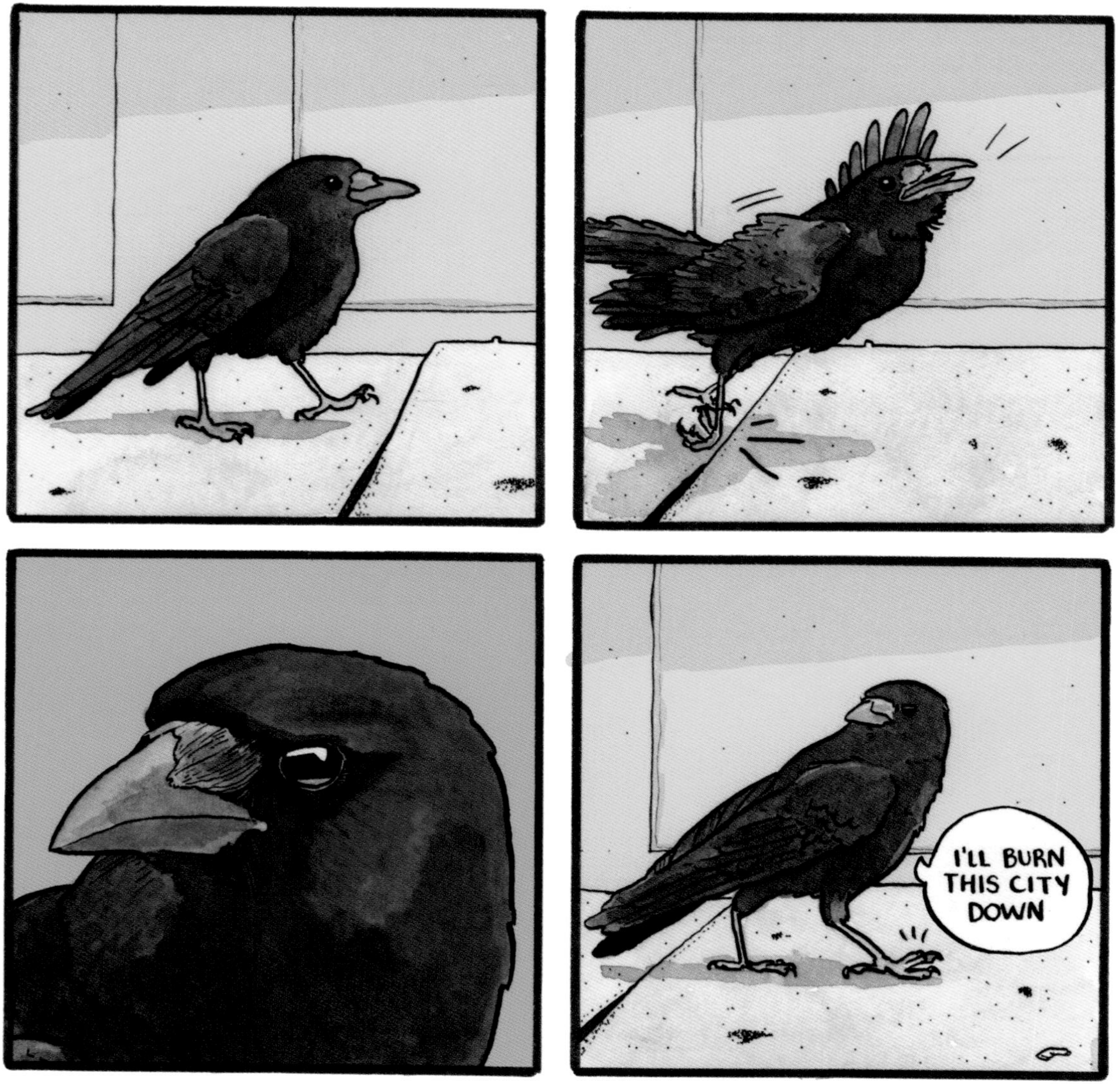
I'LL BURN THIS CITY DOWN

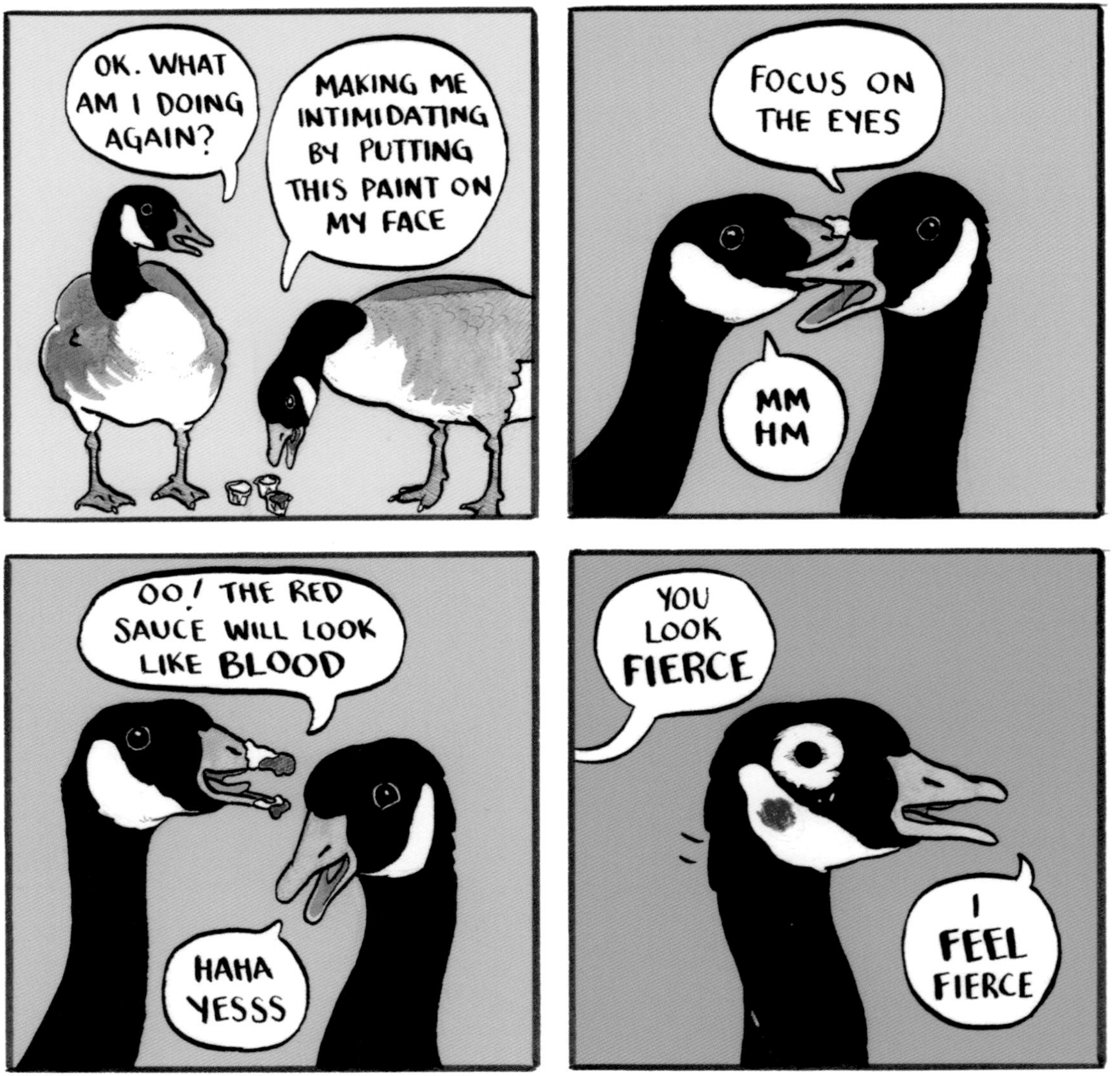
OK. WHAT AM I DOING AGAIN?
MAKING ME INTIMIDATING BY PUTTING THIS PAINT ON MY FACE
FOCUS ON THE EYES
MM HM
OO! THE RED SAUCE WILL LOOK LIKE BLOOD
HAHA YESSS
YOU LOOK FIERCE
I FEEL FIERCE

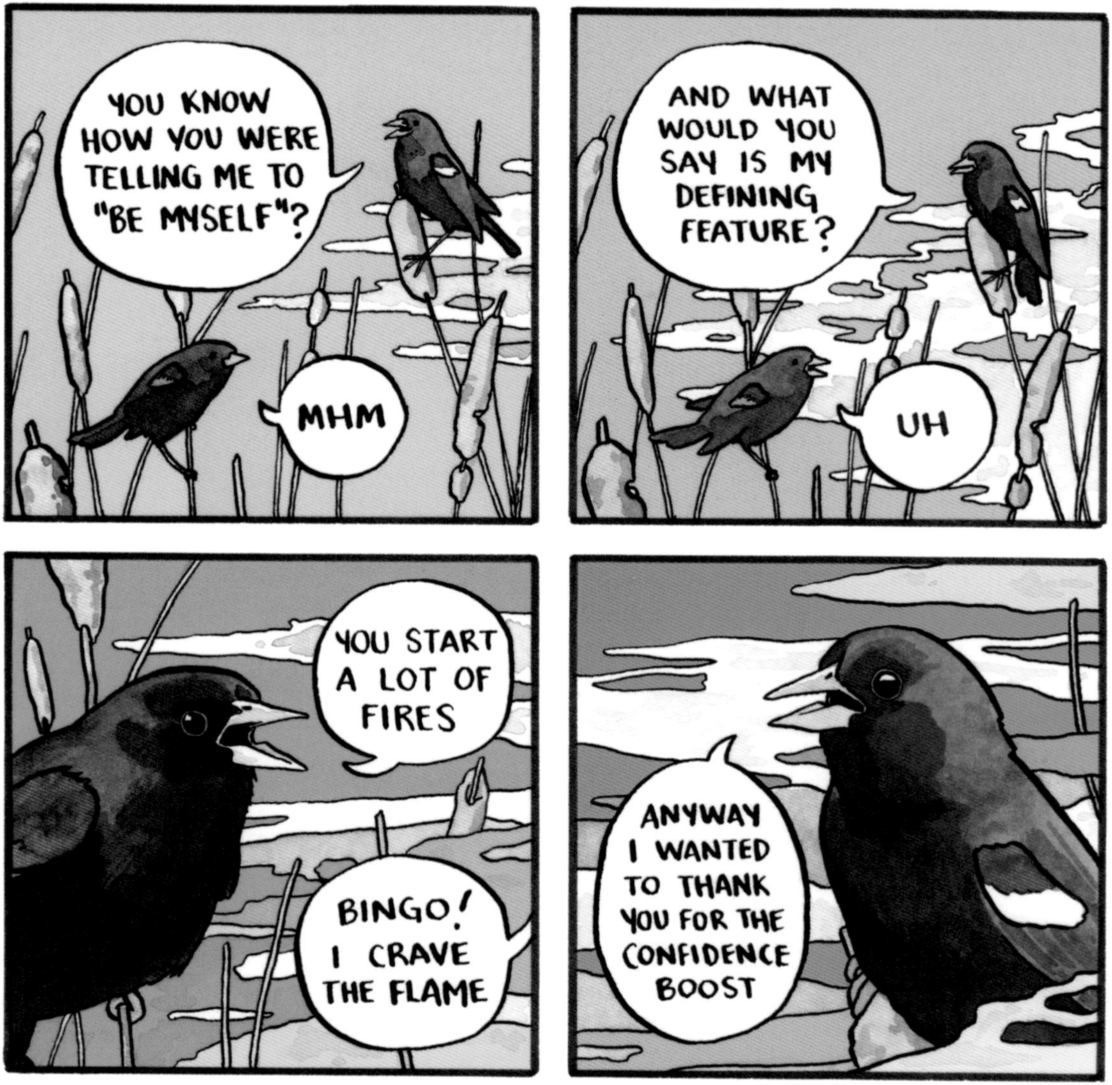
YOU KNOW HOW YOU WERE TELLING ME TO "BE MYSELF"?
MHM
AND WHAT WOULD YOU SAY IS MY DEFINING FEATURE?
UH
YOU START A LOT OF FIRES
BINGO! I CRAVE THE FLAME
ANYWAY I WANTED TO THANK YOU FOR THE CONFIDENCE BOOST

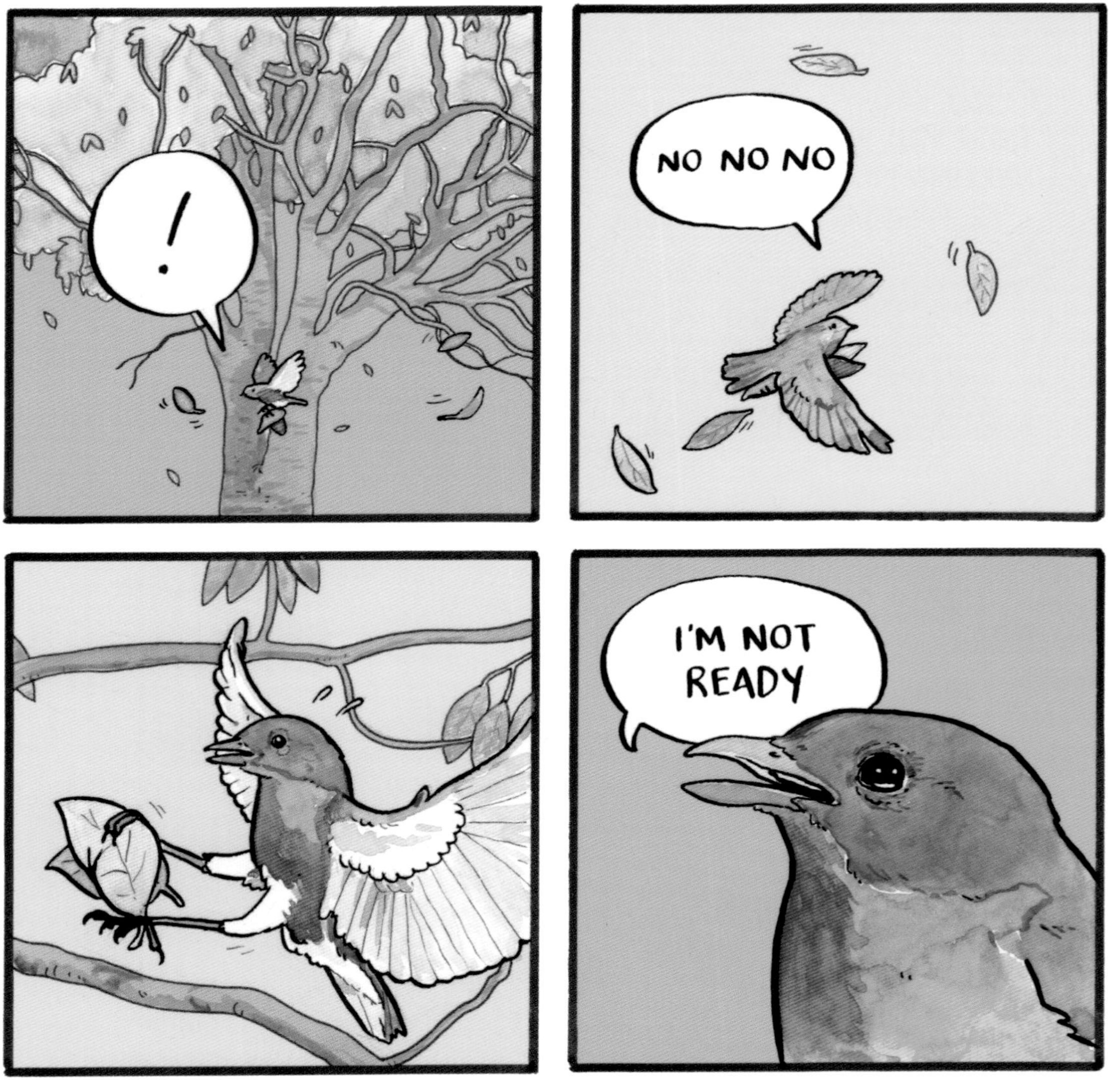
!
NO NO NO
I'M NOT READY

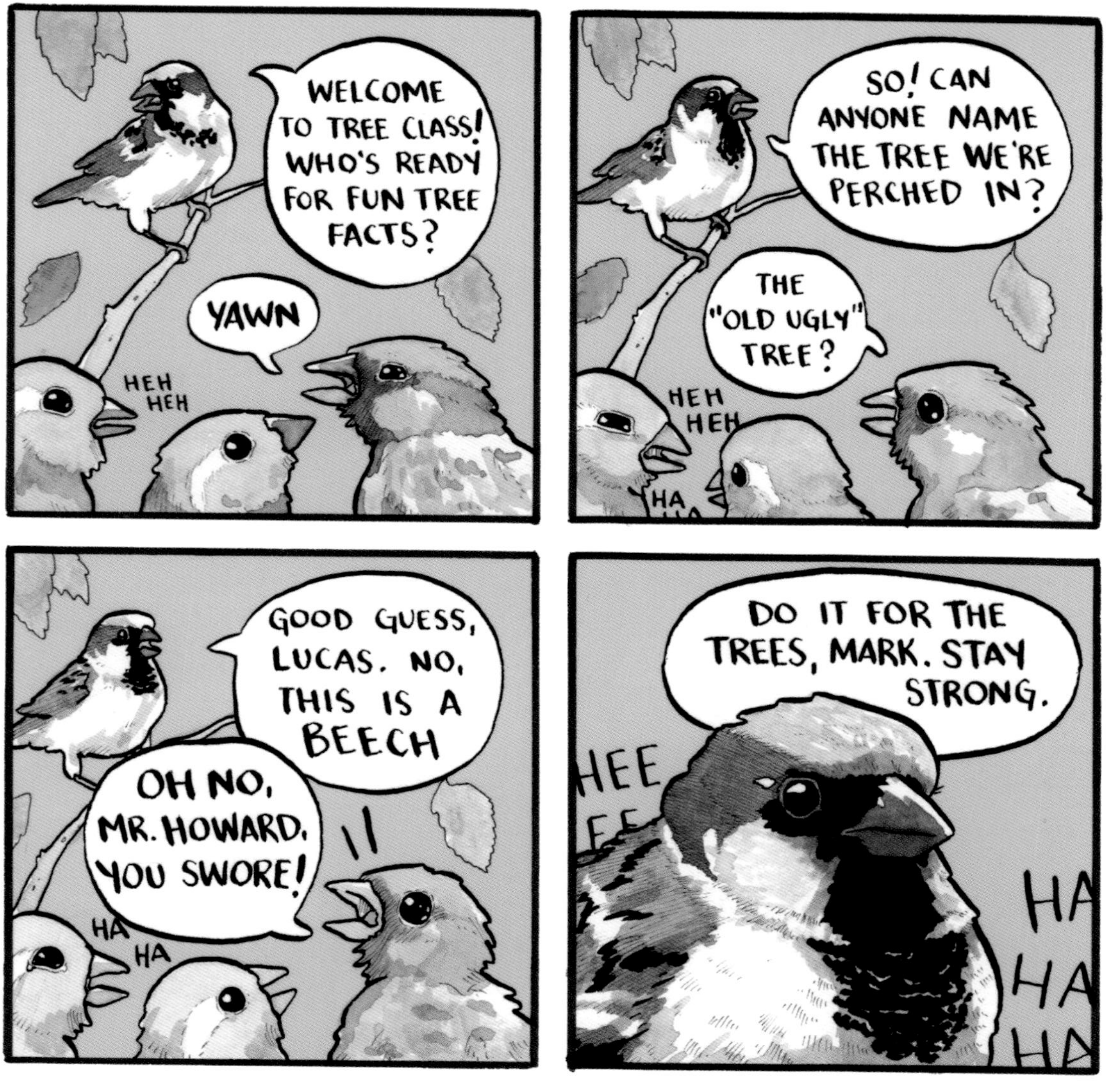
WELCOME TO TREE CLASS! WHO'S READY FOR FUN TREE FACTS?
YAWN
HEH HEH
SO! CAN ANYONE NAME THE TREE WE'RE PERCHED IN?
THE "OLD UGLY" TREE?
HEH HEH
HA
GOOD GUESS, LUCAS. NO, THIS IS A BEECH
OH NO, MR. HOWARD, YOU SWORE!
HA HA
DO IT FOR THE TREES, MARK. STAY STRONG.
HEE
HA HA

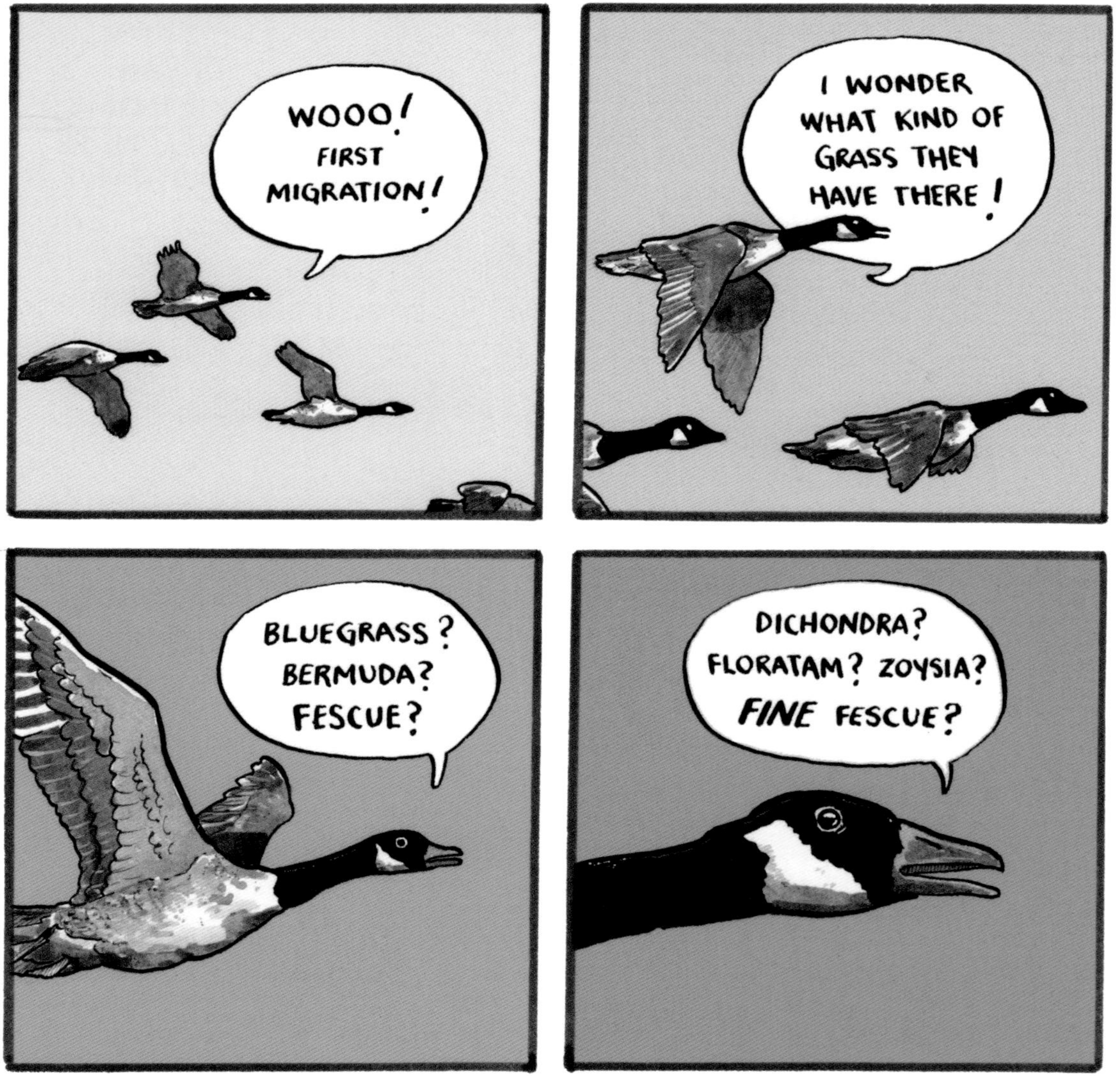
WOOO! FIRST MIGRATION!
I WONDER WHAT KIND OF GRASS THEY HAVE THERE!
BLUEGRASS? BERMUDA? FESCUE?
DICHONDRA? FLORATAM? ZOYSIA? *FINE* FESCUE?

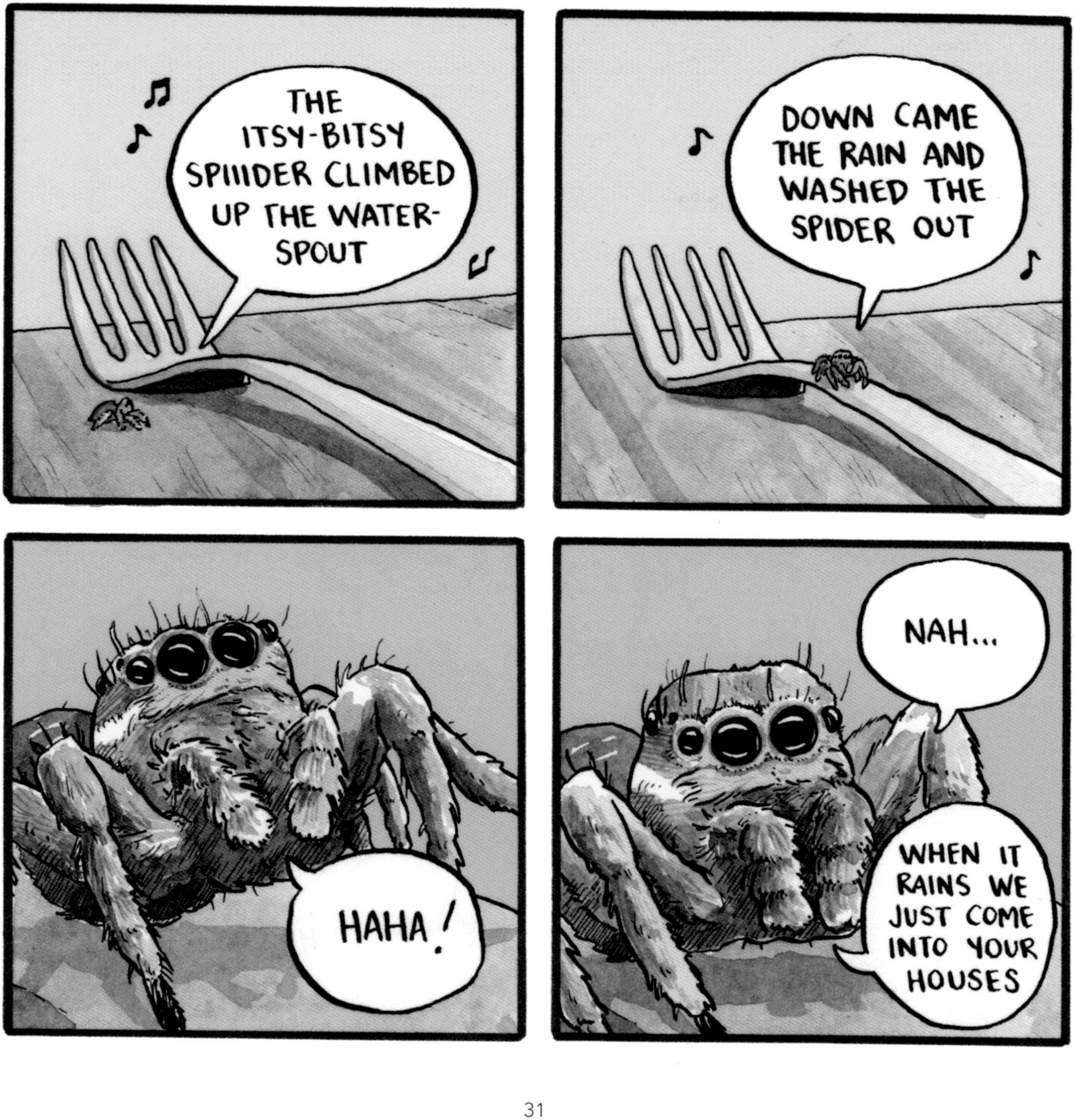
THE ITSY-BITSY SPIIIDER CLIMBED UP THE WATER-SPOUT
DOWN CAME THE RAIN AND WASHED THE SPIDER OUT
HAHA!
NAH...
WHEN IT RAINS WE JUST COME INTO YOUR HOUSES

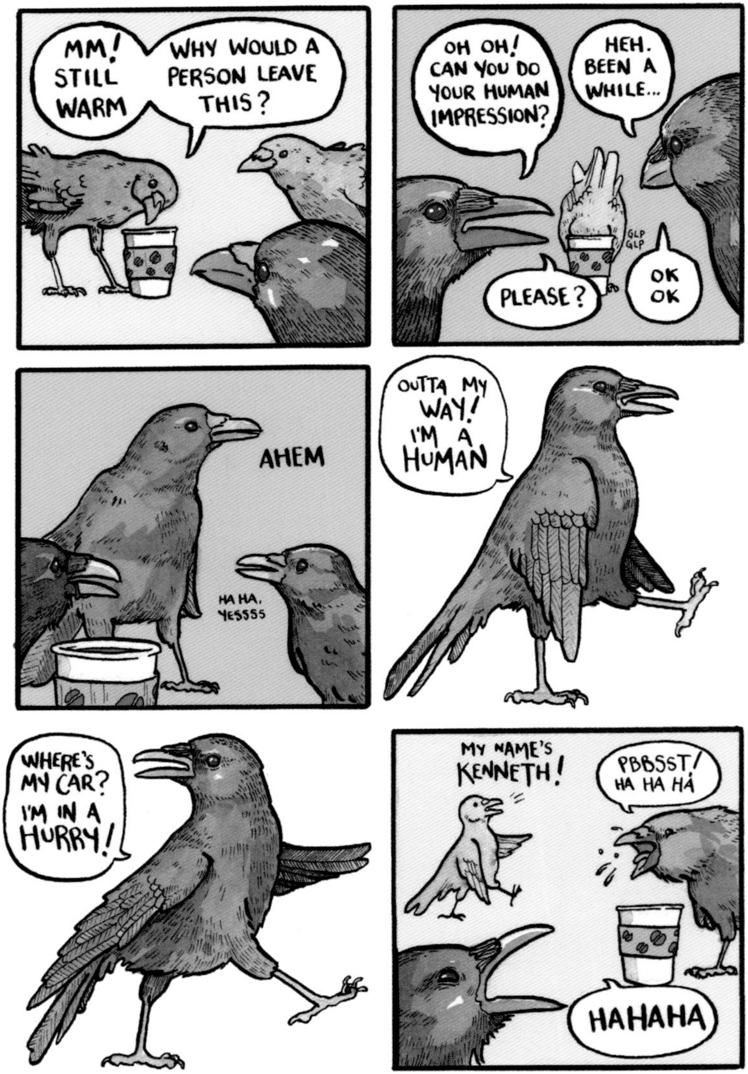
MM! STILL WARM
WHY WOULD A PERSON LEAVE THIS?
OH OH! CAN YOU DO YOUR HUMAN IMPRESSION?
HEH. BEEN A WHILE...
GLP GLP
PLEASE?
OK OK
AHEM
HA HA. YESSSS
OUTTA MY WAY! I'M A HUMAN
WHERE'S MY CAR? I'M IN A HURRY!
MY NAME'S KENNETH!
PBBSST! HA HA HA
HAHAHA

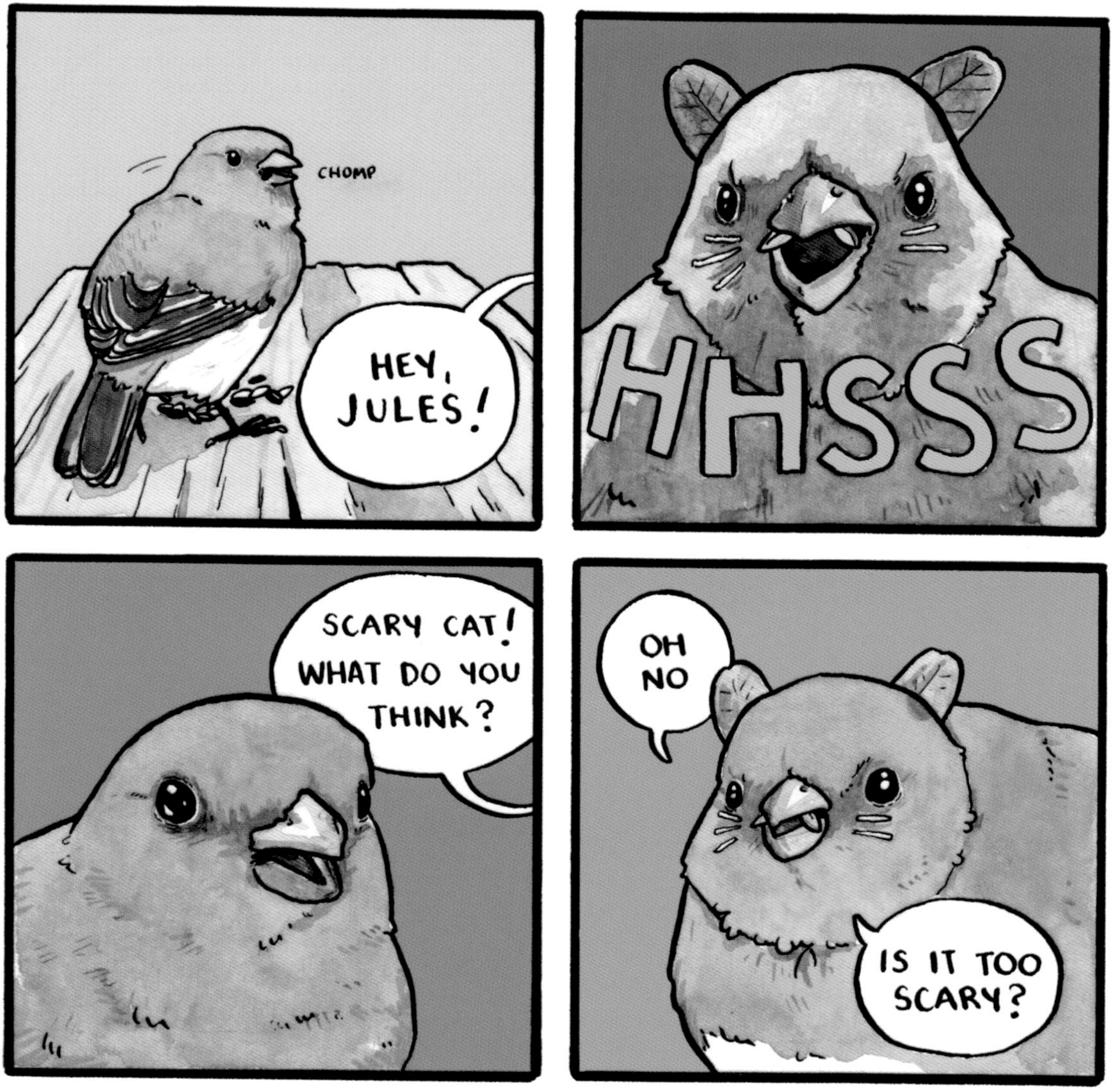
CHOMP
HEY, JULES!
HHSSS
SCARY CAT! WHAT DO YOU THINK?
OH NO
IS IT TOO SCARY?

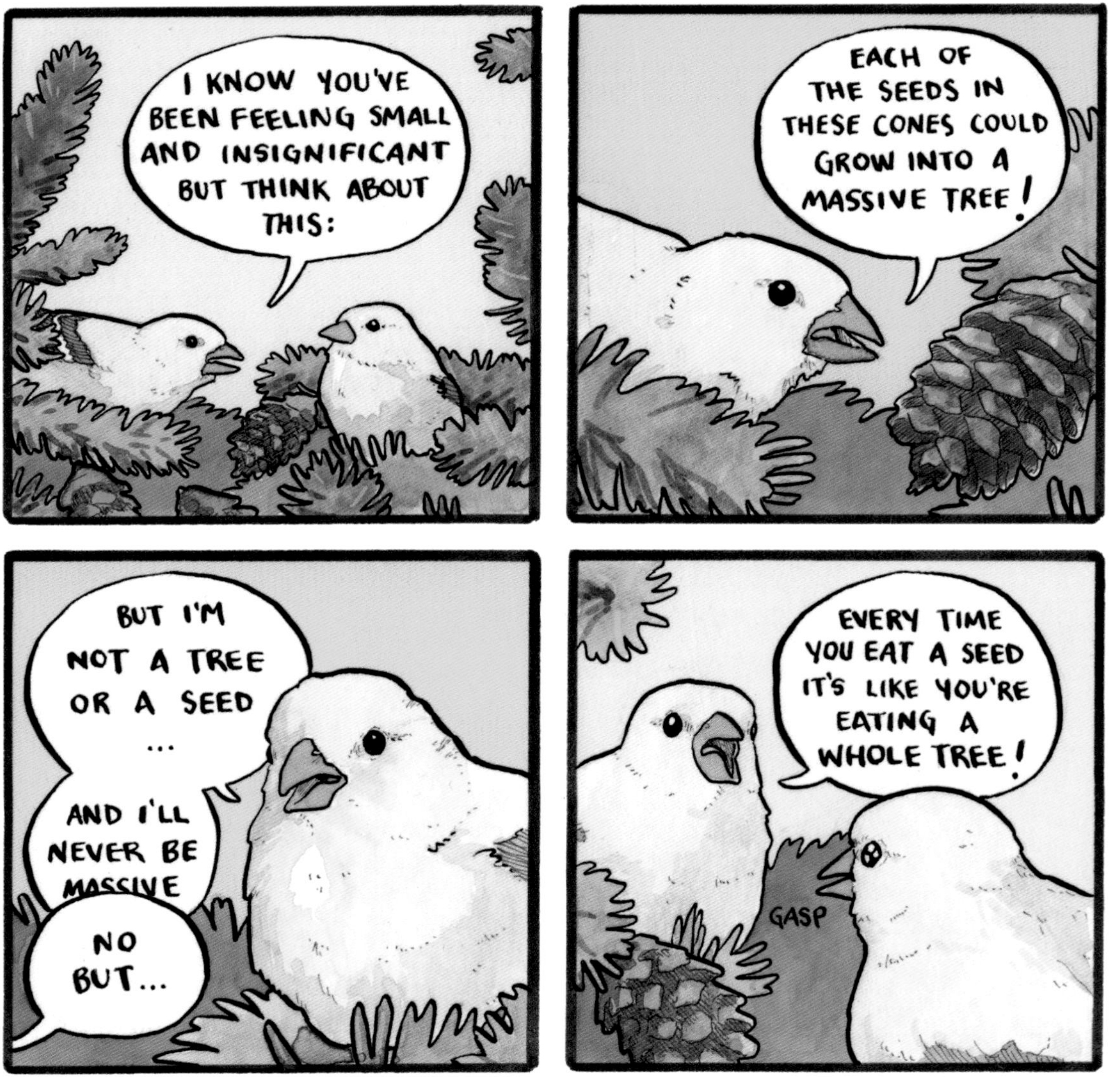
I KNOW YOU'VE BEEN FEELING SMALL AND INSIGNIFICANT BUT THINK ABOUT THIS:
EACH OF THE SEEDS IN THESE CONES COULD GROW INTO A MASSIVE TREE!
BUT I'M NOT A TREE OR A SEED ...
AND I'LL NEVER BE MASSIVE
NO BUT...
EVERY TIME YOU EAT A SEED IT'S LIKE YOU'RE EATING A WHOLE TREE!
GASP

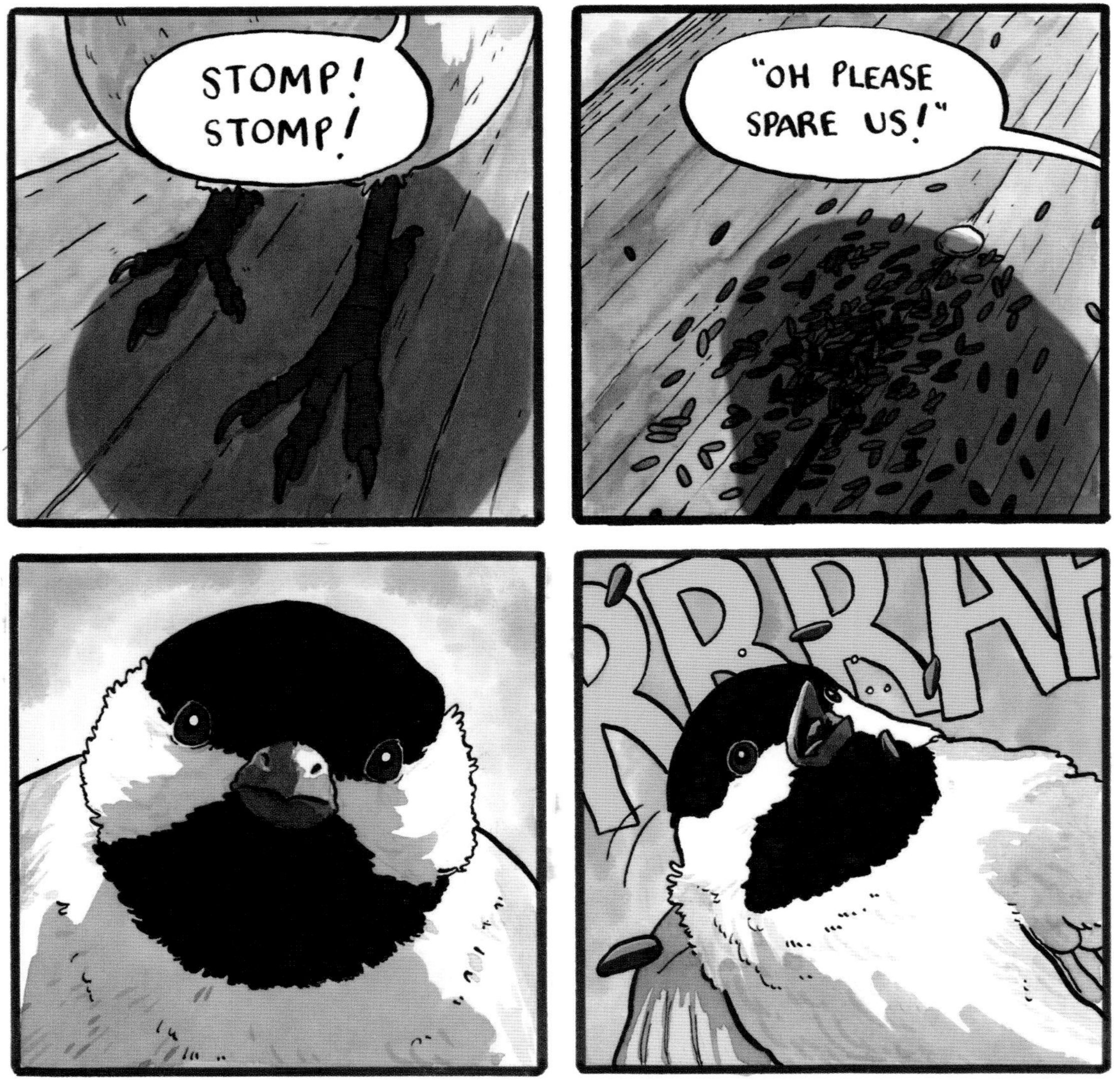
STOMP! STOMP!
"OH PLEASE SPARE US!"

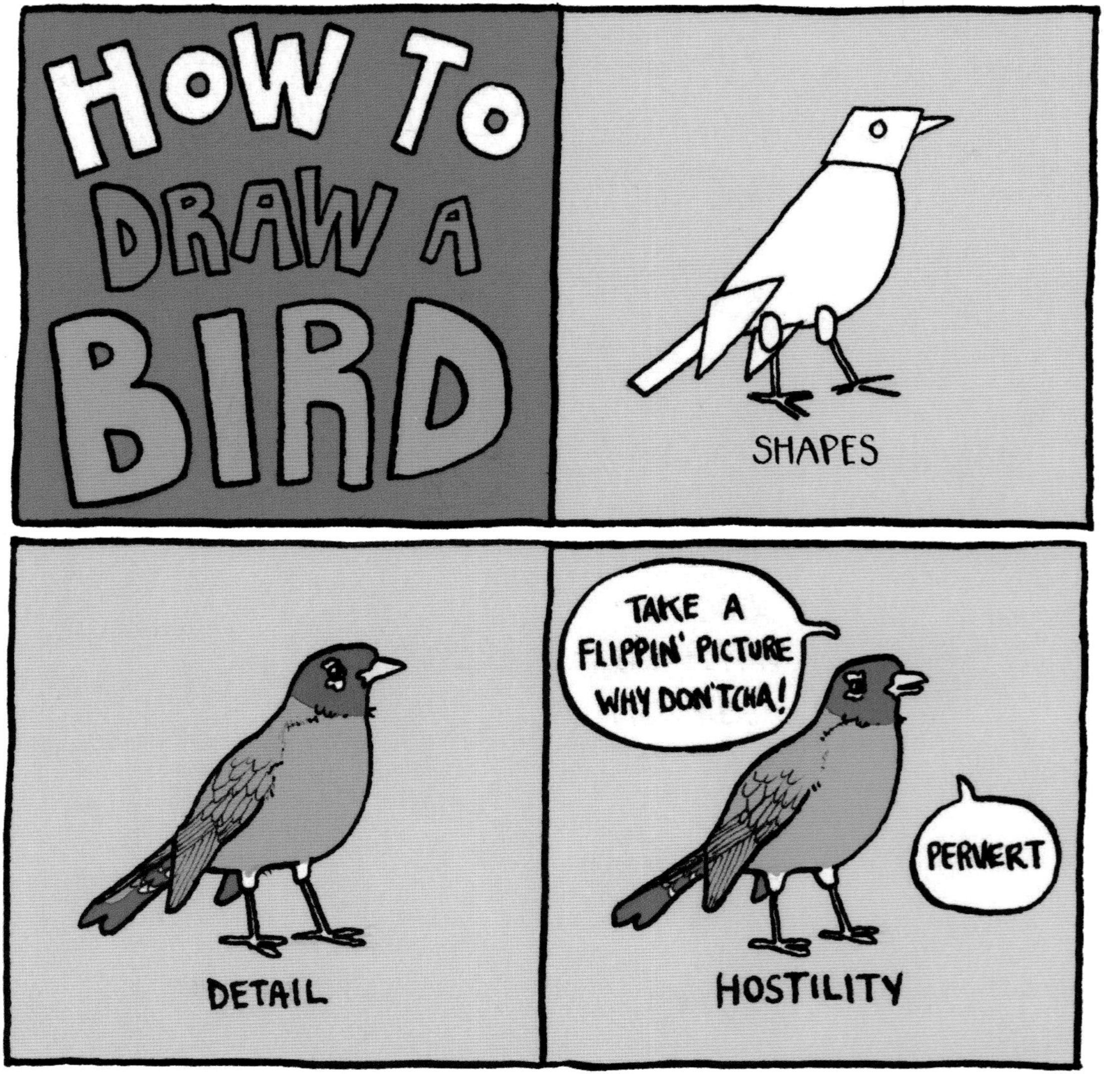
HOW TO DRAW A BIRD
SHAPES
DETAIL
TAKE A FLIPPIN' PICTURE WHY DON'TCHA!
PERVERT
HOSTILITY

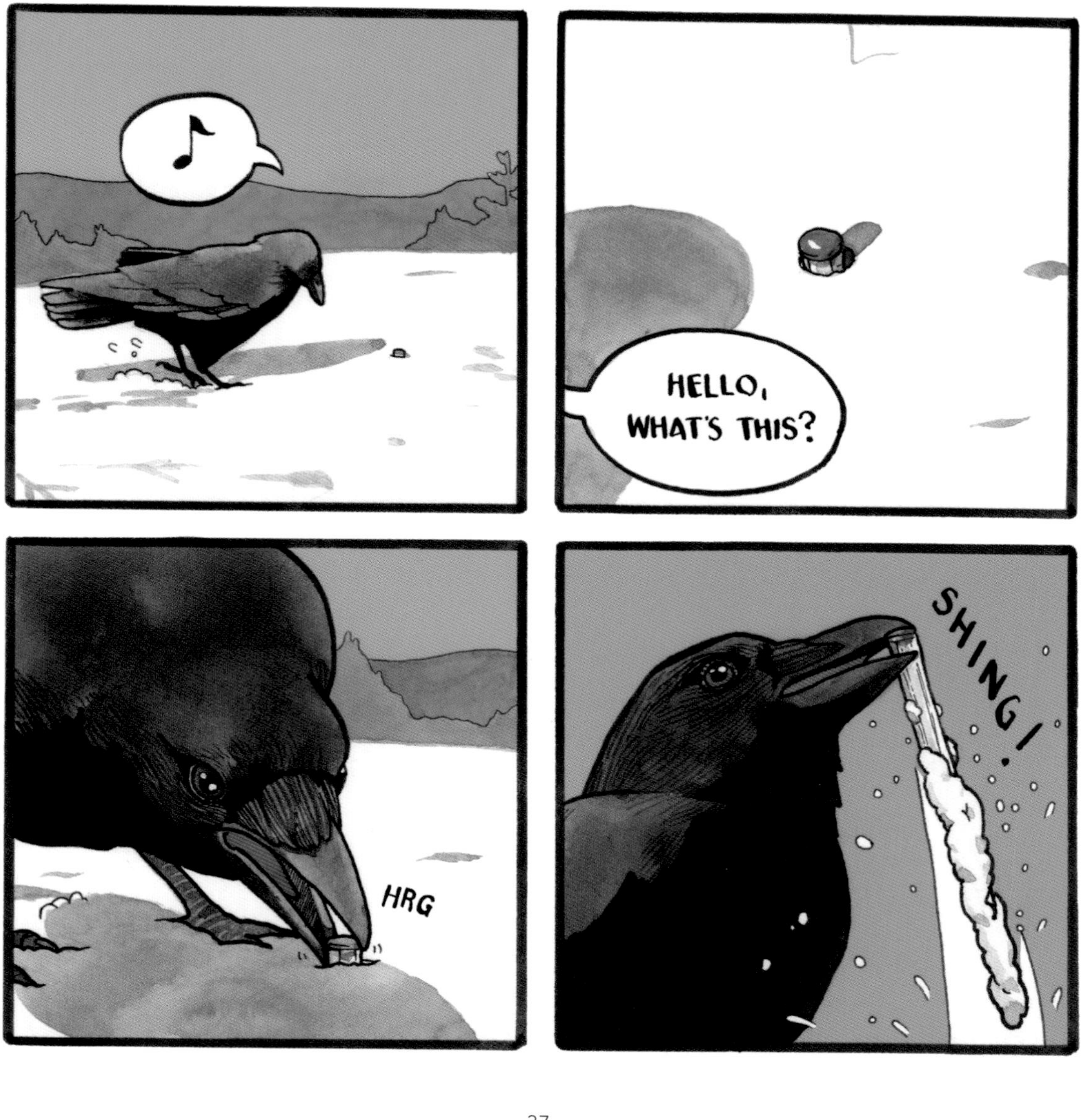
♪
HELLO, WHAT'S THIS?
HRG
SHING!

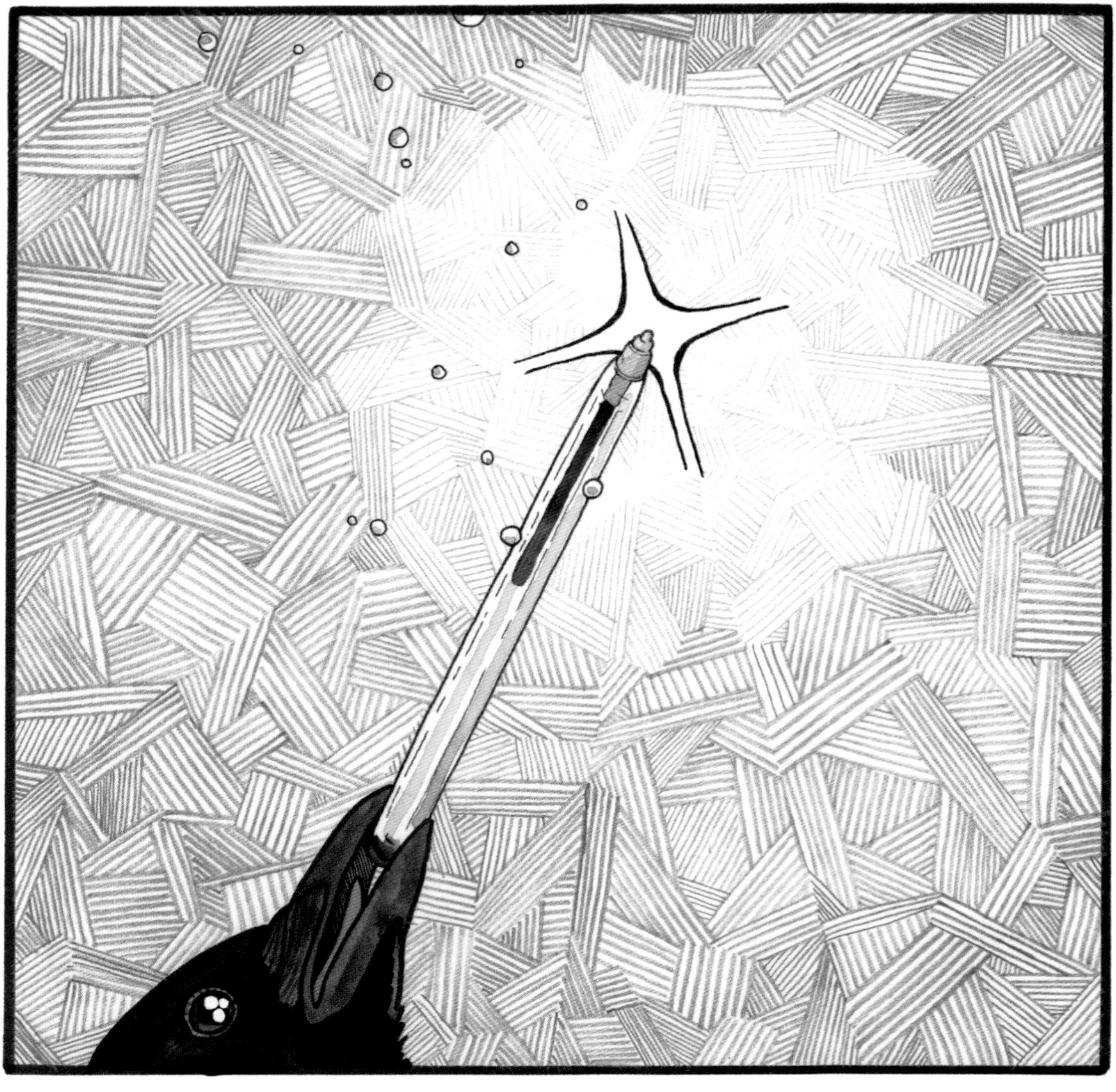

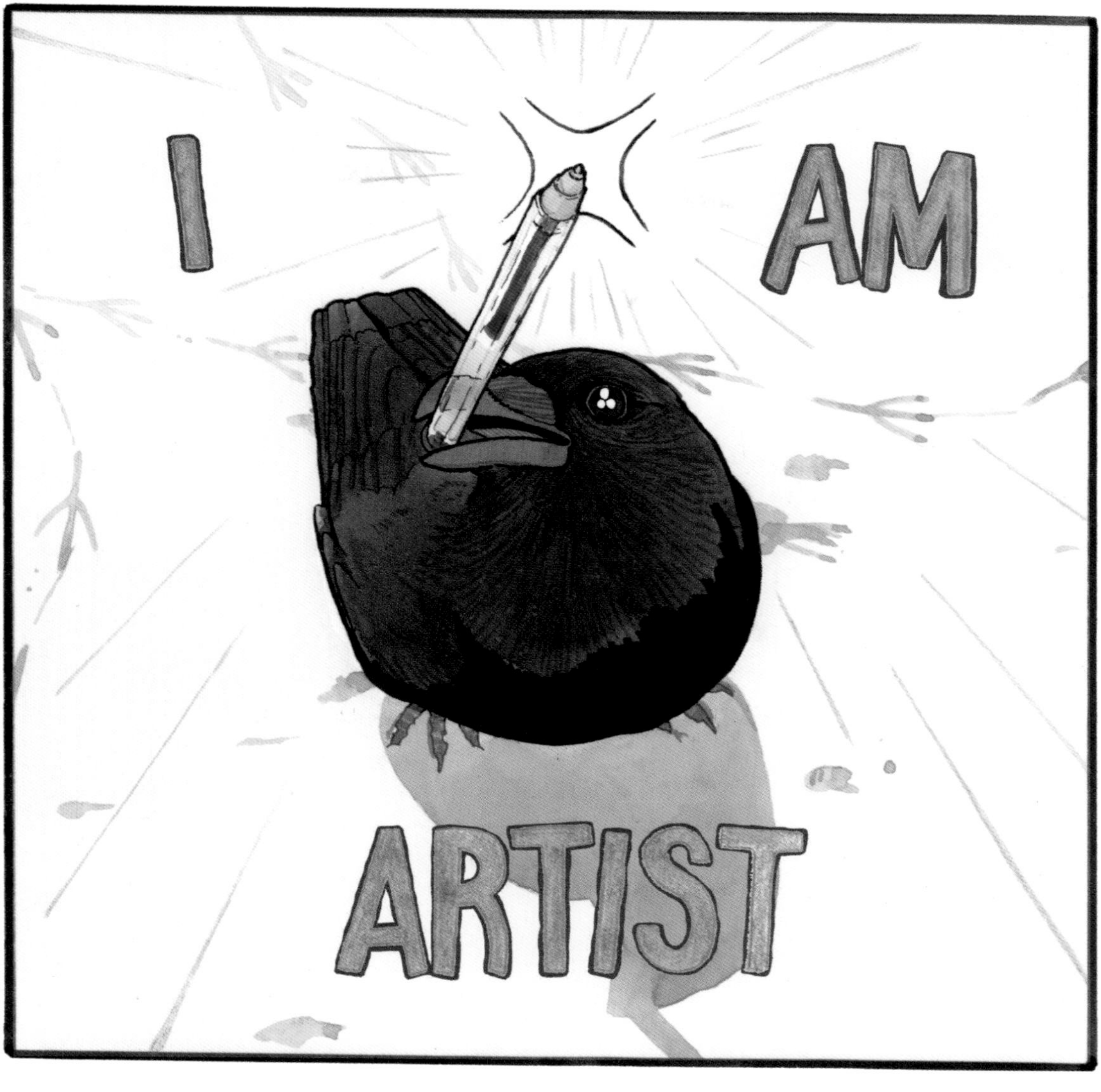
I AM
ARTIST

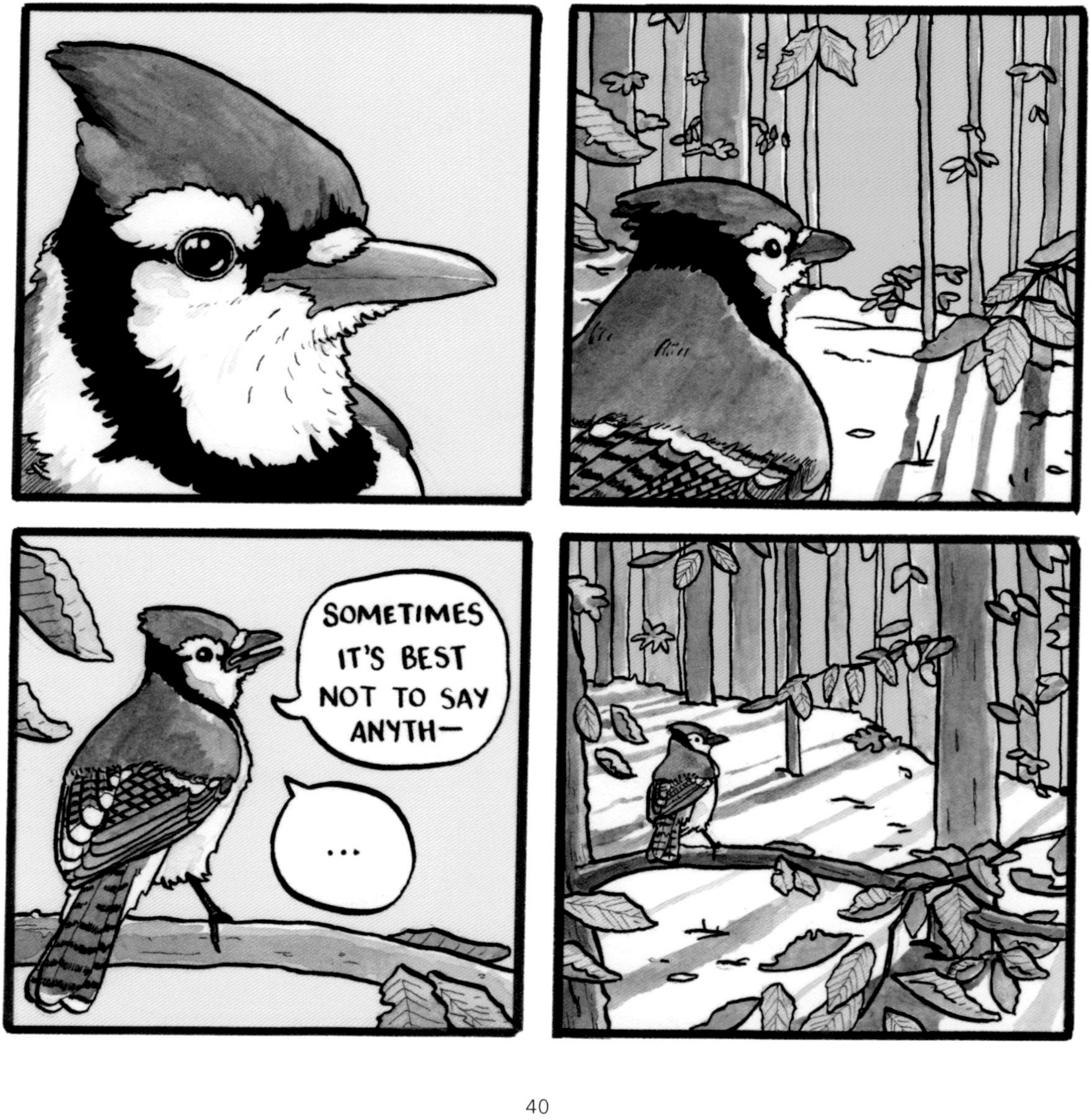
SOMETIMES IT'S BEST NOT TO SAY ANYTH—
...

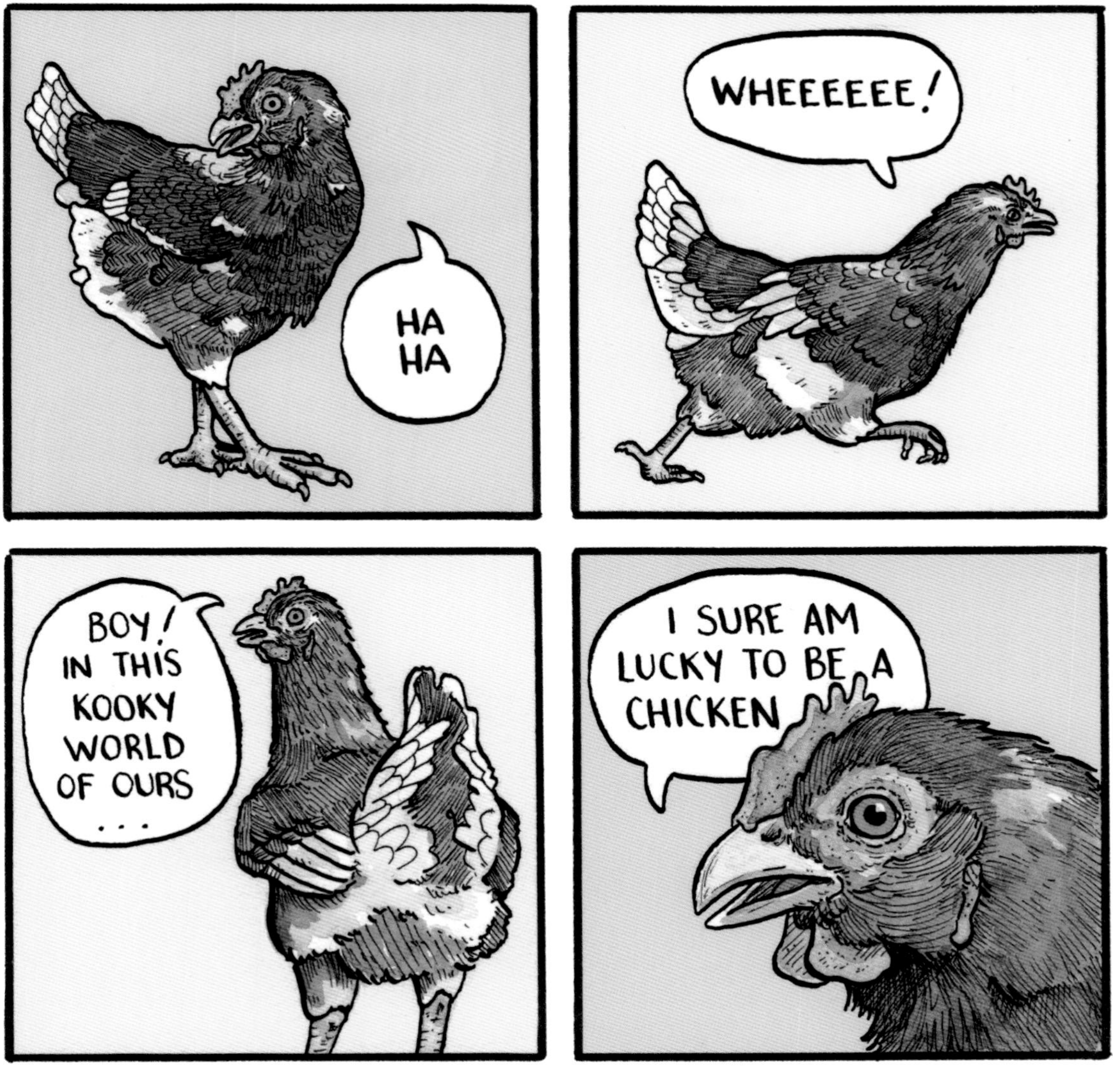
HA HA
WHEEEEEE!
BOY! IN THIS KOOKY WORLD OF OURS . . .
I SURE AM LUCKY TO BE A CHICKEN

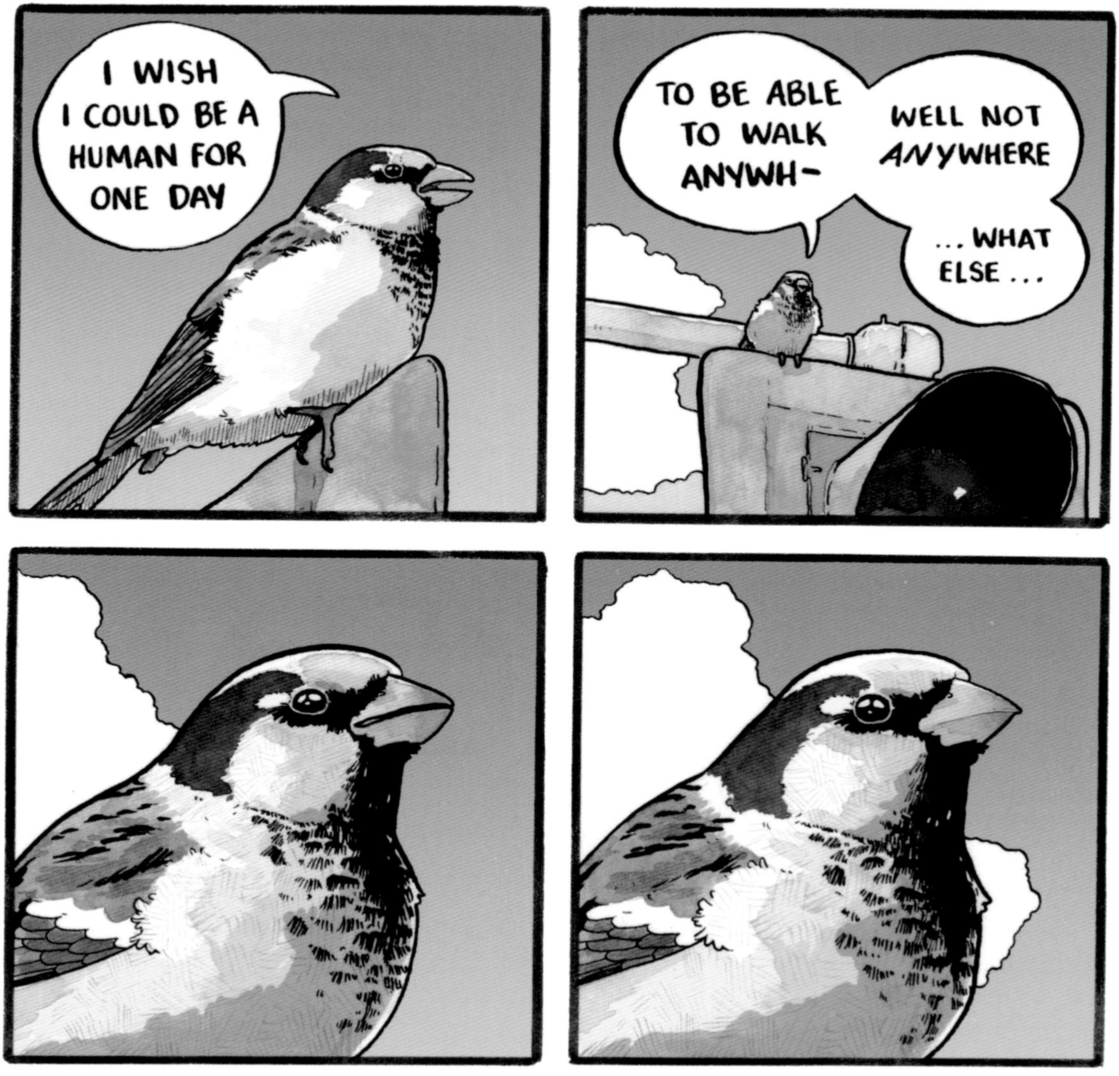
I WISH I COULD BE A HUMAN FOR ONE DAY
TO BE ABLE TO WALK ANYWH-
WELL NOT *ANYWHERE*
...WHAT ELSE...

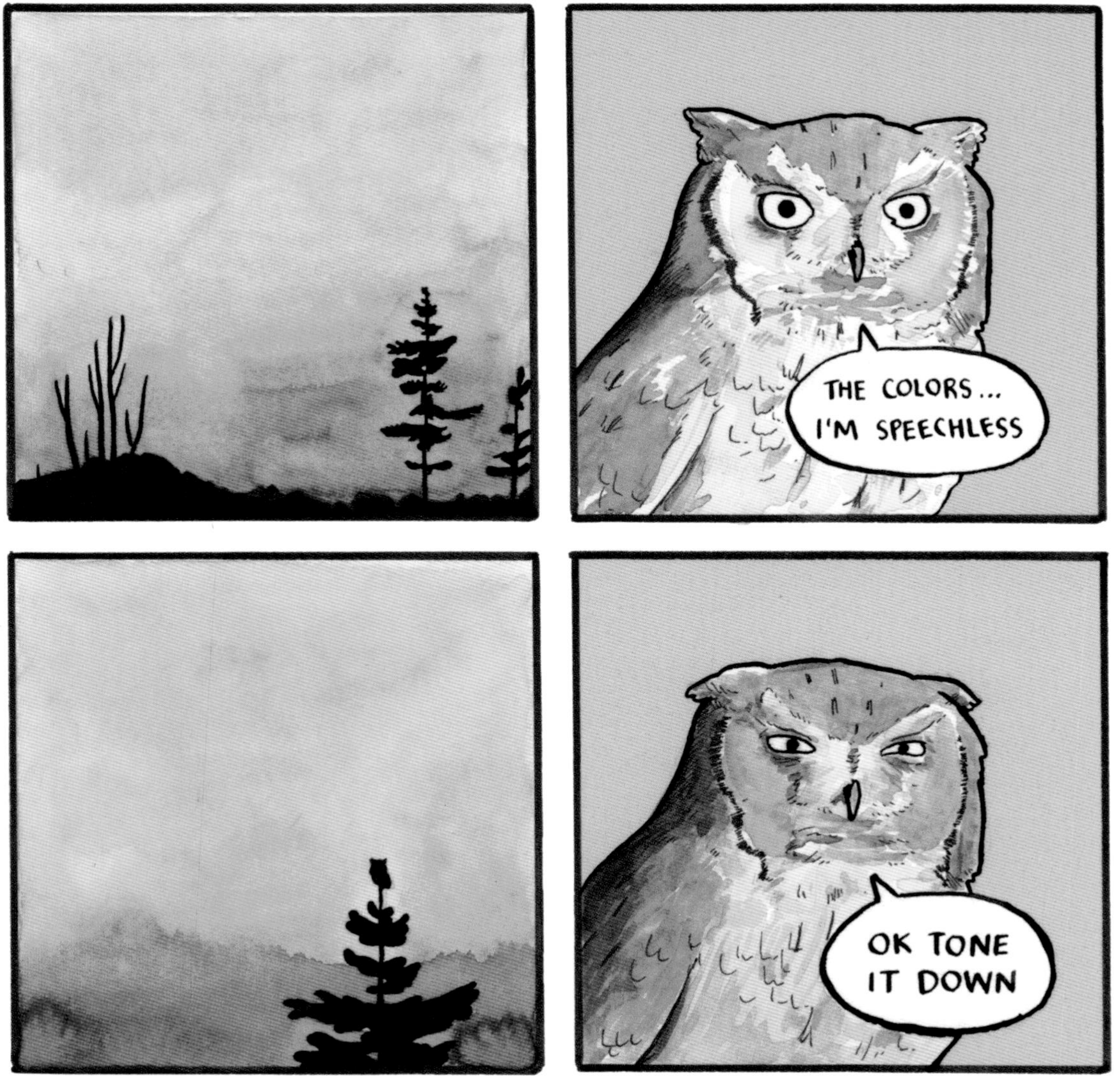
THE COLORS...
I'M SPEECHLESS
OK TONE
IT DOWN

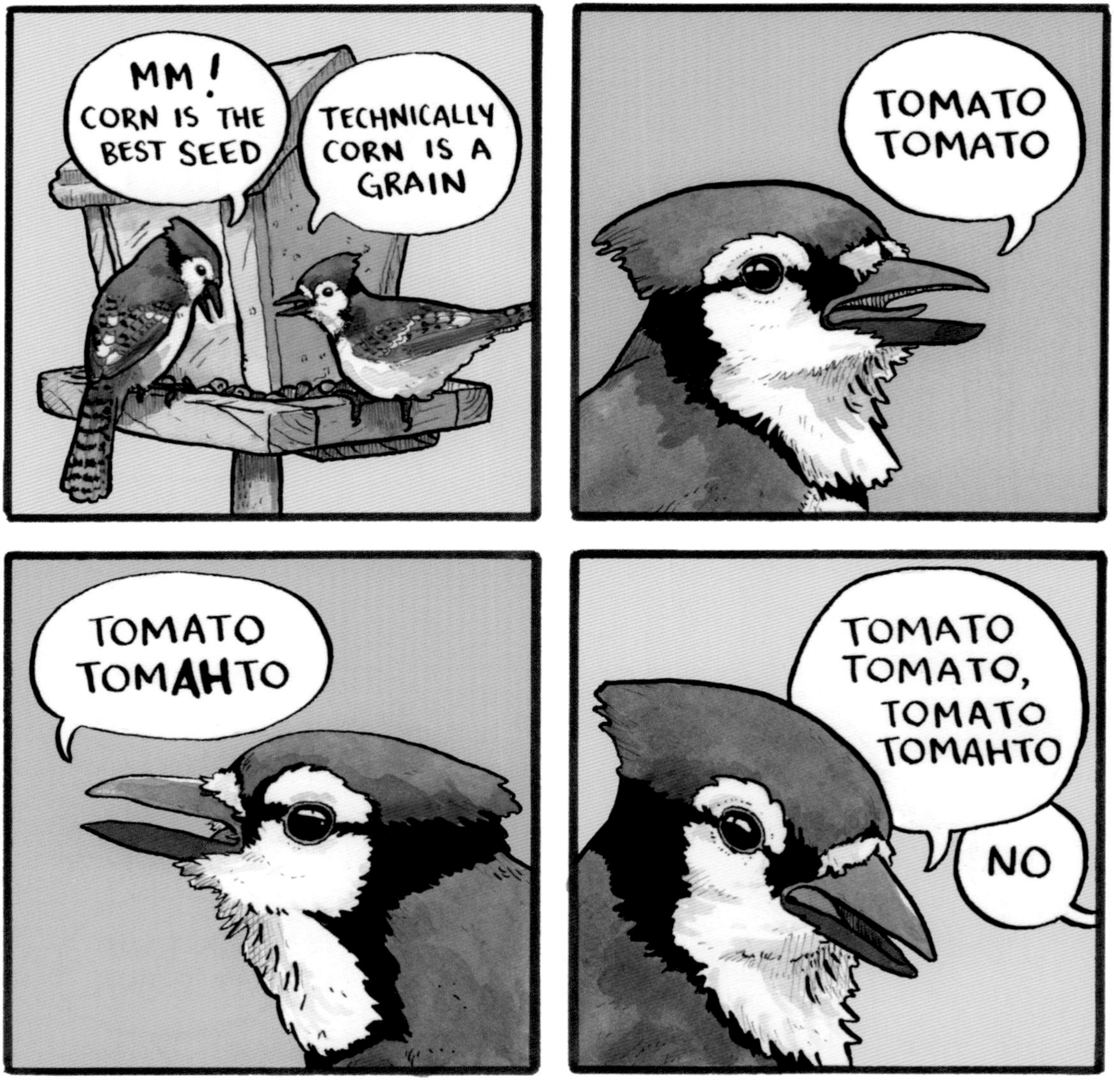
MM! CORN IS THE BEST SEED
TECHNICALLY CORN IS A GRAIN
TOMATO TOMATO
TOMATO TOMAHTO
TOMATO TOMATO, TOMATO TOMAHTO
NO

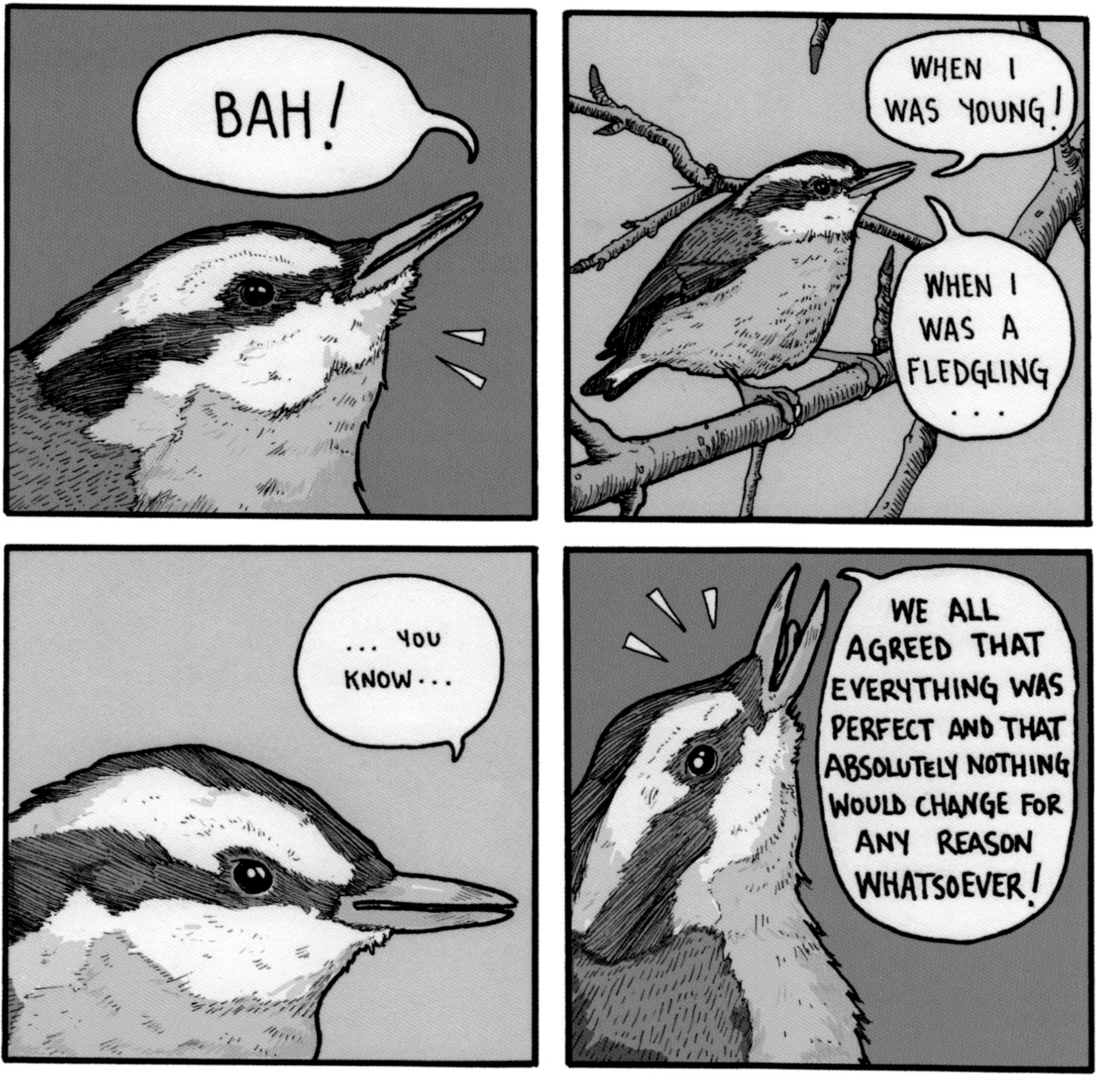
BAH!
WHEN I WAS YOUNG!
WHEN I WAS A FLEDGLING . . .
... YOU KNOW...
WE ALL AGREED THAT EVERYTHING WAS PERFECT AND THAT ABSOLUTELY NOTHING WOULD CHANGE FOR ANY REASON WHATSOEVER!

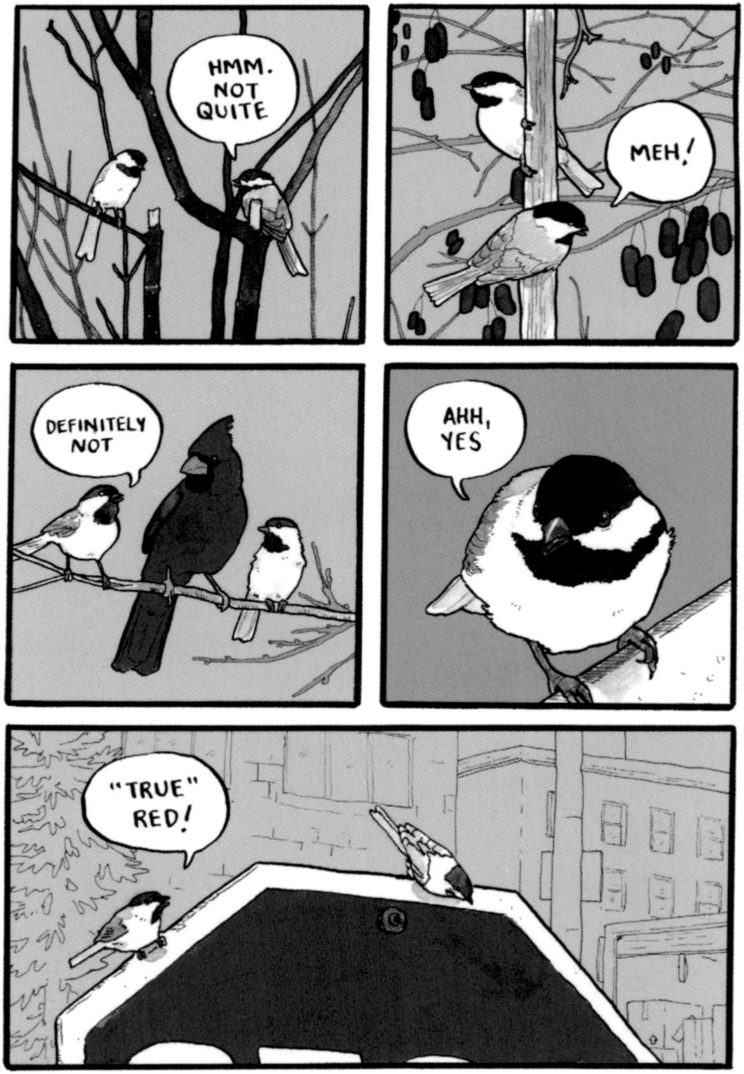
HMM. NOT QUITE
MEH!
DEFINITELY NOT
AHH, YES
"TRUE" RED!

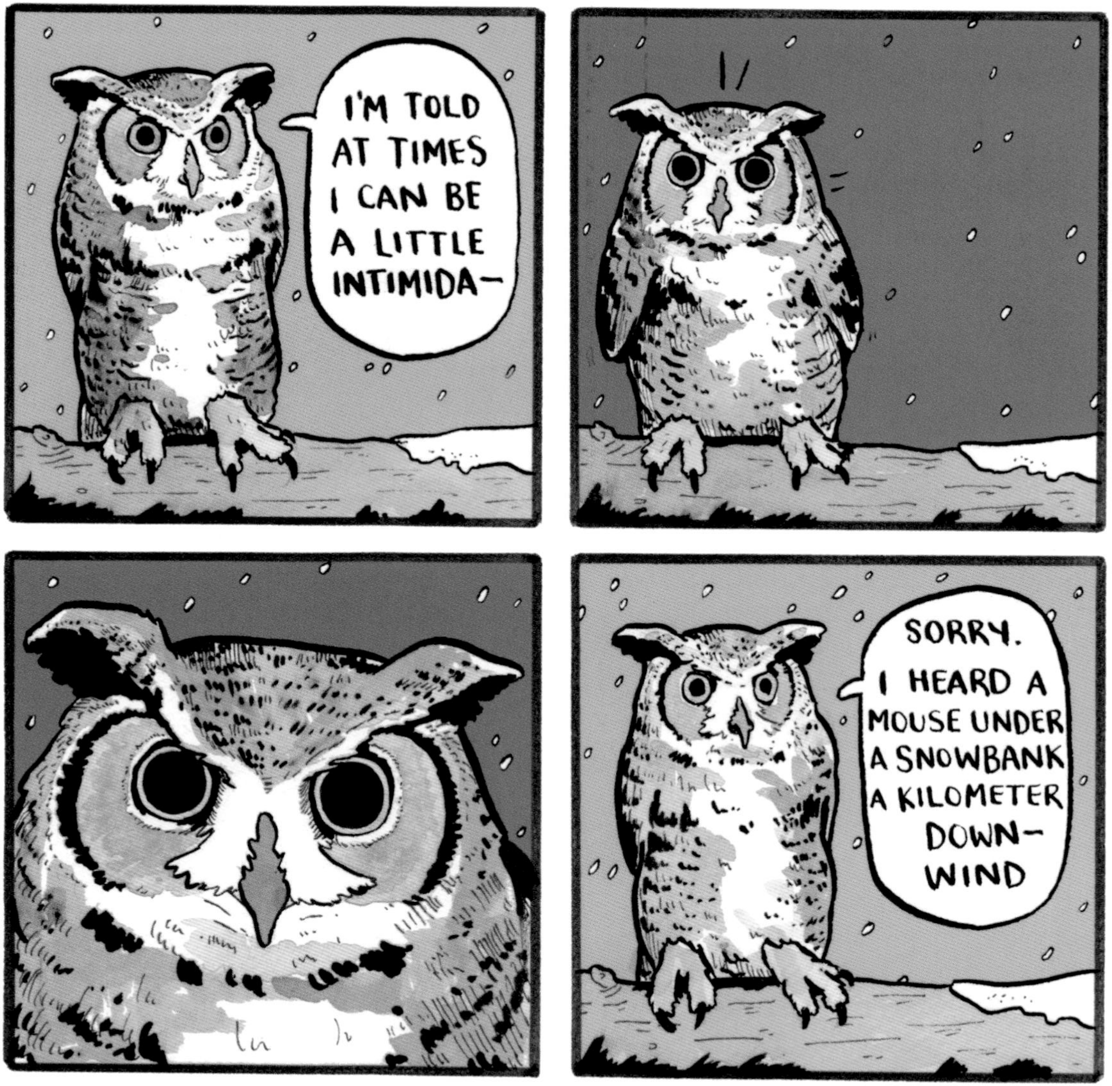
I'M TOLD AT TIMES I CAN BE A LITTLE INTIMIDA–
SORRY. I HEARD A MOUSE UNDER A SNOWBANK A KILOMETER DOWN-WIND

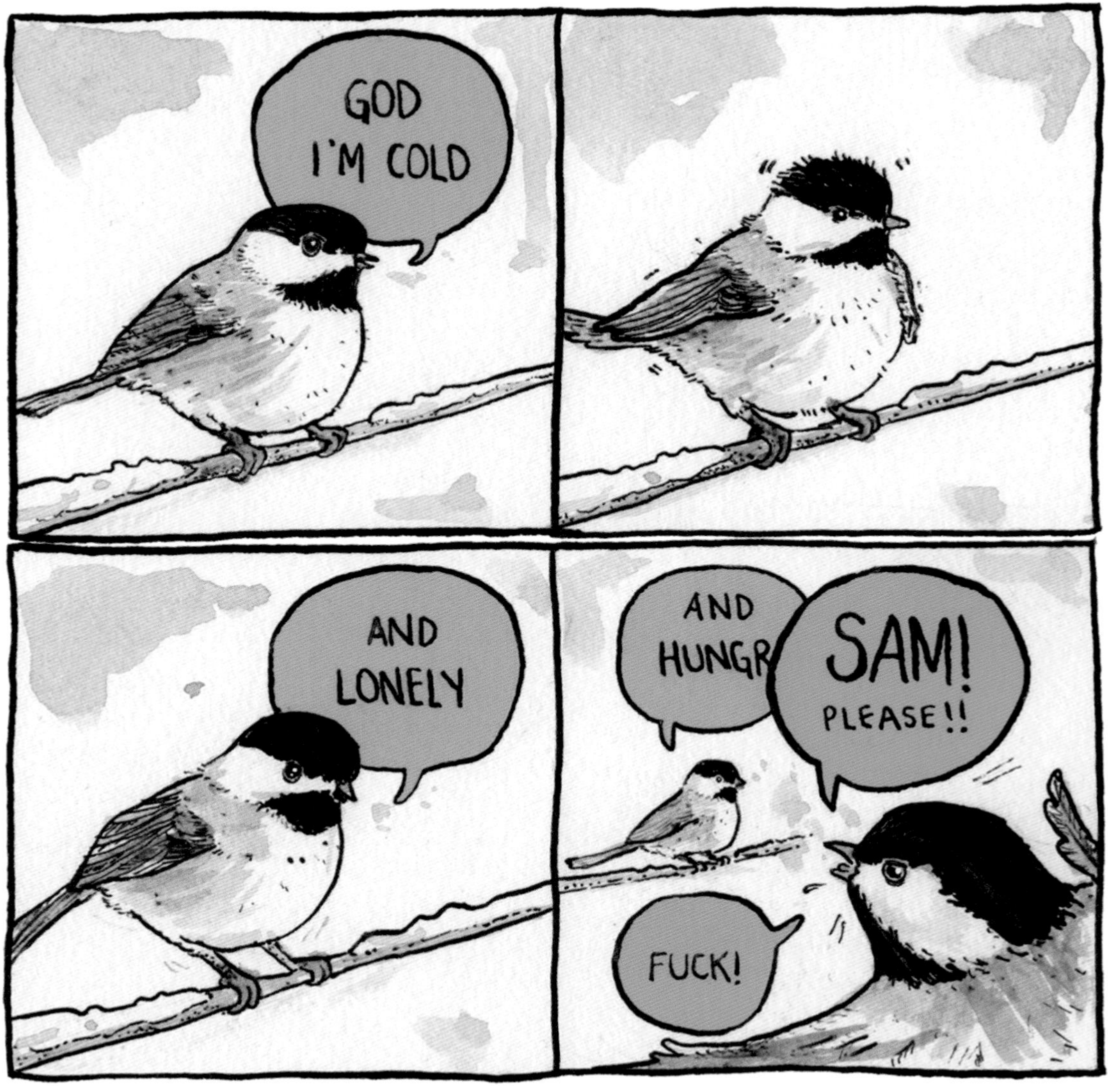
GOD I'M COLD
AND LONELY
AND HUNGR
SAM! PLEASE!!
FUCK!

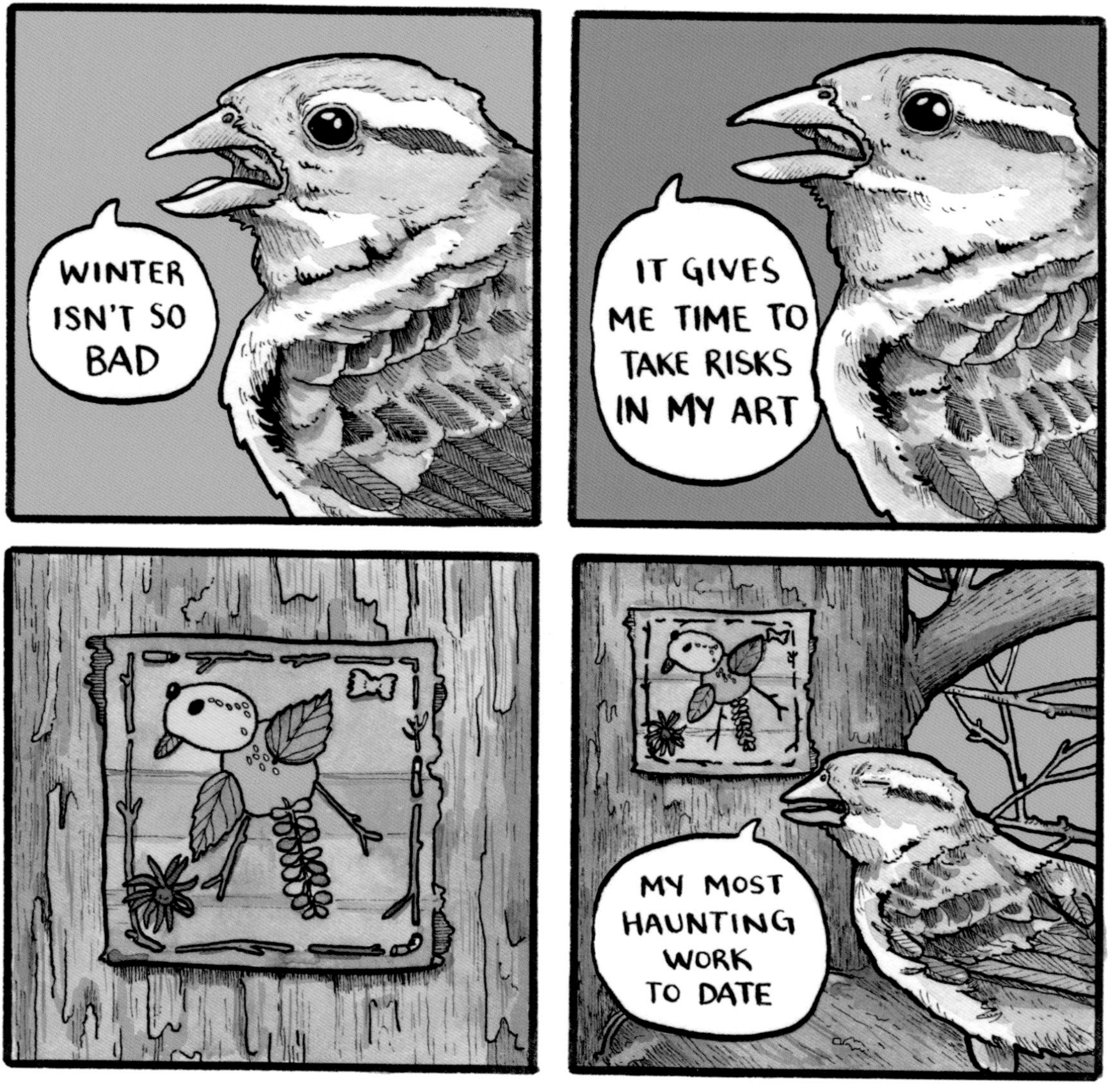
WINTER ISN'T SO BAD
IT GIVES ME TIME TO TAKE RISKS IN MY ART
MY MOST HAUNTING WORK TO DATE

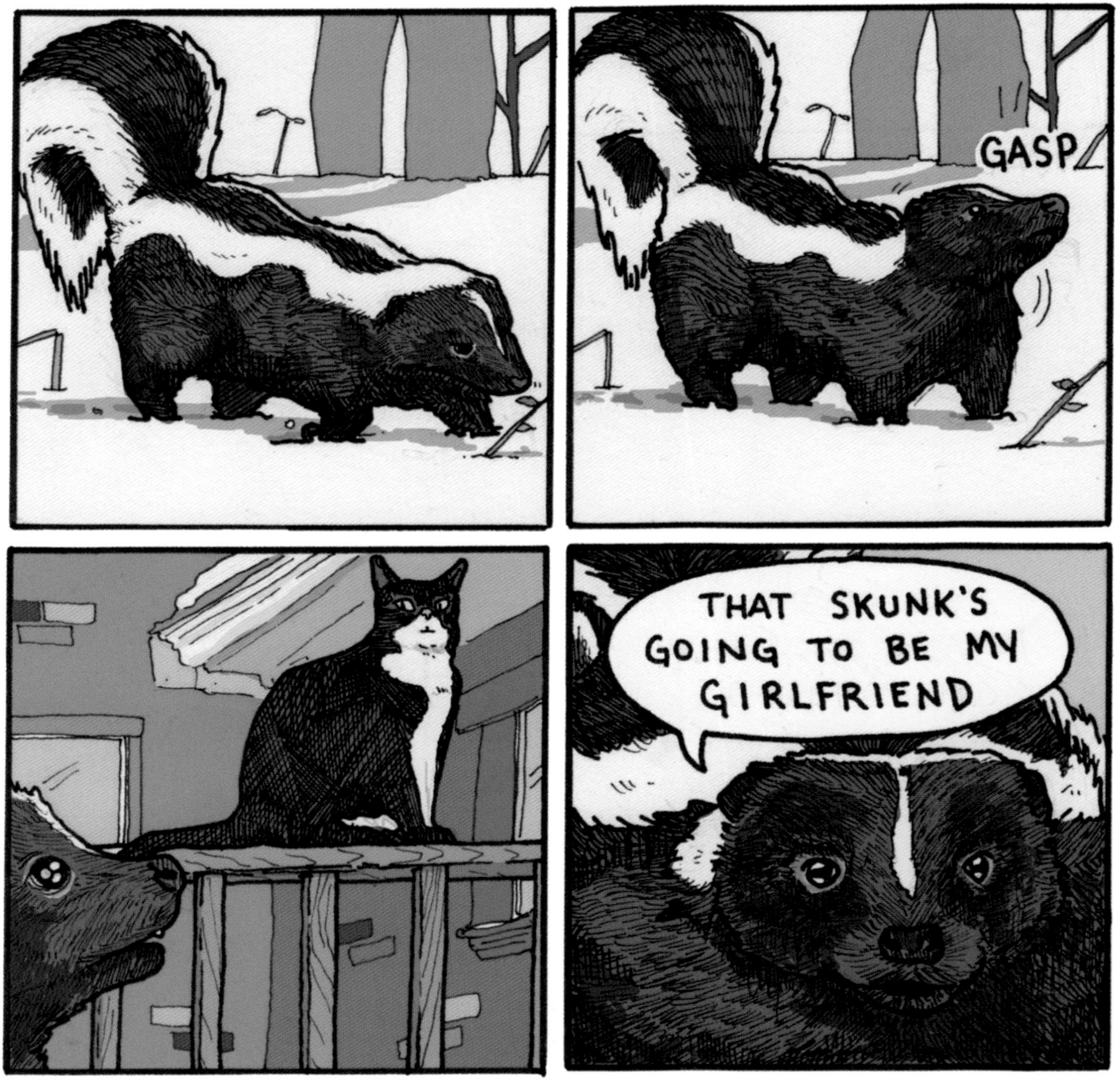
GASP
THAT SKUNK'S GOING TO BE MY GIRLFRIEND

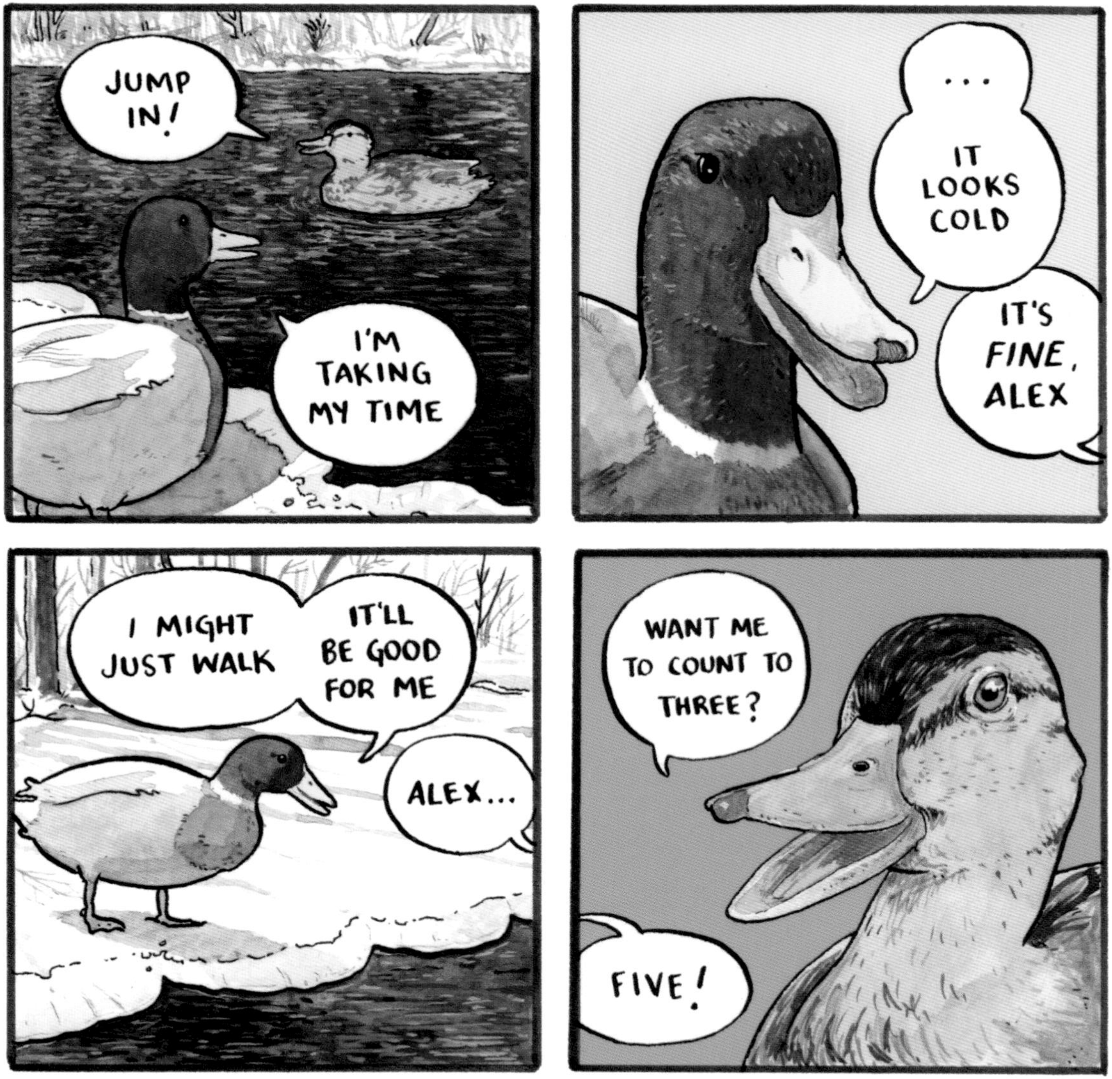
JUMP IN!
I'M TAKING MY TIME
...
IT LOOKS COLD
IT'S FINE, ALEX
I MIGHT JUST WALK
IT'LL BE GOOD FOR ME
ALEX...
WANT ME TO COUNT TO THREE?
FIVE!

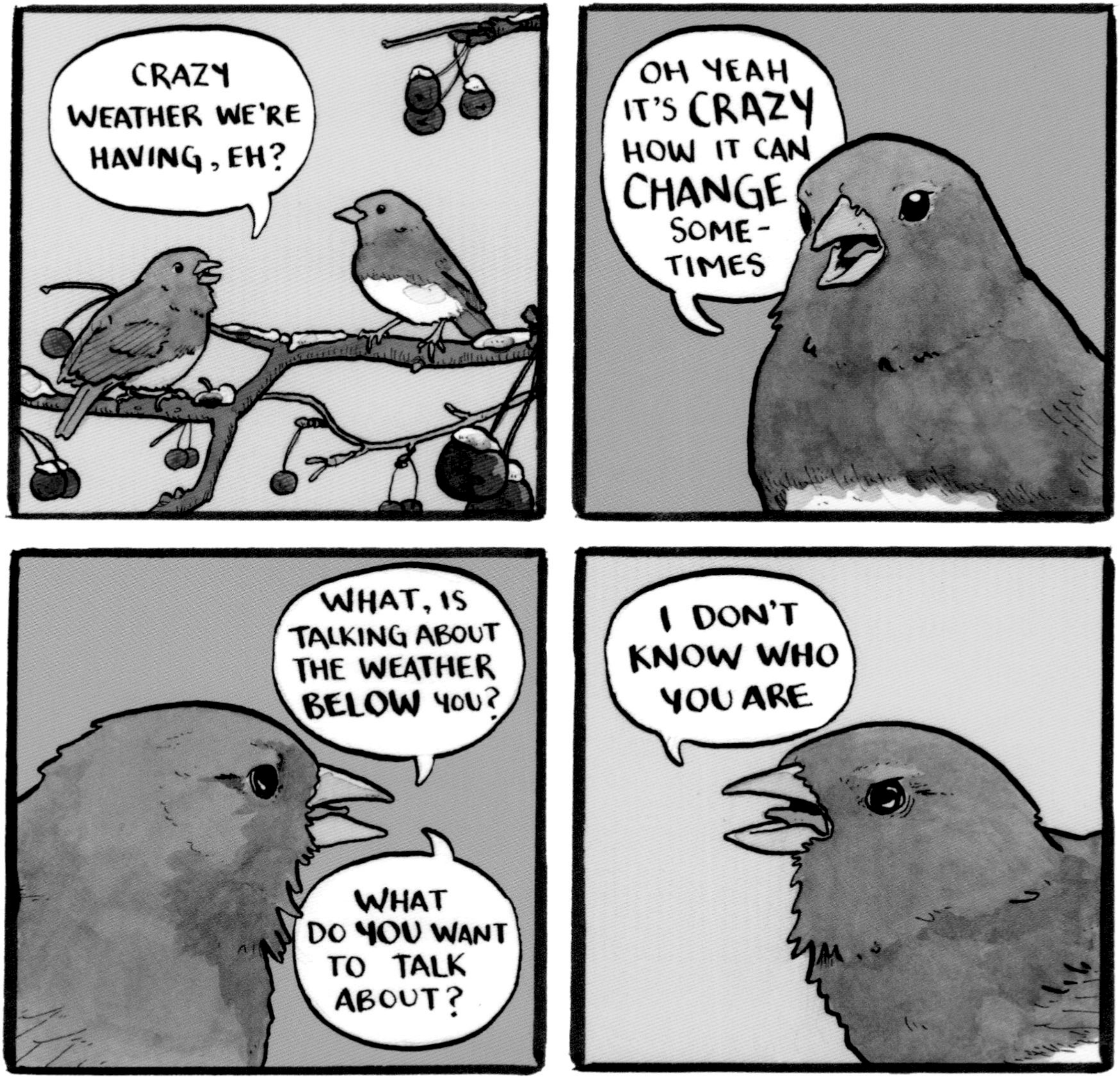
CRAZY WEATHER WE'RE HAVING, EH?
OH YEAH IT'S CRAZY HOW IT CAN CHANGE SOME-TIMES
WHAT, IS TALKING ABOUT THE WEATHER BELOW YOU?
WHAT DO YOU WANT TO TALK ABOUT?
I DON'T KNOW WHO YOU ARE

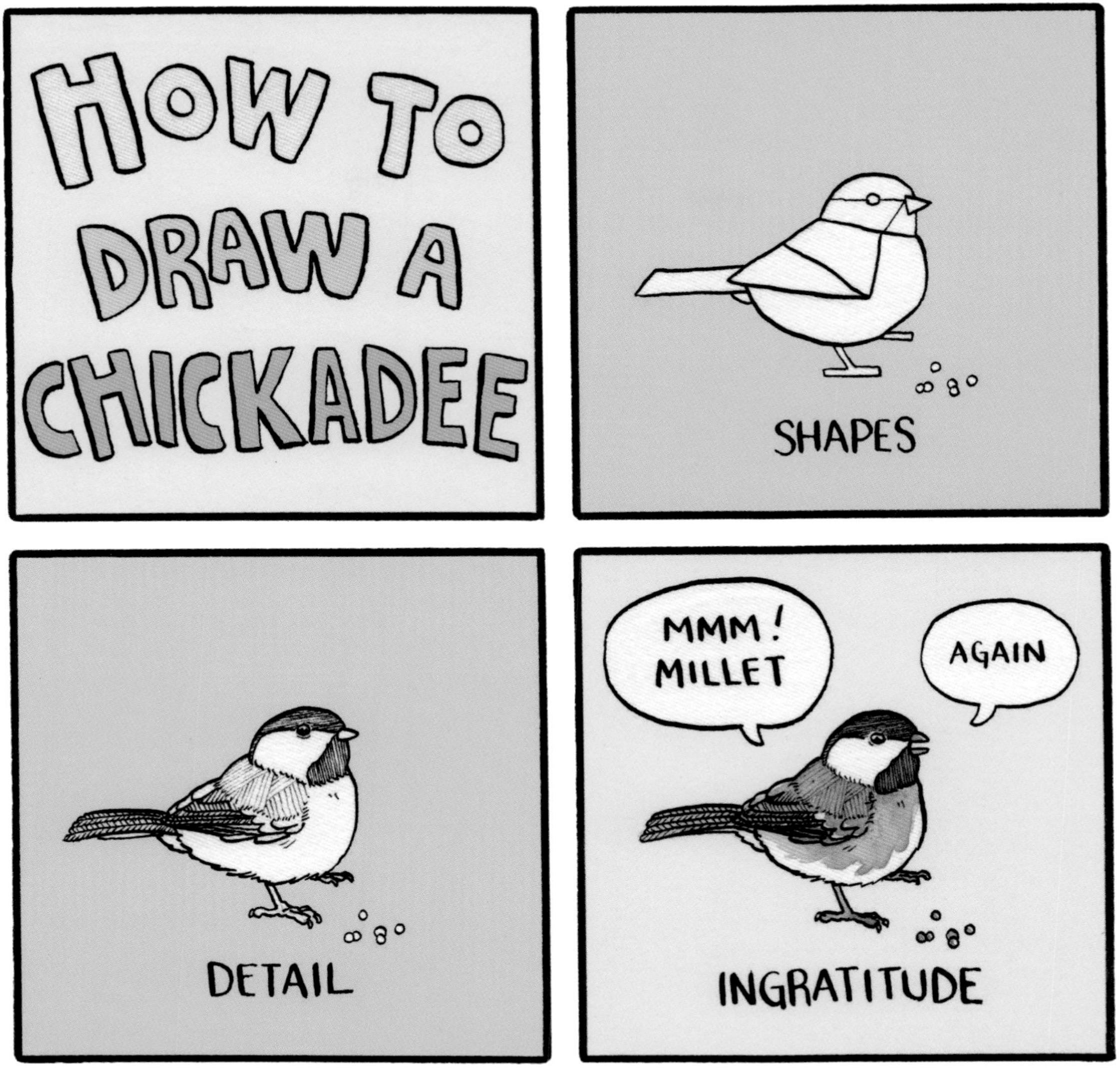
HOW TO DRAW A CHICKADEE
SHAPES
DETAIL
MMM! MILLET
AGAIN
INGRATITUDE

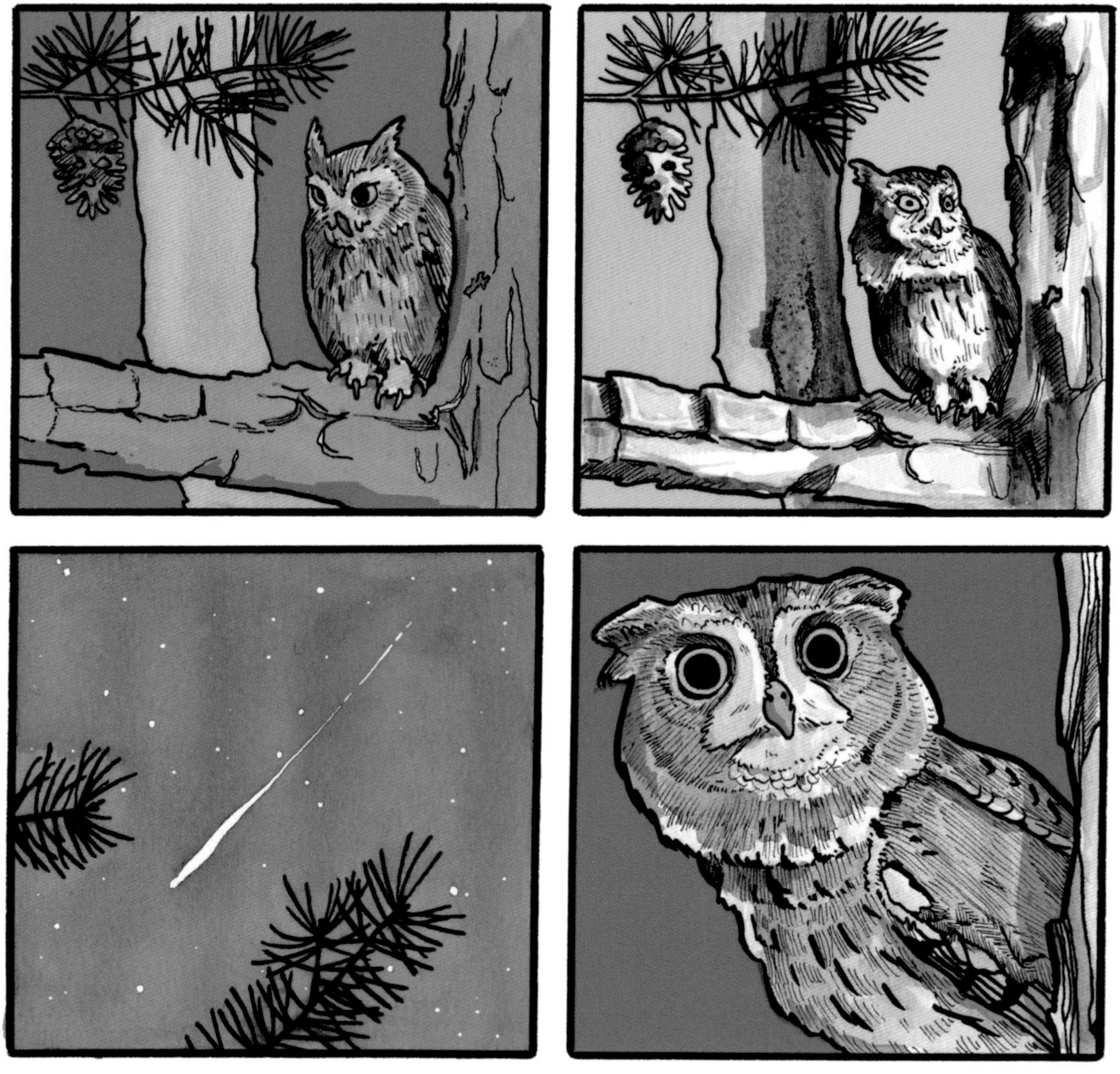

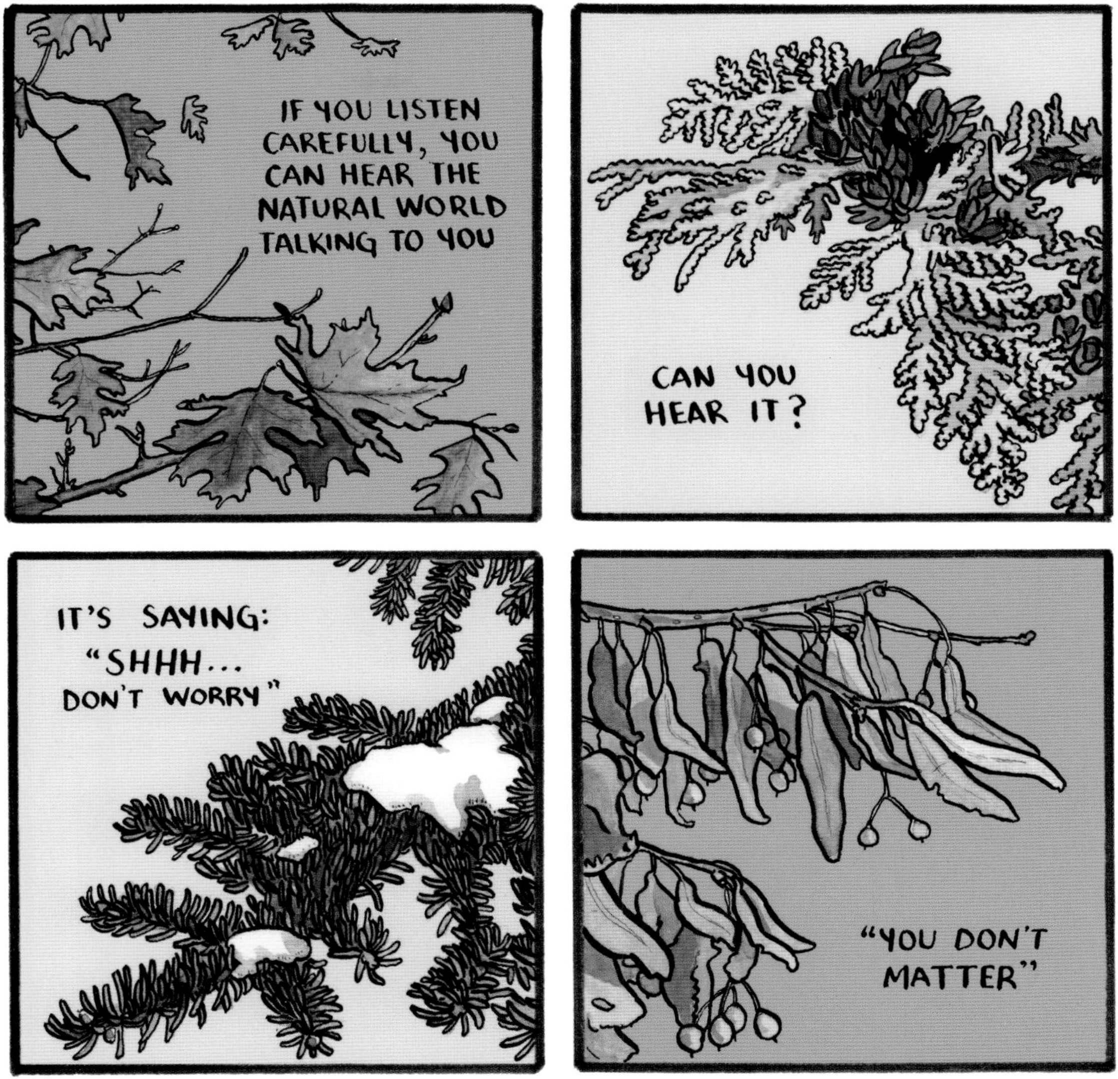
IF YOU LISTEN CAREFULLY, YOU CAN HEAR THE NATURAL WORLD TALKING TO YOU
CAN YOU HEAR IT?
IT'S SAYING:
"SHHH... DON'T WORRY"
"YOU DON'T MATTER"

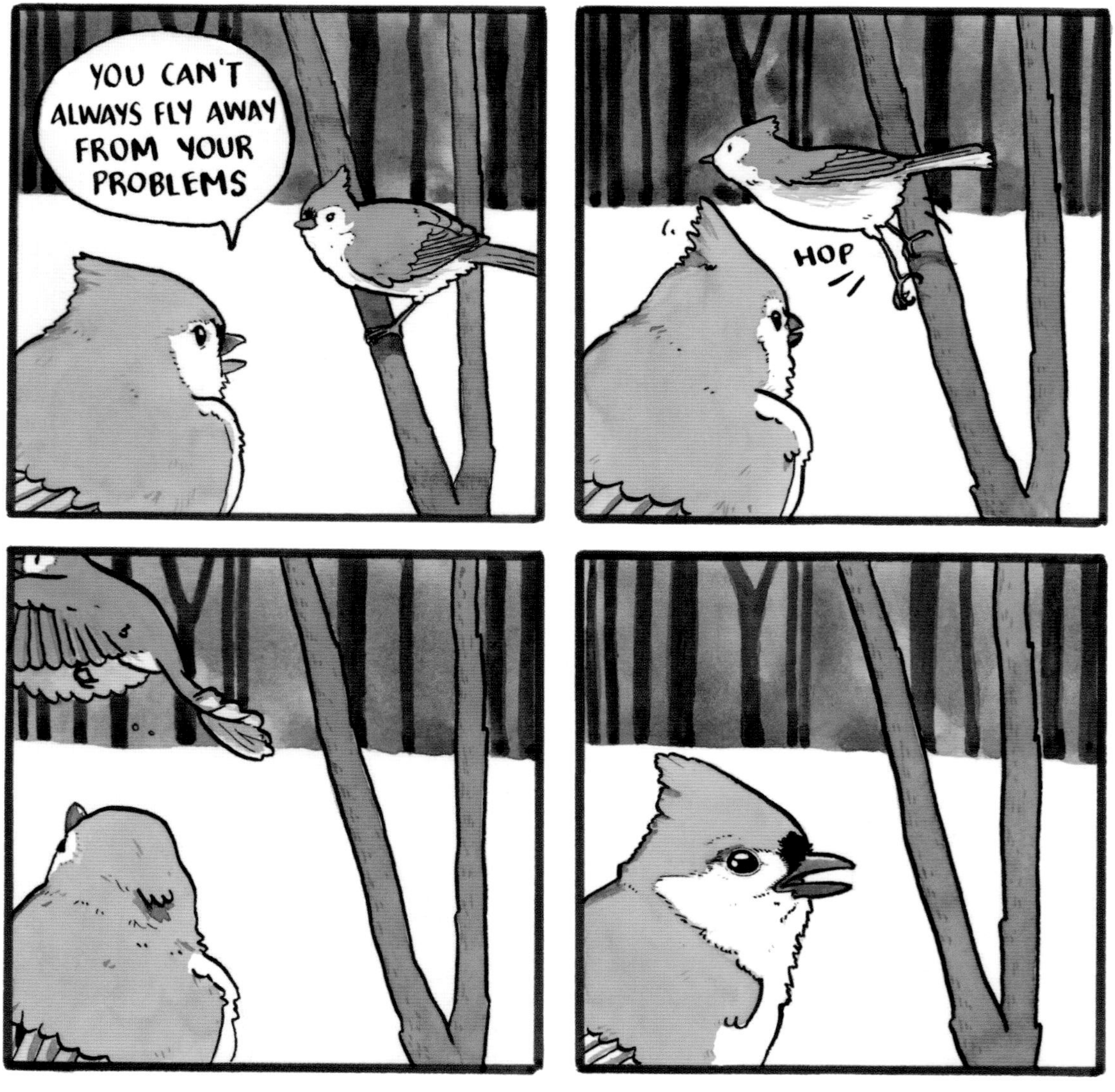
YOU CAN'T ALWAYS FLY AWAY FROM YOUR PROBLEMS
HOP

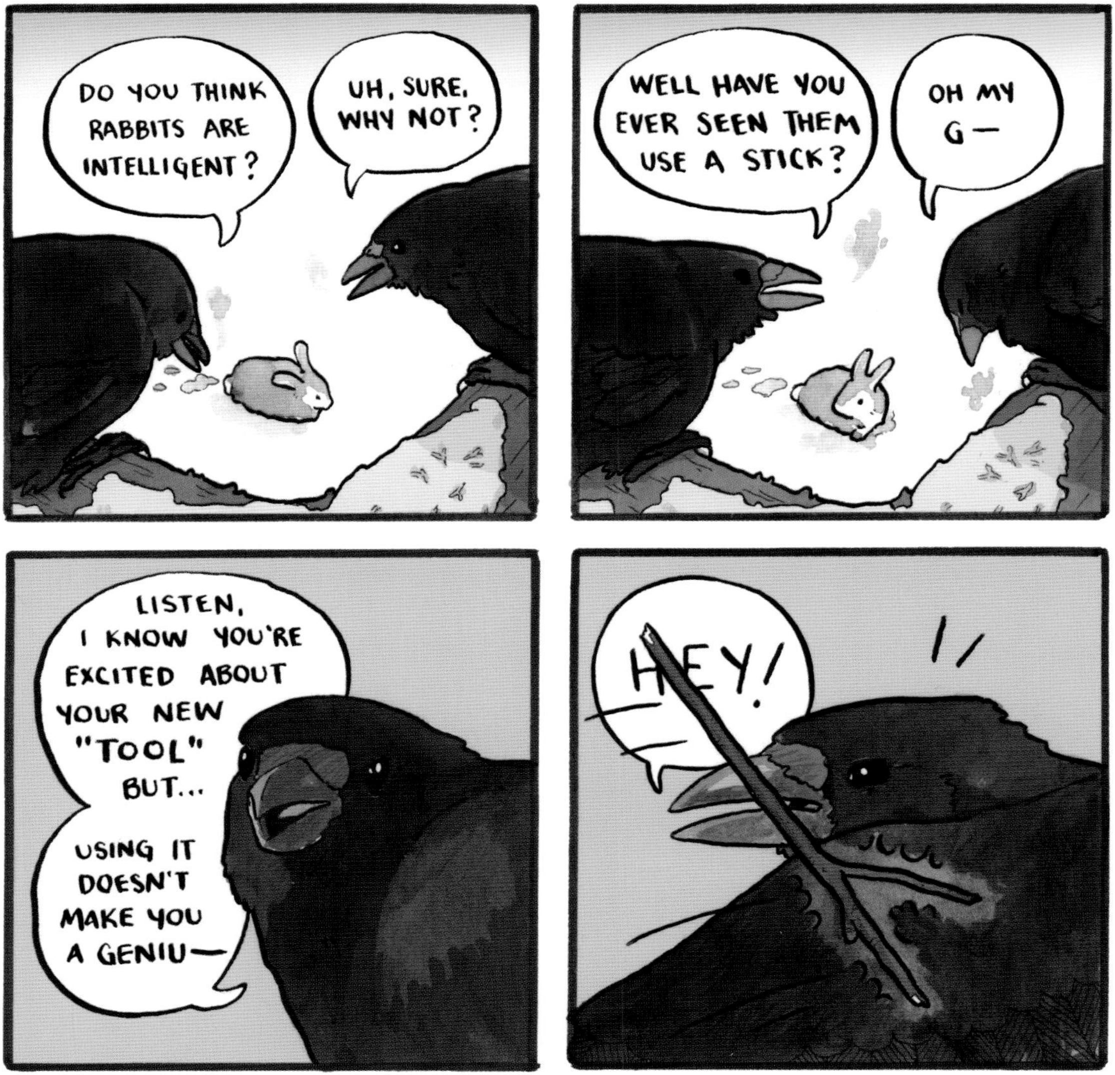
DO YOU THINK RABBITS ARE INTELLIGENT?
UH, SURE, WHY NOT?
WELL HAVE YOU EVER SEEN THEM USE A STICK?
OH MY G—
LISTEN, I KNOW YOU'RE EXCITED ABOUT YOUR NEW "TOOL" BUT...
USING IT DOESN'T MAKE YOU A GENIU—
HEY!

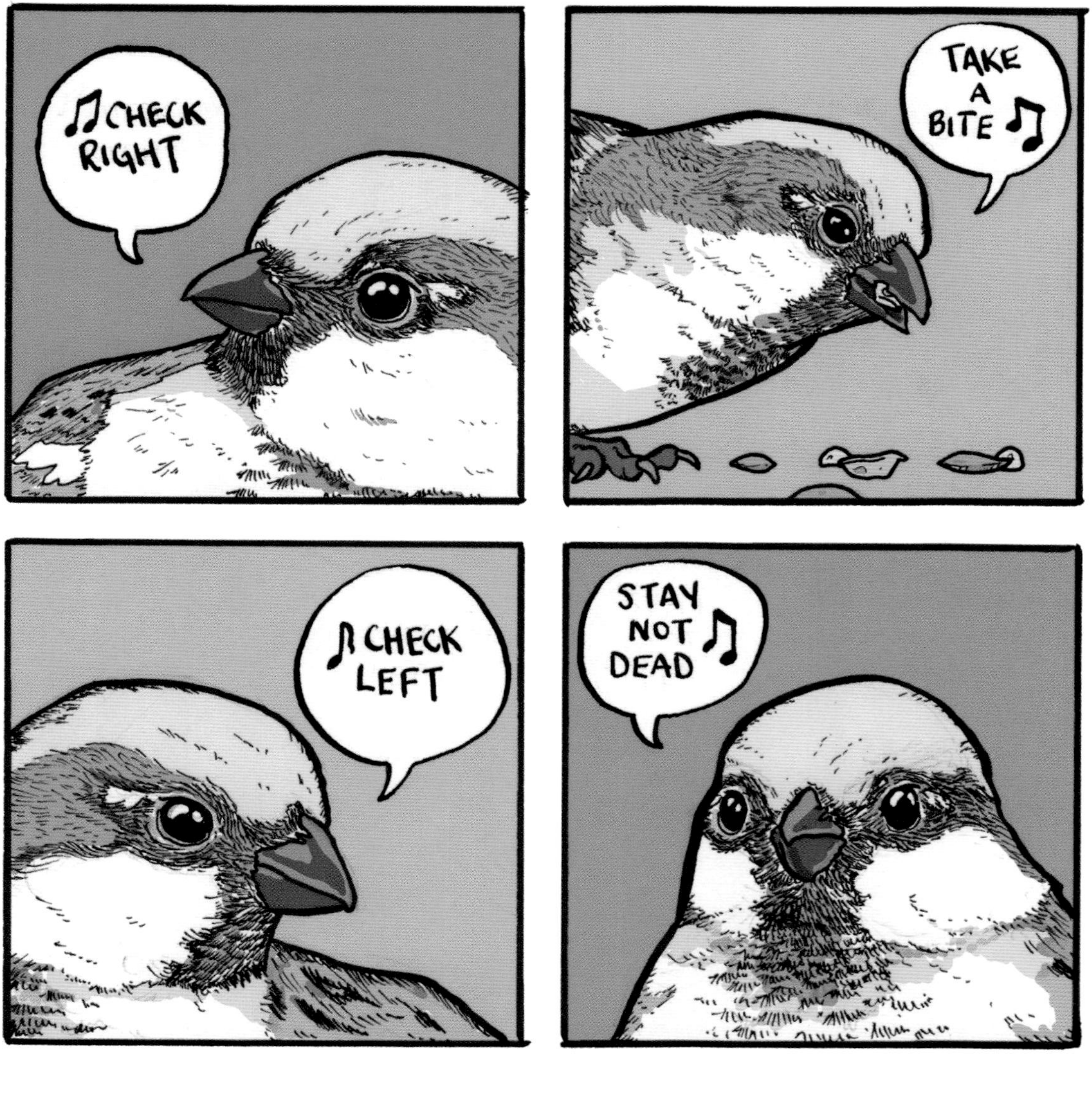
♫ CHECK RIGHT
TAKE A BITE ♫
♫ CHECK LEFT
STAY NOT DEAD ♫

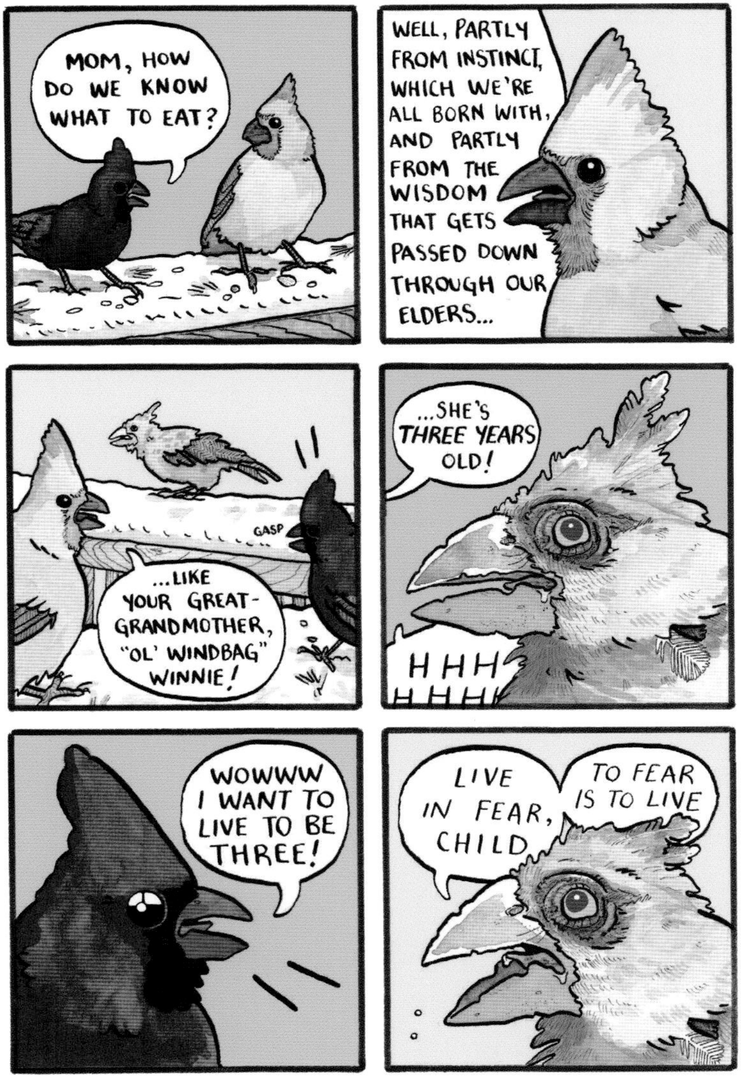
MOM, HOW DO WE KNOW WHAT TO EAT?
WELL, PARTLY FROM INSTINCT, WHICH WE'RE ALL BORN WITH, AND PARTLY FROM THE WISDOM THAT GETS PASSED DOWN THROUGH OUR ELDERS...
...LIKE YOUR GREAT-GRANDMOTHER, "OL' WINDBAG" WINNIE!
GASP
...SHE'S THREE YEARS OLD!
HHH HHH
WOWWW I WANT TO LIVE TO BE THREE!
LIVE IN FEAR, CHILD
TO FEAR IS TO LIVE

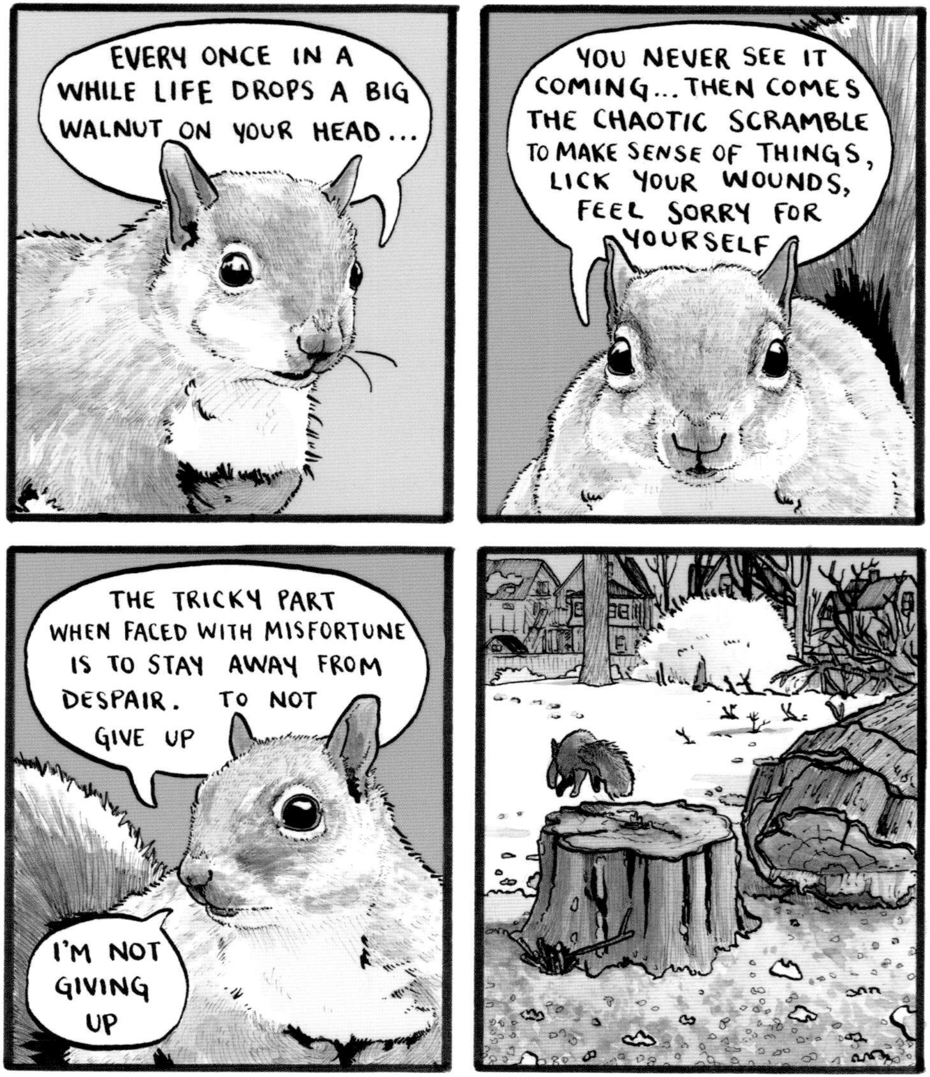
EVERY ONCE IN A WHILE LIFE DROPS A BIG WALNUT ON YOUR HEAD...
YOU NEVER SEE IT COMING... THEN COMES THE CHAOTIC SCRAMBLE TO MAKE SENSE OF THINGS, LICK YOUR WOUNDS, FEEL SORRY FOR YOURSELF
THE TRICKY PART WHEN FACED WITH MISFORTUNE IS TO STAY AWAY FROM DESPAIR. TO NOT GIVE UP
I'M NOT GIVING UP

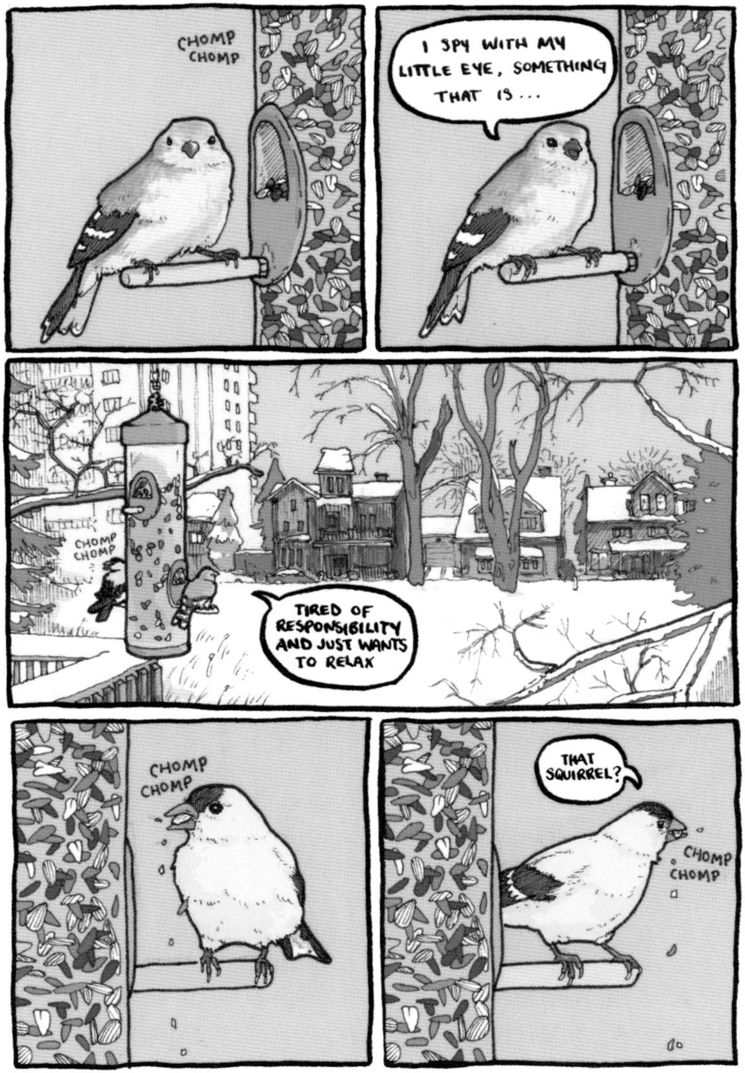
CHOMP CHOMP
I SPY WITH MY LITTLE EYE, SOMETHING THAT IS...
CHOMP CHOMP
TIRED OF RESPONSIBILITY AND JUST WANTS TO RELAX
CHOMP CHOMP
THAT SQUIRREL?
CHOMP CHOMP

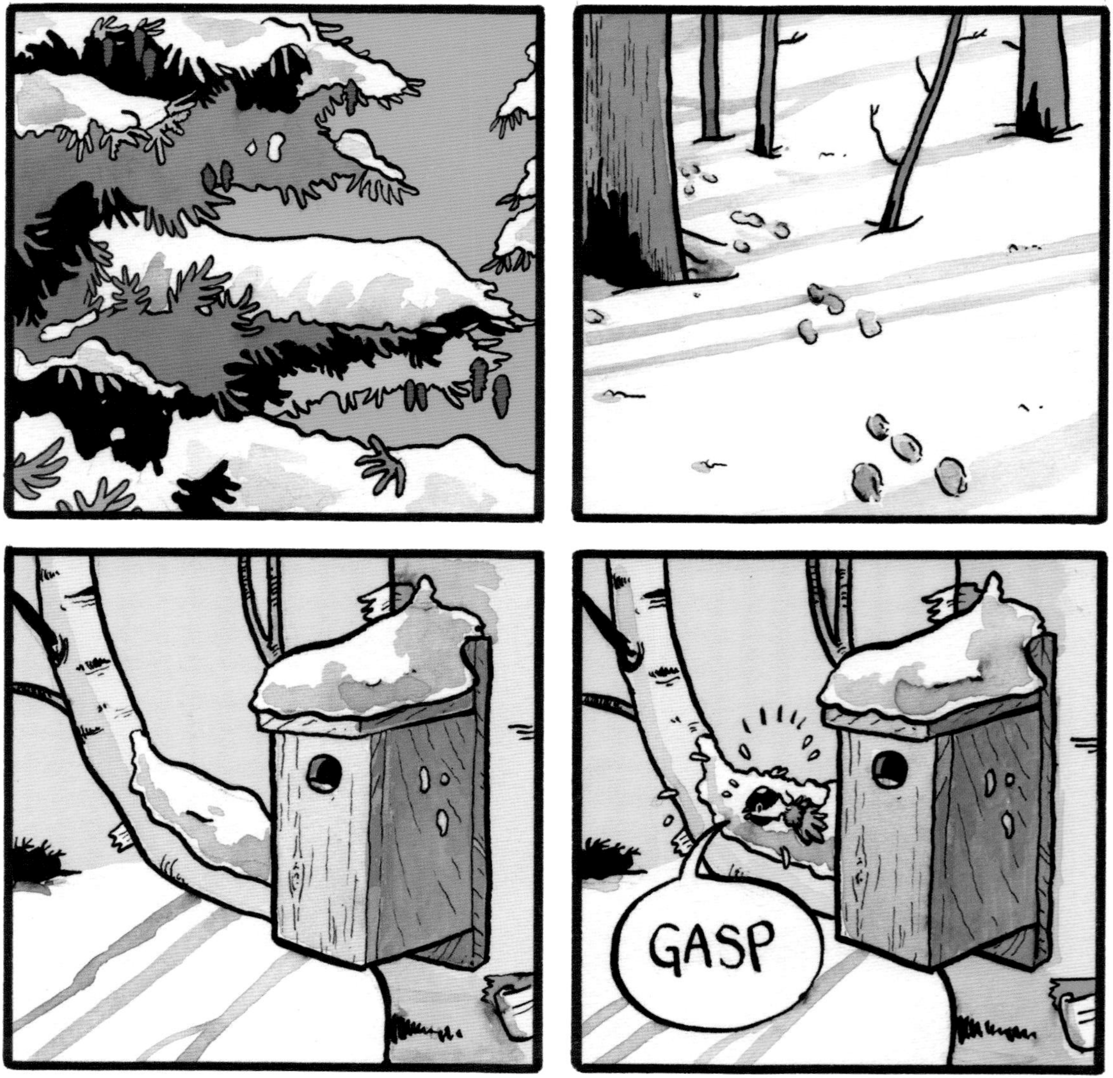
GASP

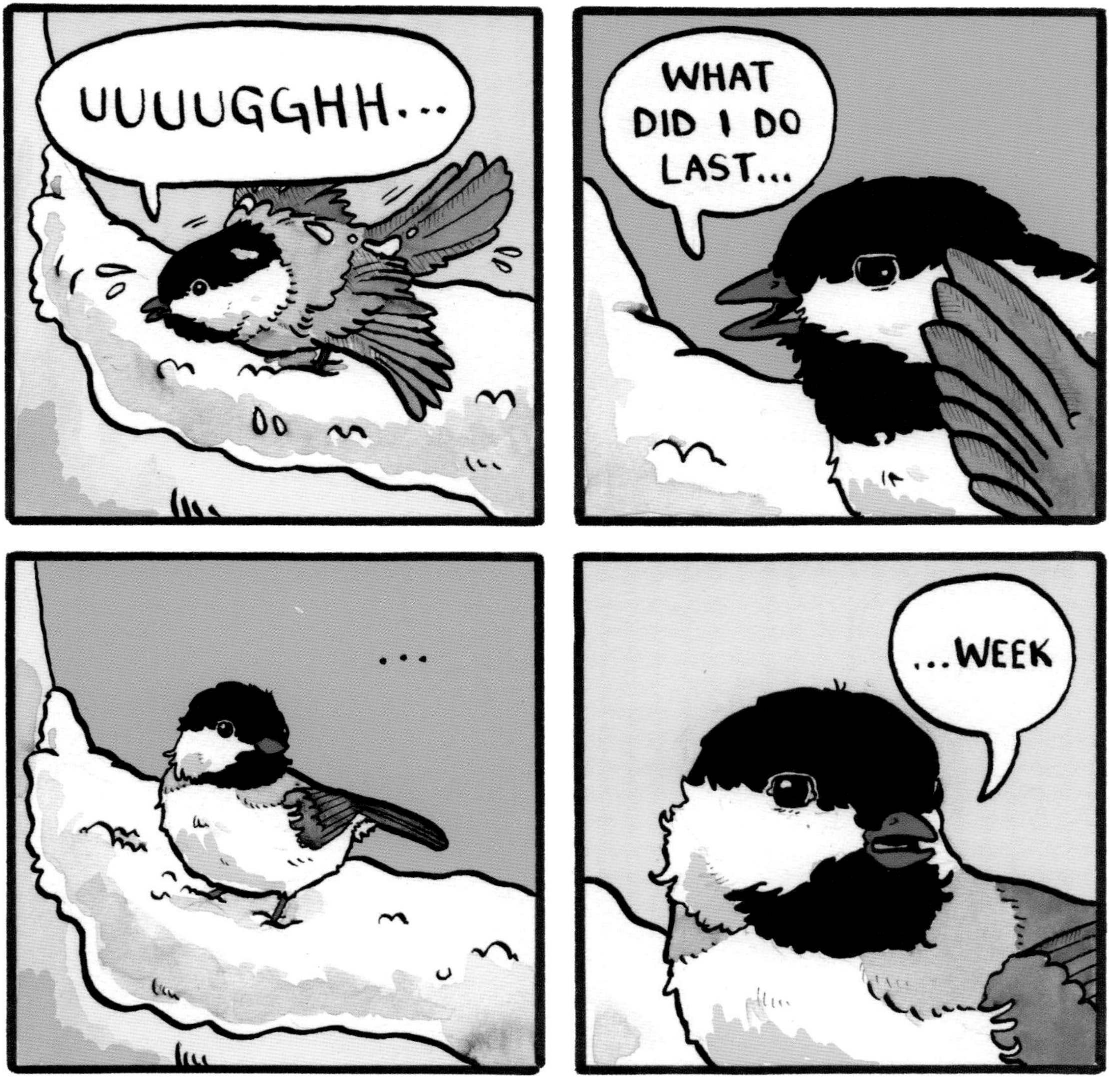
UUUUGGHH...
WHAT DID I DO LAST...
...
...WEEK

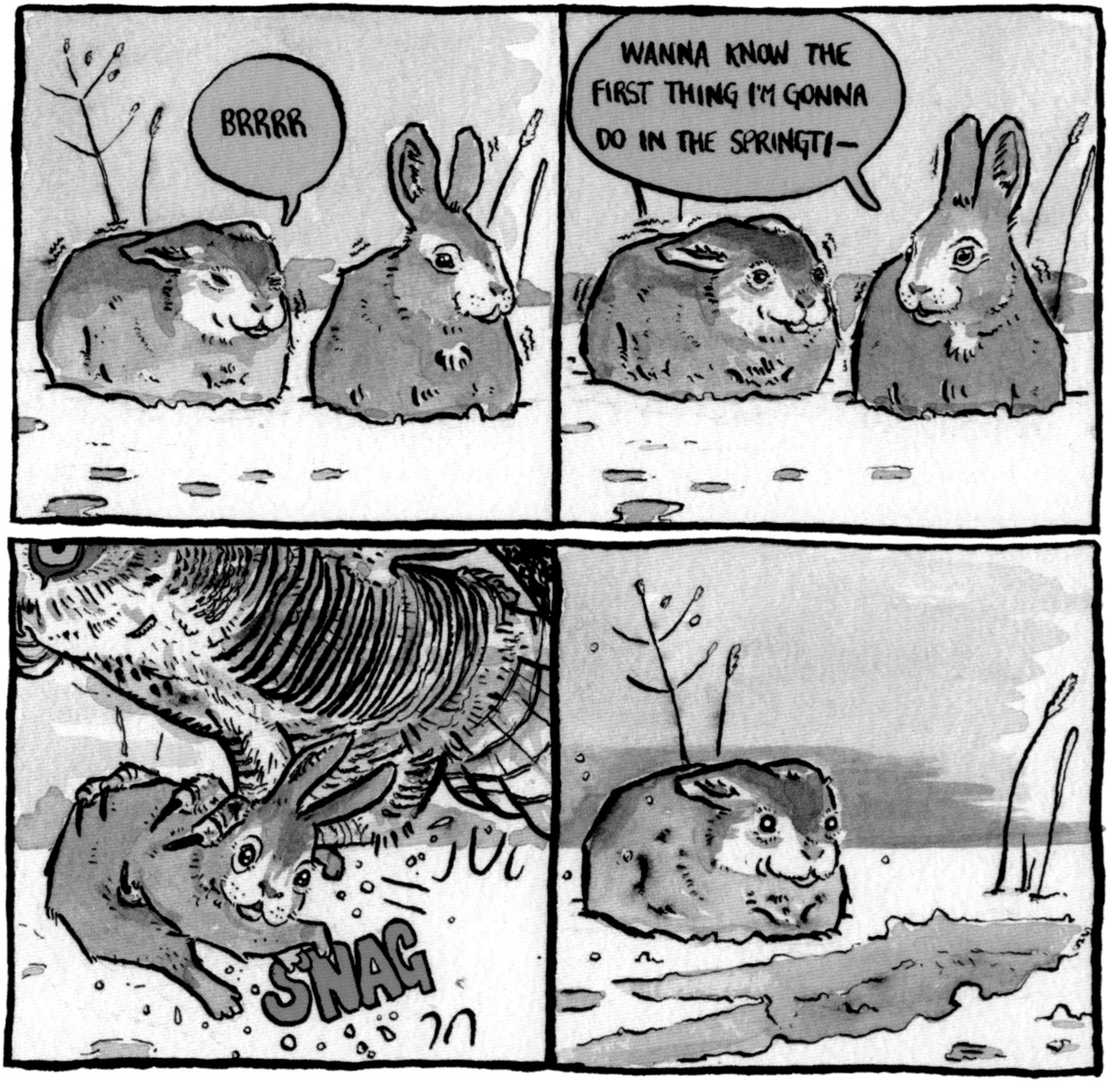
BRRRR
WANNA KNOW THE FIRST THING I'M GONNA DO IN THE SPRINGTI—
SNAG

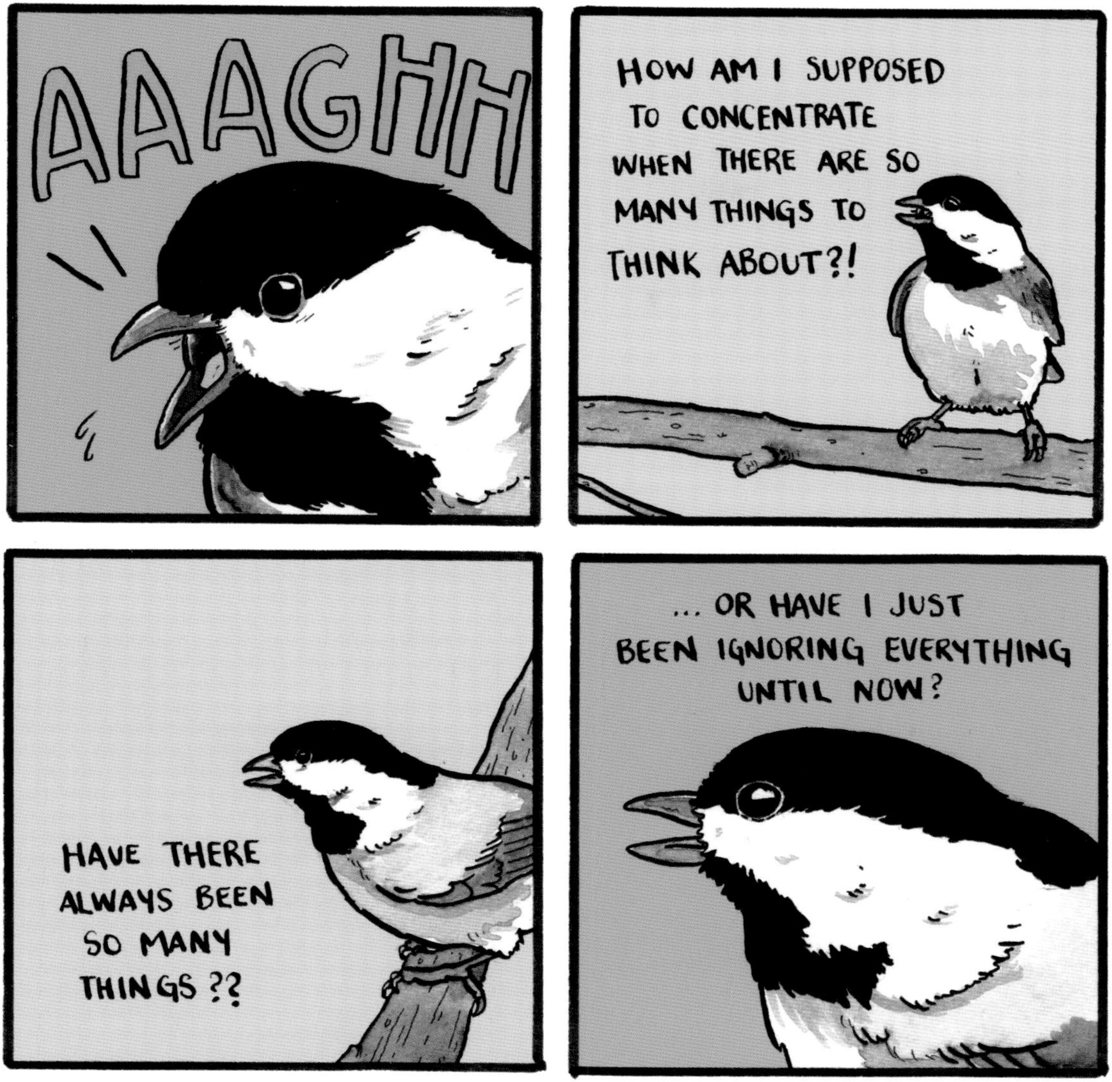
AAAGHH
HOW AM I SUPPOSED TO CONCENTRATE WHEN THERE ARE SO MANY THINGS TO THINK ABOUT?!
HAVE THERE ALWAYS BEEN SO MANY THINGS??
... OR HAVE I JUST BEEN IGNORING EVERYTHING UNTIL NOW?

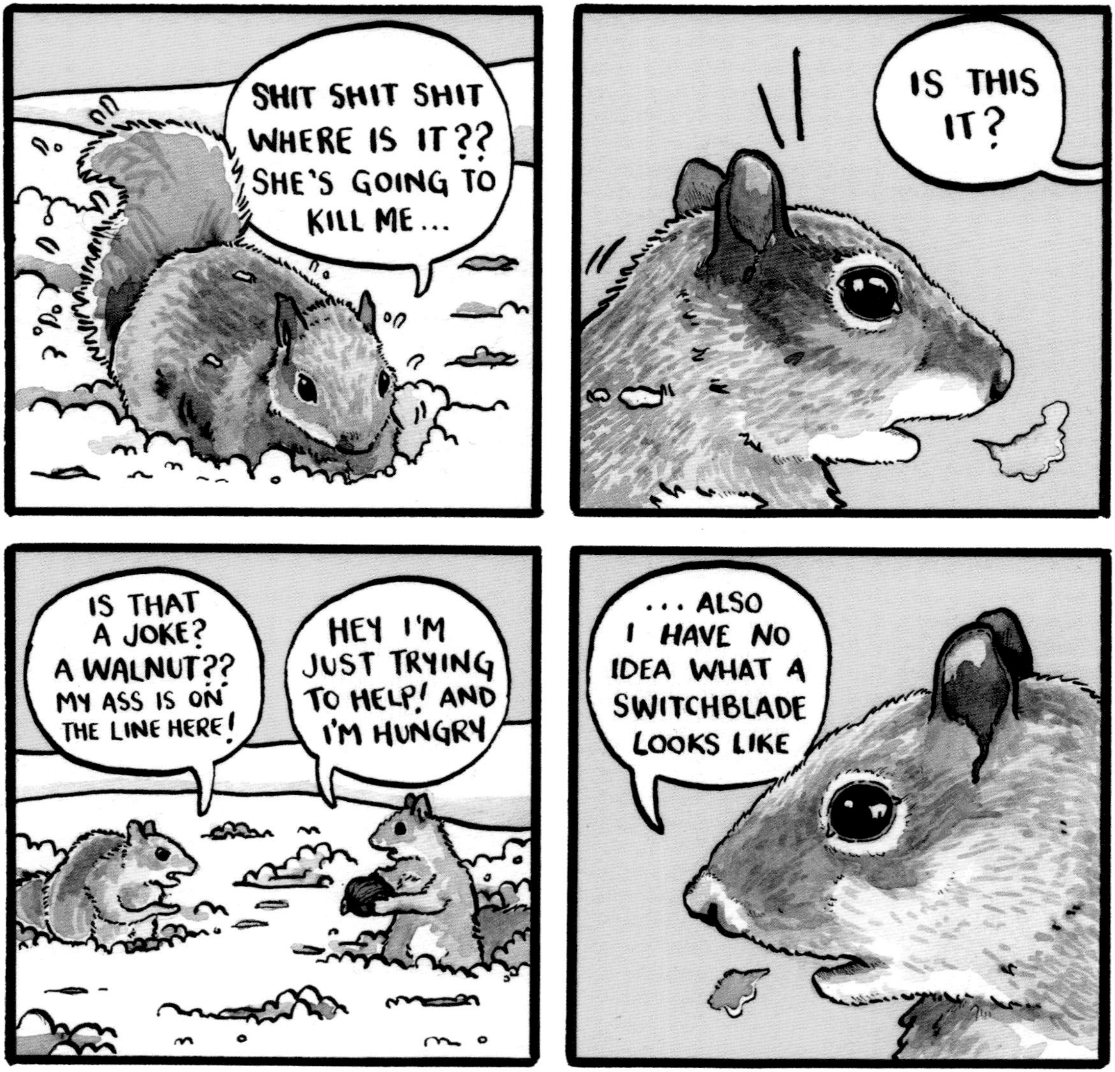
SHIT SHIT SHIT WHERE IS IT?? SHE'S GOING TO KILL ME...
IS THIS IT?
IS THAT A JOKE? A WALNUT?? MY ASS IS ON THE LINE HERE!
HEY I'M JUST TRYING TO HELP! AND I'M HUNGRY
... ALSO I HAVE NO IDEA WHAT A SWITCHBLADE LOOKS LIKE

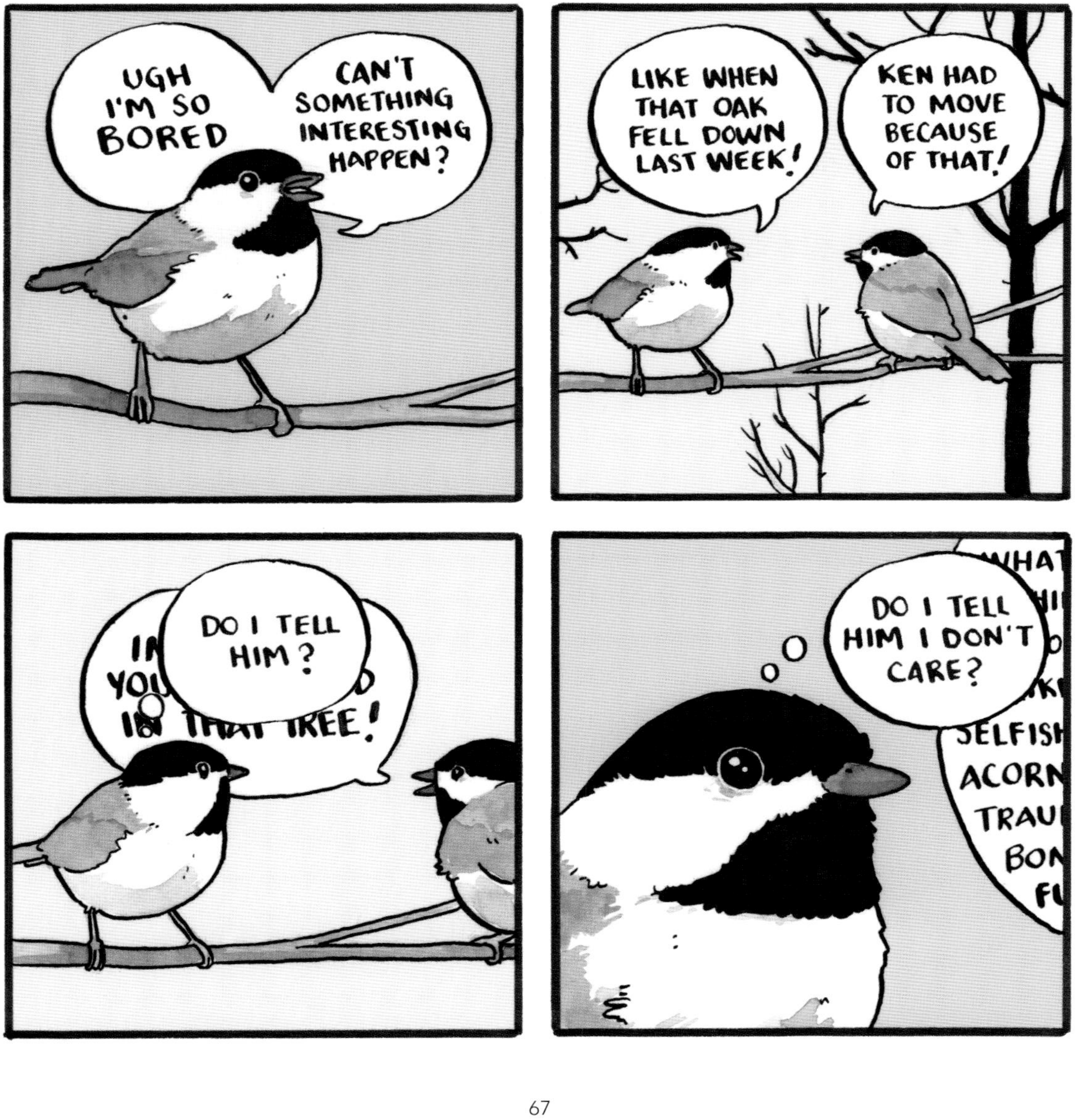
UGH I'M SO BORED
CAN'T SOMETHING INTERESTING HAPPEN?
LIKE WHEN THAT OAK FELL DOWN LAST WEEK!
KEN HAD TO MOVE BECAUSE OF THAT!
DO I TELL HIM?
DO I TELL HIM I DON'T CARE?

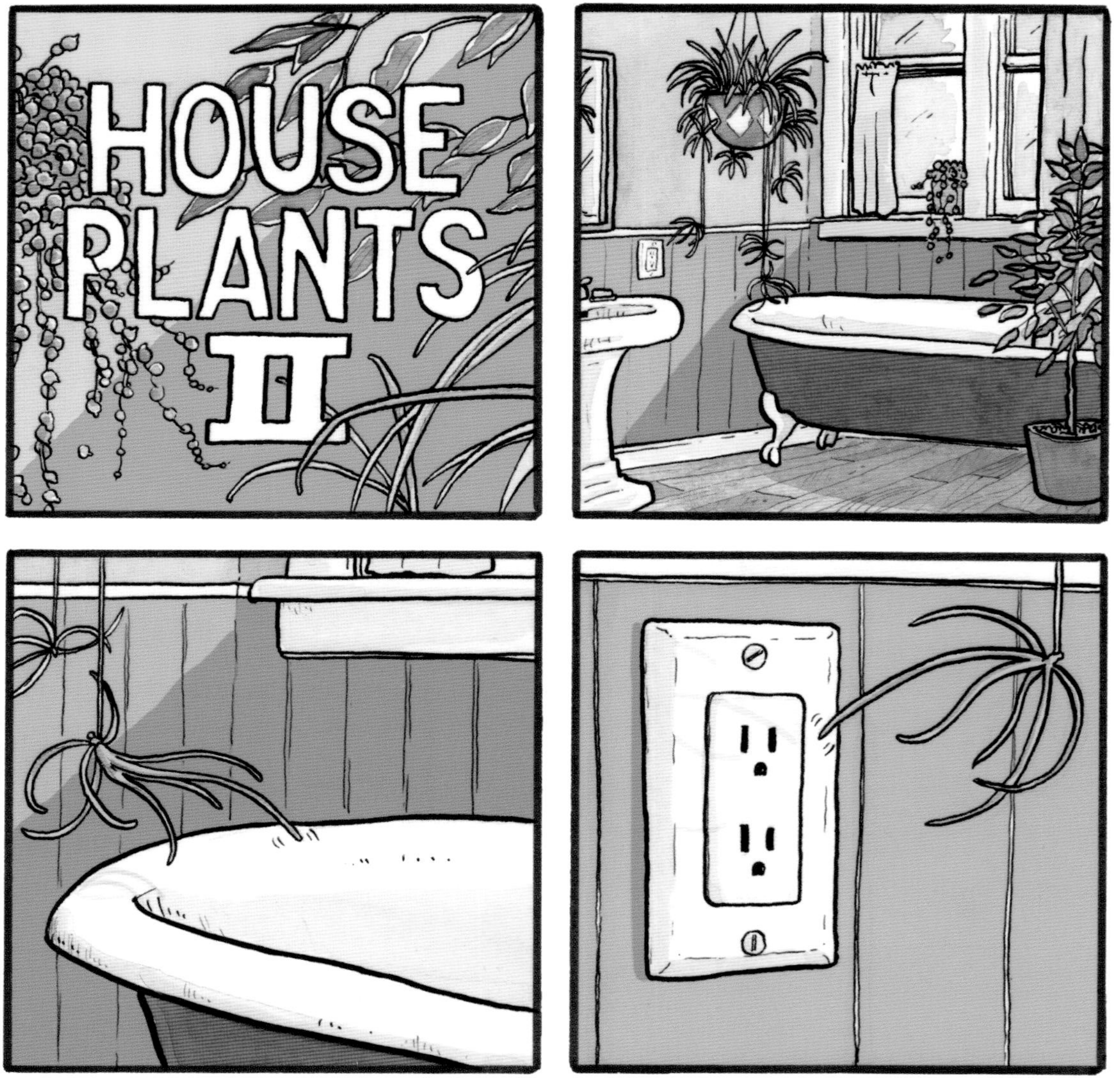
HOUSE
PLANTS
II

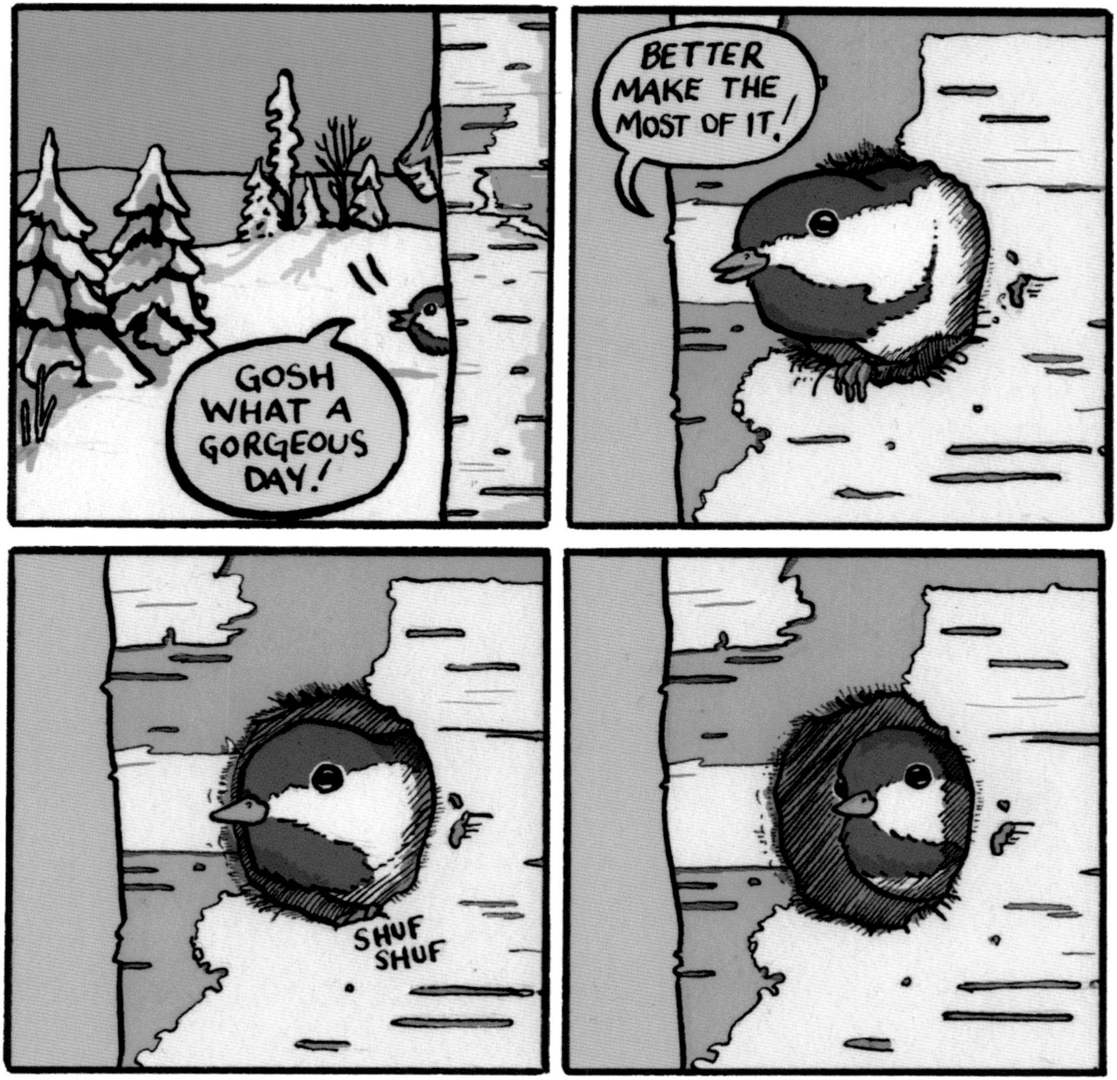
GOSH WHAT A GORGEOUS DAY!
BETTER MAKE THE MOST OF IT!
SHUF SHUF

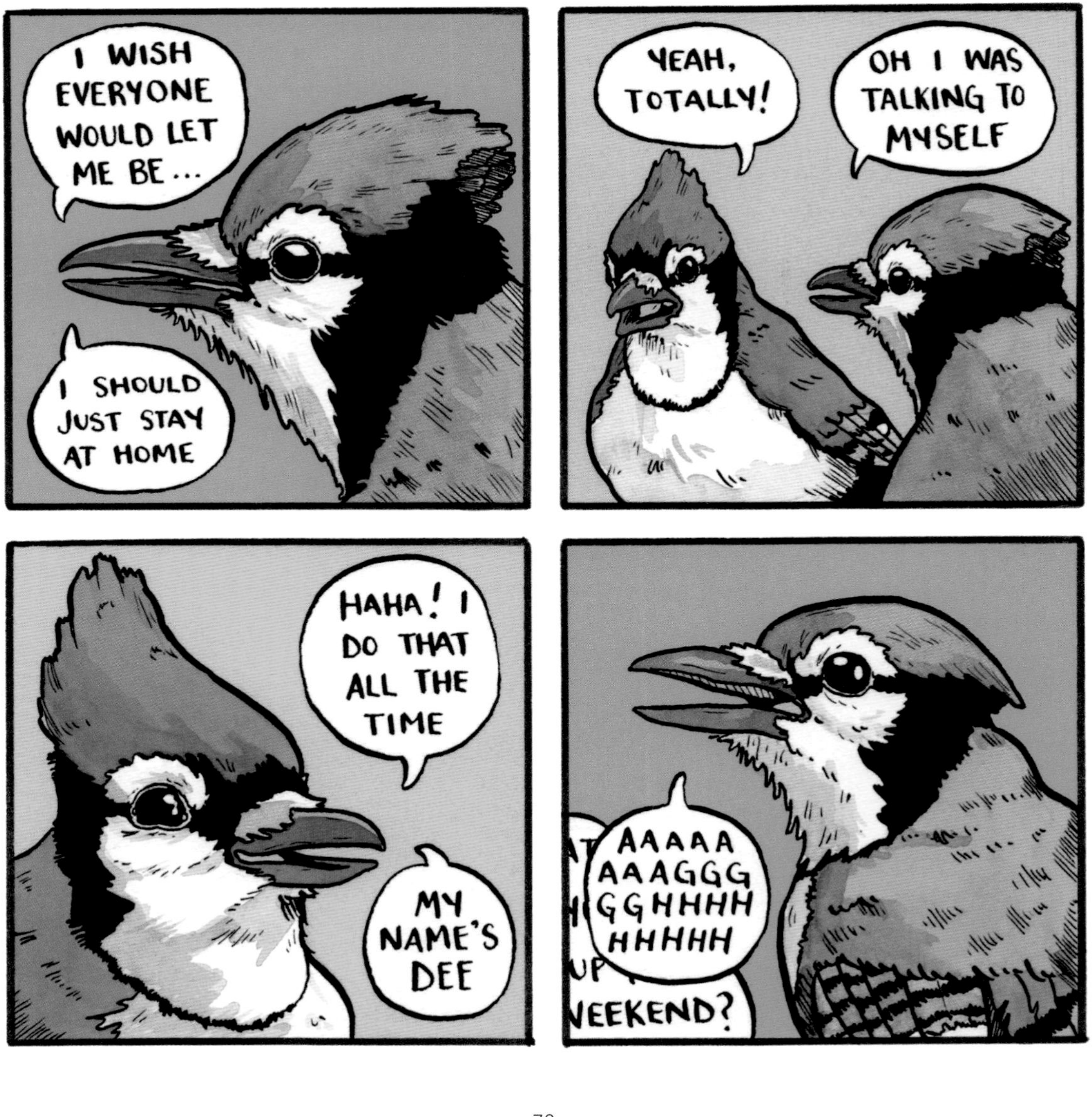
I WISH EVERYONE WOULD LET ME BE...
I SHOULD JUST STAY AT HOME
YEAH, TOTALLY!
OH I WAS TALKING TO MYSELF
HAHA! I DO THAT ALL THE TIME
MY NAME'S DEE
AAAAA AAAGGG GGHHHH HHHHH

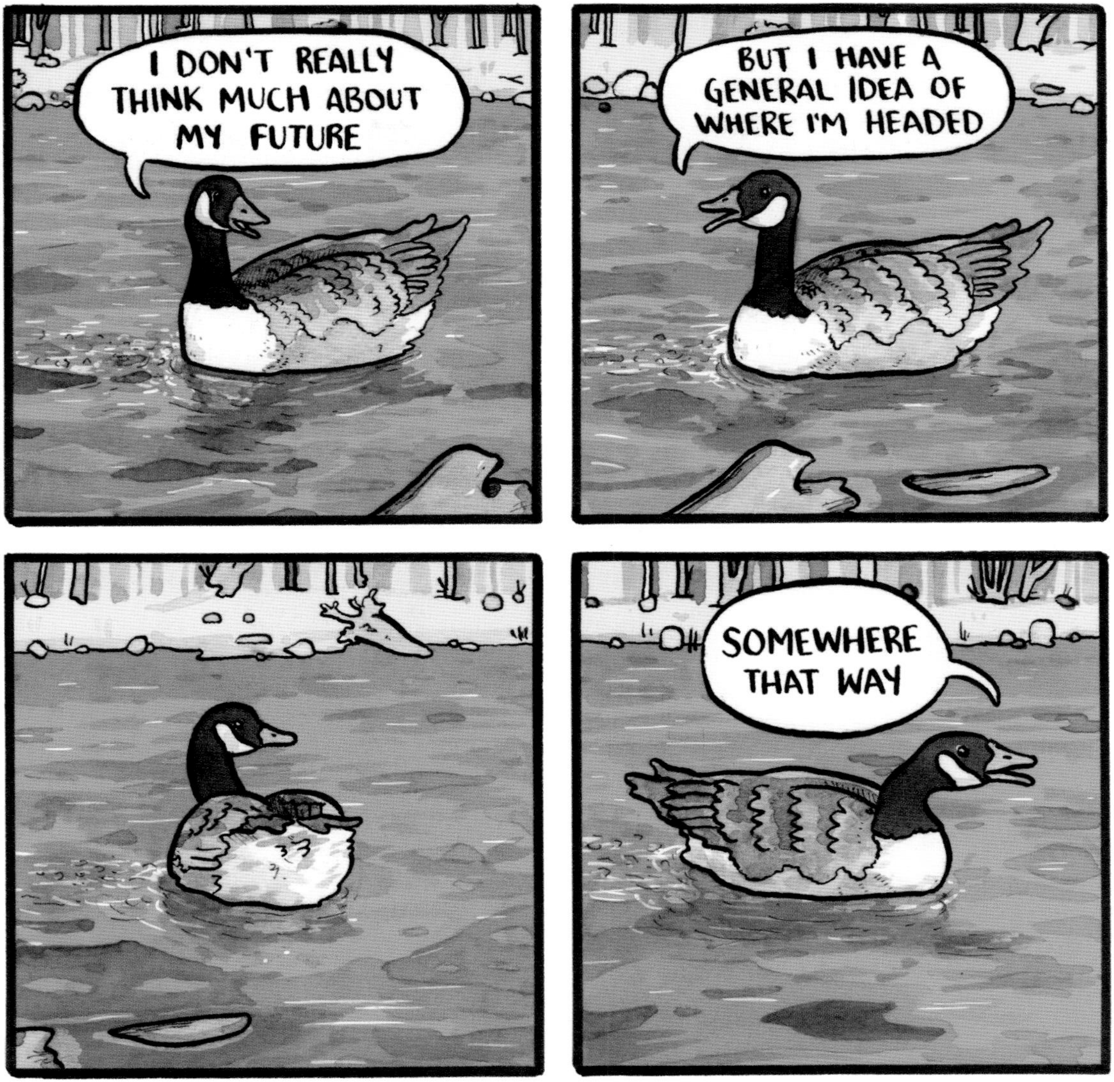
I DON'T REALLY THINK MUCH ABOUT MY FUTURE
BUT I HAVE A GENERAL IDEA OF WHERE I'M HEADED
SOMEWHERE THAT WAY

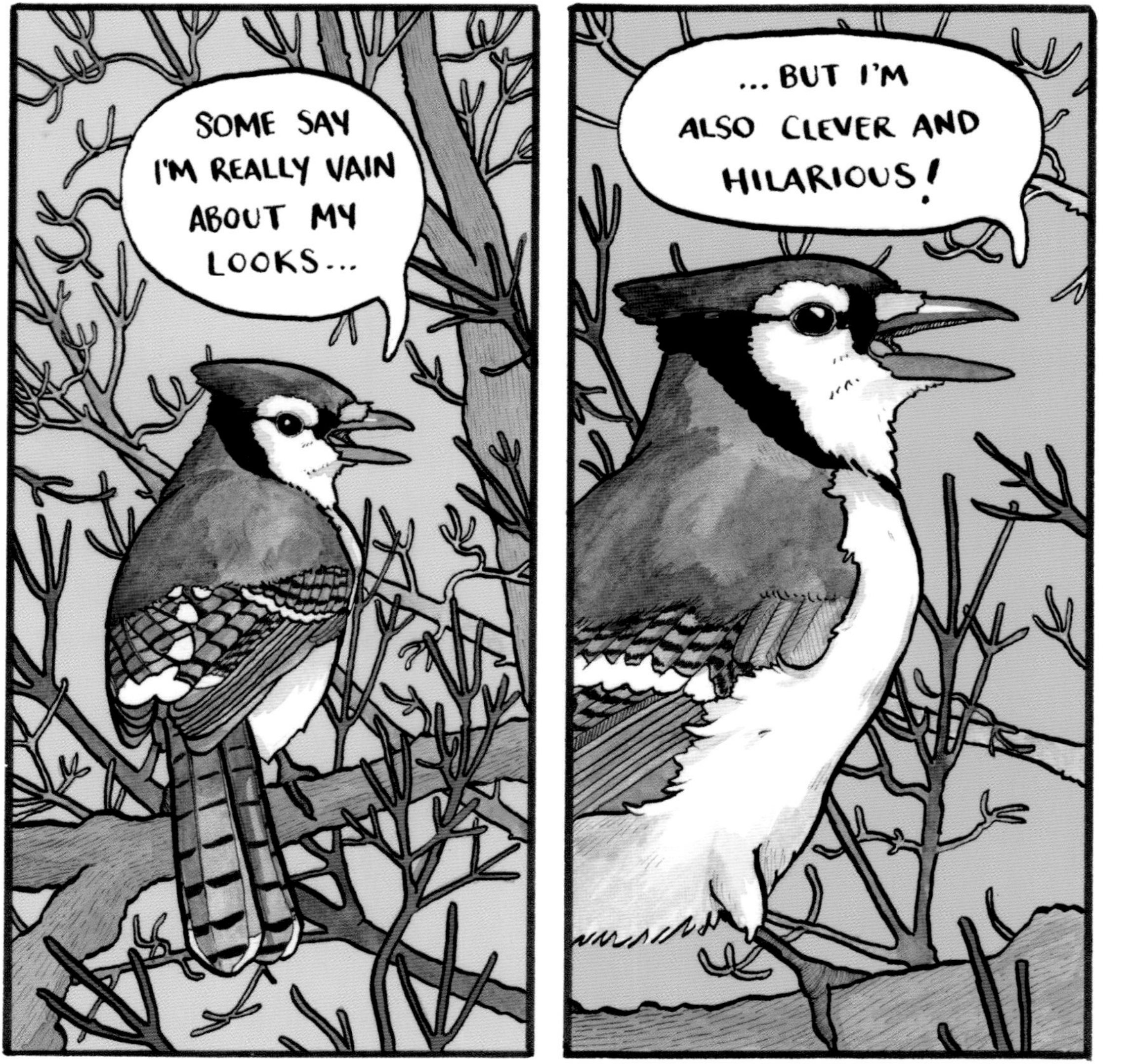
SOME SAY I'M REALLY VAIN ABOUT MY LOOKS...
...BUT I'M ALSO CLEVER AND HILARIOUS!

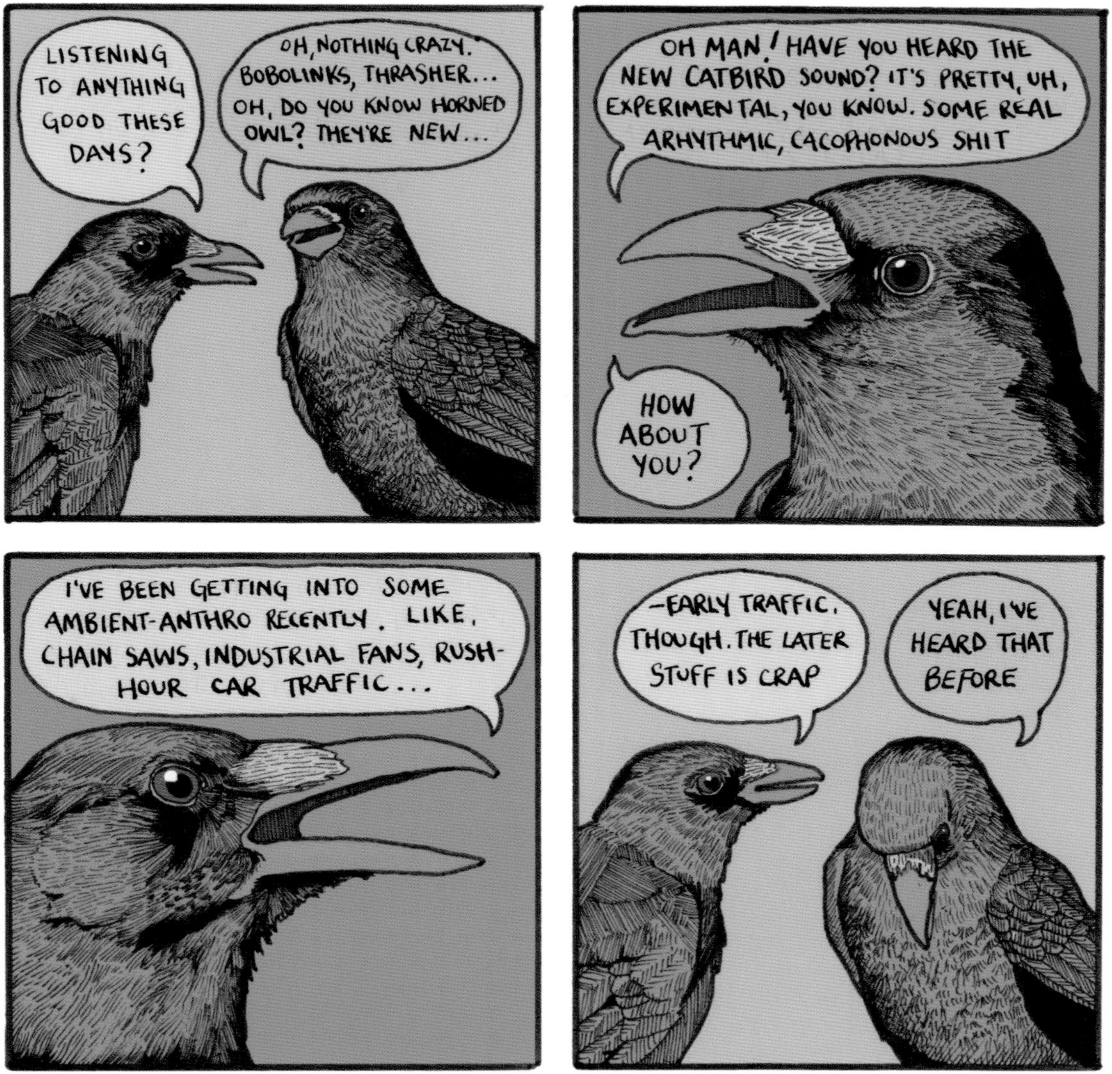
LISTENING TO ANYTHING GOOD THESE DAYS?
OH, NOTHING CRAZY. BOBOLINKS, THRASHER... OH, DO YOU KNOW HORNED OWL? THEY'RE NEW...
OH MAN! HAVE YOU HEARD THE NEW CATBIRD SOUND? IT'S PRETTY, UH, EXPERIMENTAL, YOU KNOW. SOME REAL ARHYTHMIC, CACOPHONOUS SHIT
HOW ABOUT YOU?
I'VE BEEN GETTING INTO SOME AMBIENT-ANTHRO RECENTLY. LIKE, CHAIN SAWS, INDUSTRIAL FANS, RUSH-HOUR CAR TRAFFIC...
—EARLY TRAFFIC, THOUGH. THE LATER STUFF IS CRAP
YEAH, I'VE HEARD THAT BEFORE

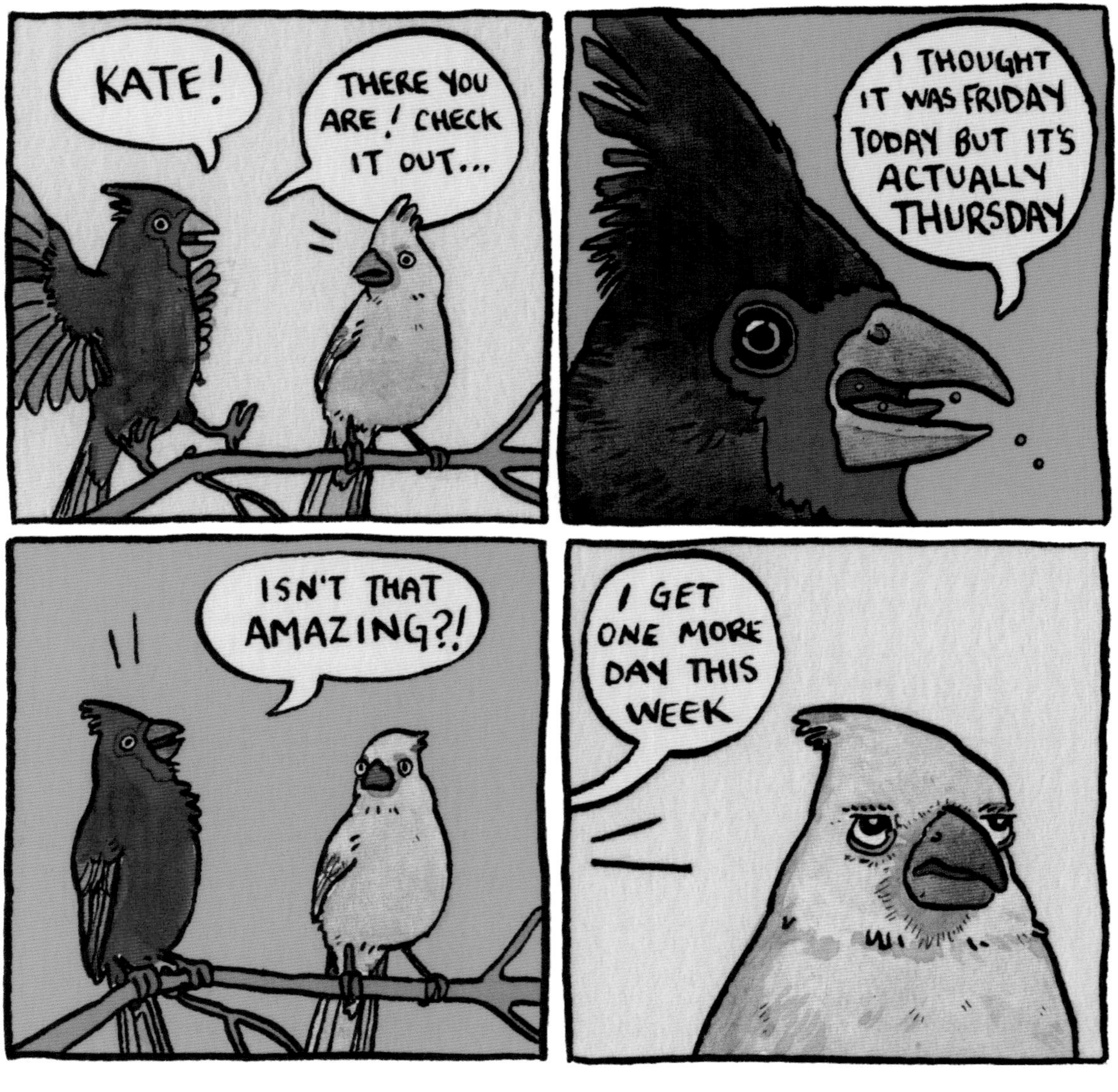
KATE!
THERE YOU ARE! CHECK IT OUT...
I THOUGHT IT WAS FRIDAY TODAY BUT IT'S ACTUALLY THURSDAY
ISN'T THAT AMAZING?!
I GET ONE MORE DAY THIS WEEK

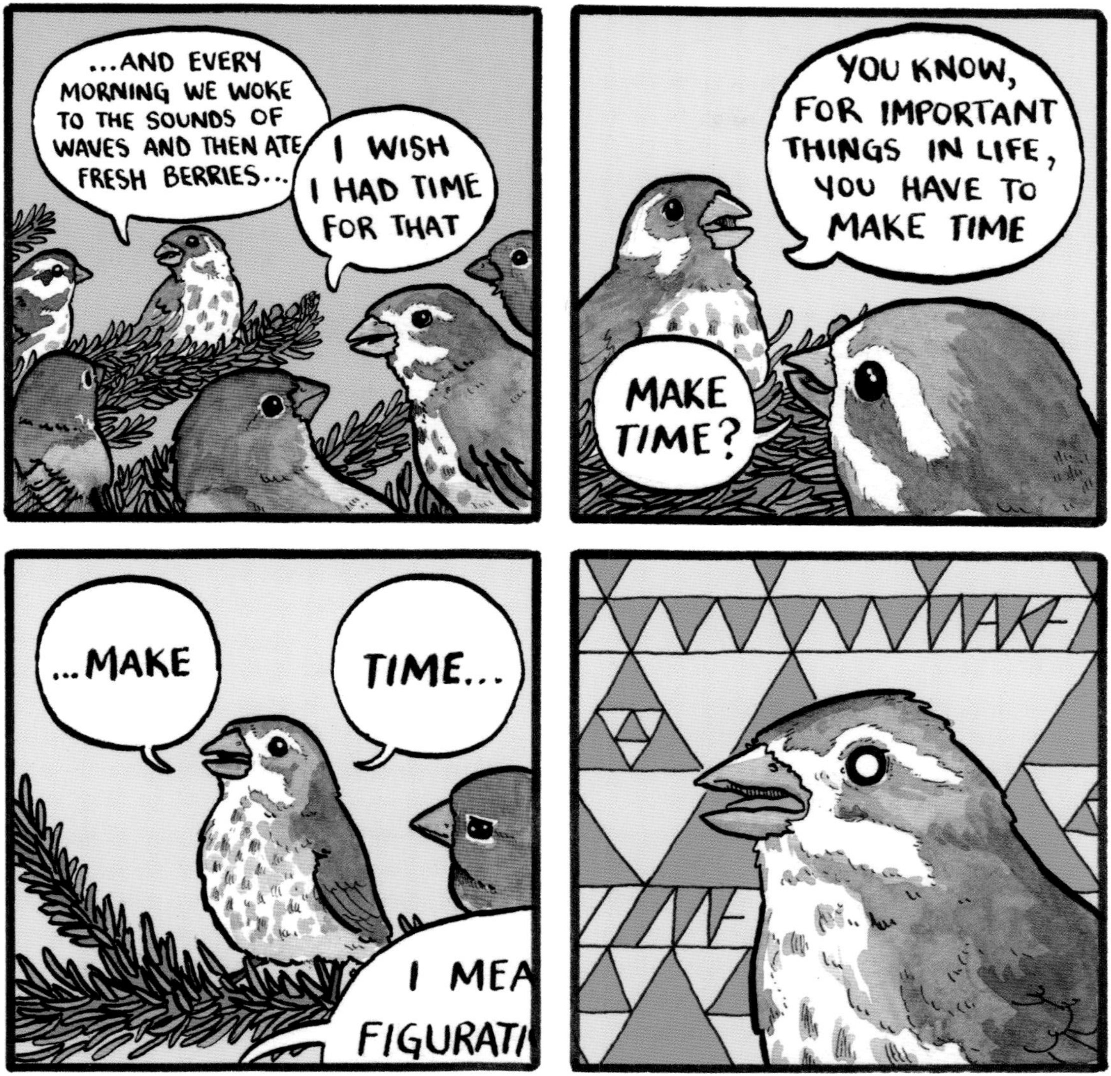
...AND EVERY MORNING WE WOKE TO THE SOUNDS OF WAVES AND THEN ATE FRESH BERRIES...
I WISH I HAD TIME FOR THAT
YOU KNOW, FOR IMPORTANT THINGS IN LIFE, YOU HAVE TO MAKE TIME
MAKE TIME?
...MAKE
TIME...
I MEA
FIGURATI

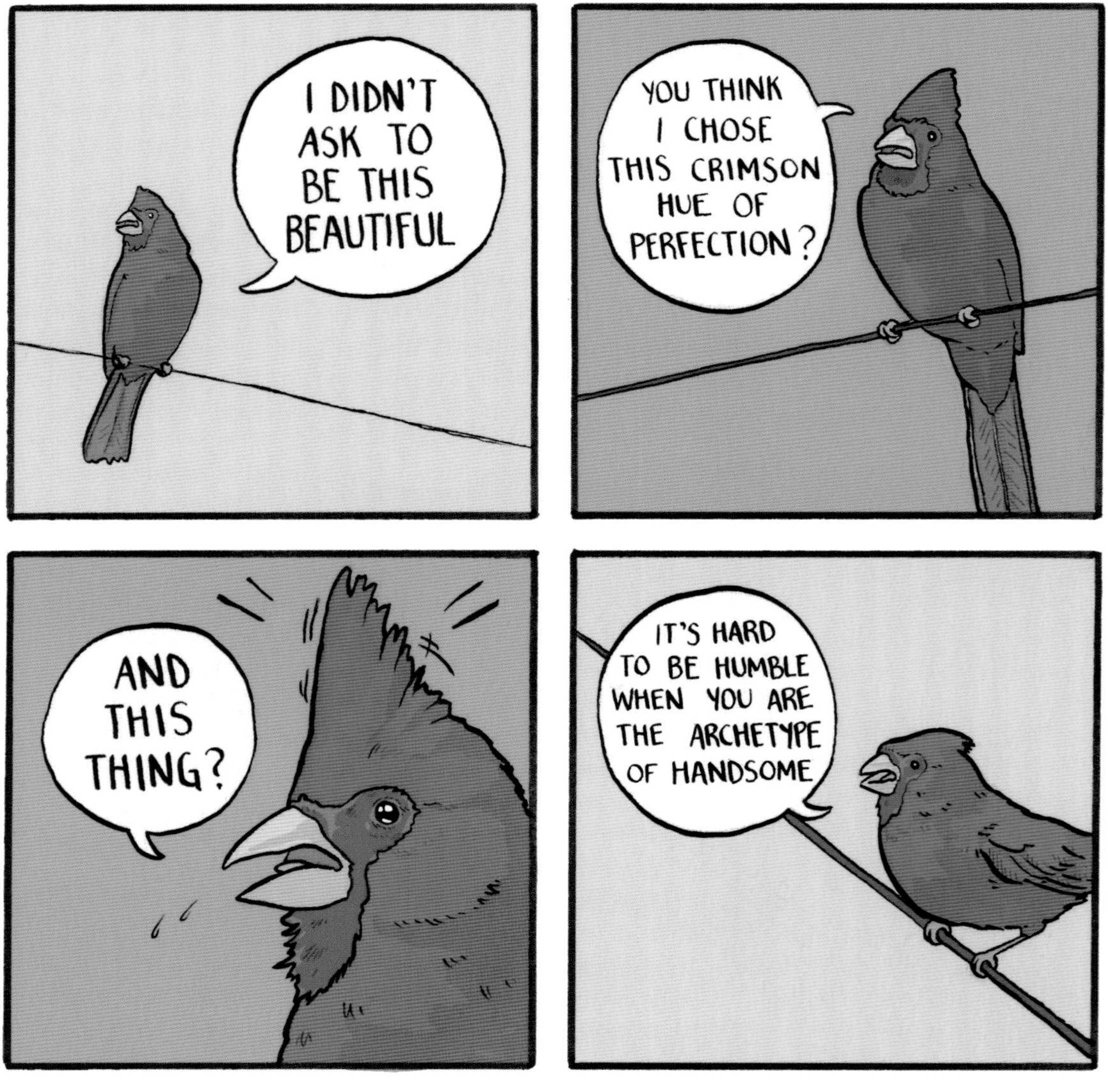
I DIDN'T ASK TO BE THIS BEAUTIFUL
YOU THINK I CHOSE THIS CRIMSON HUE OF PERFECTION?
AND THIS THING?
IT'S HARD TO BE HUMBLE WHEN YOU ARE THE ARCHETYPE OF HANDSOME

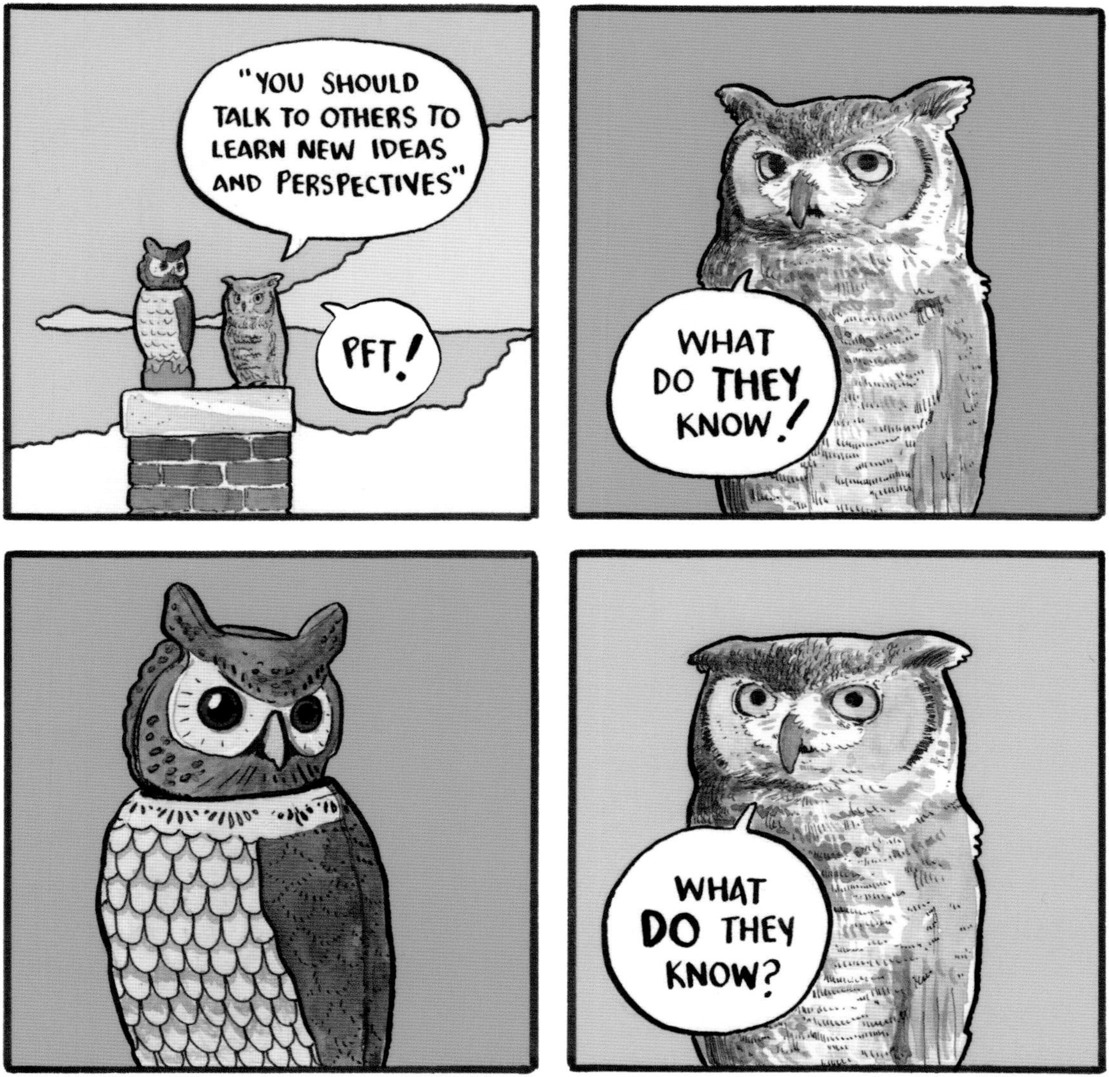
"YOU SHOULD TALK TO OTHERS TO LEARN NEW IDEAS AND PERSPECTIVES"
PFT!
WHAT DO **THEY** KNOW!
WHAT **DO** THEY KNOW?

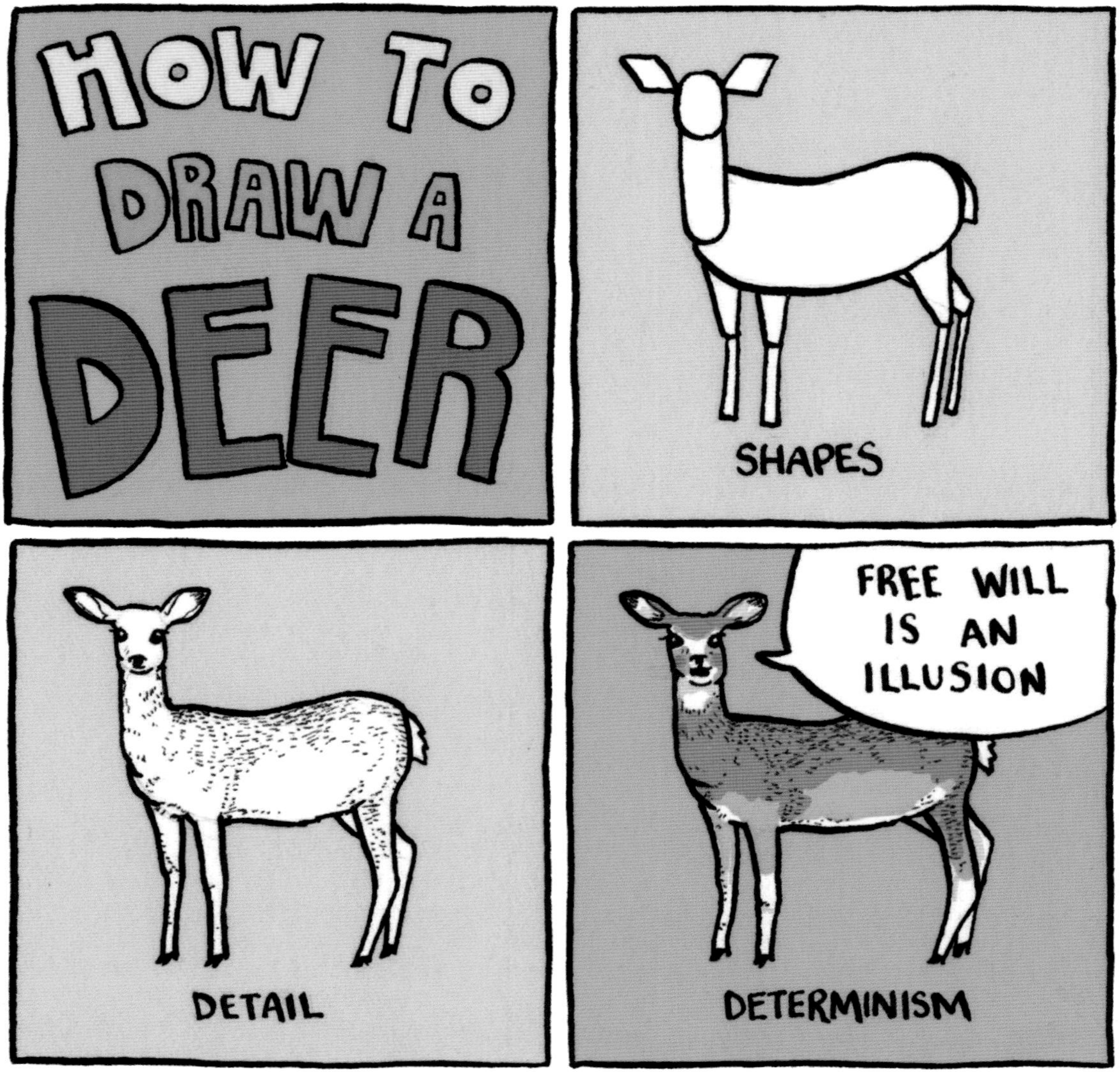
HOW TO DRAW A DEER
SHAPES
DETAIL
FREE WILL IS AN ILLUSION
DETERMINISM

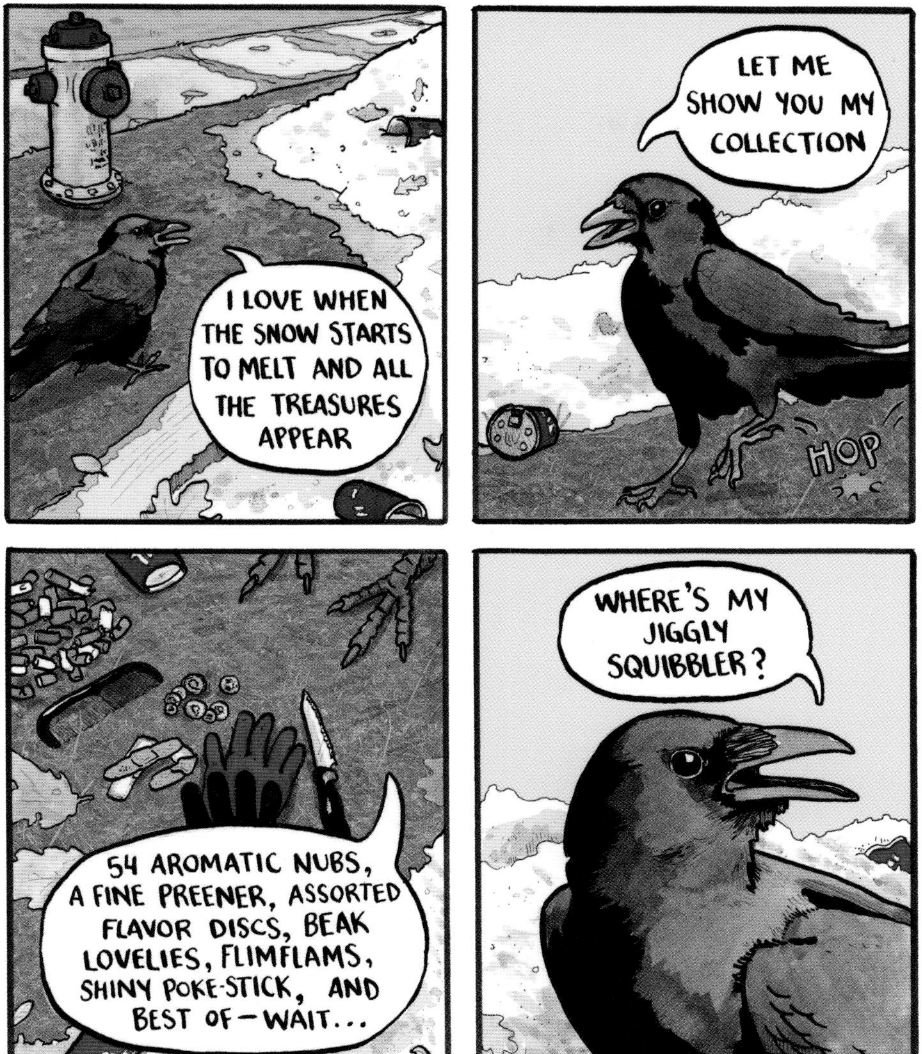
I LOVE WHEN THE SNOW STARTS TO MELT AND ALL THE TREASURES APPEAR
LET ME SHOW YOU MY COLLECTION
HOP
54 AROMATIC NUBS, A FINE PREENER, ASSORTED FLAVOR DISCS, BEAK LOVELIES, FLIMFLAMS, SHINY POKE-STICK, AND BEST OF—WAIT...
WHERE'S MY JIGGLY SQUIBBLER?

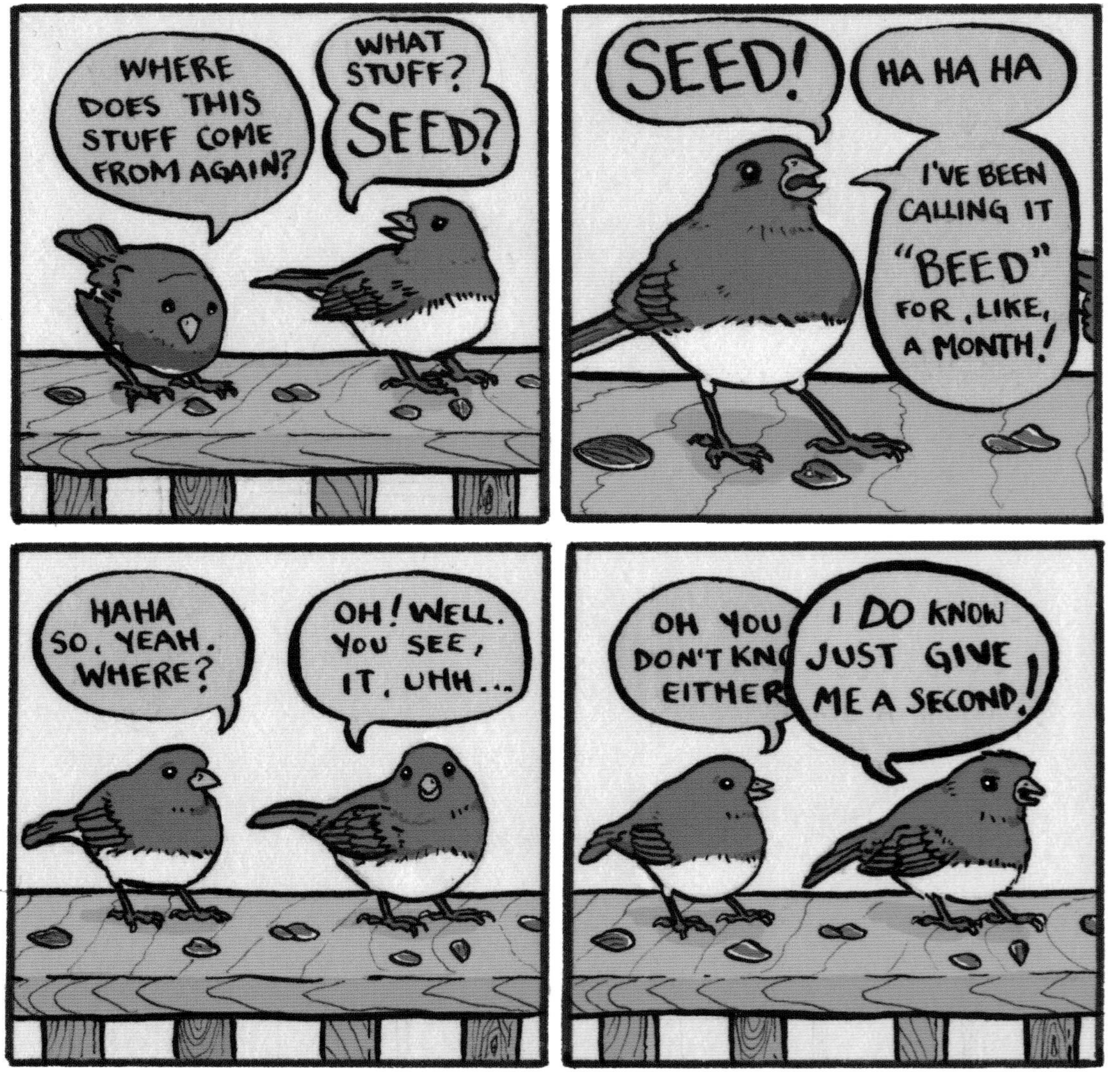
WHERE DOES THIS STUFF COME FROM AGAIN?
WHAT STUFF? SEED?
SEED!
HA HA HA
I'VE BEEN CALLING IT "BEED" FOR, LIKE, A MONTH!
HAHA SO, YEAH. WHERE?
OH! WELL. YOU SEE, IT, UHH...
OH YOU DON'T KN EITHER
I DO KNOW JUST GIVE ME A SECOND!

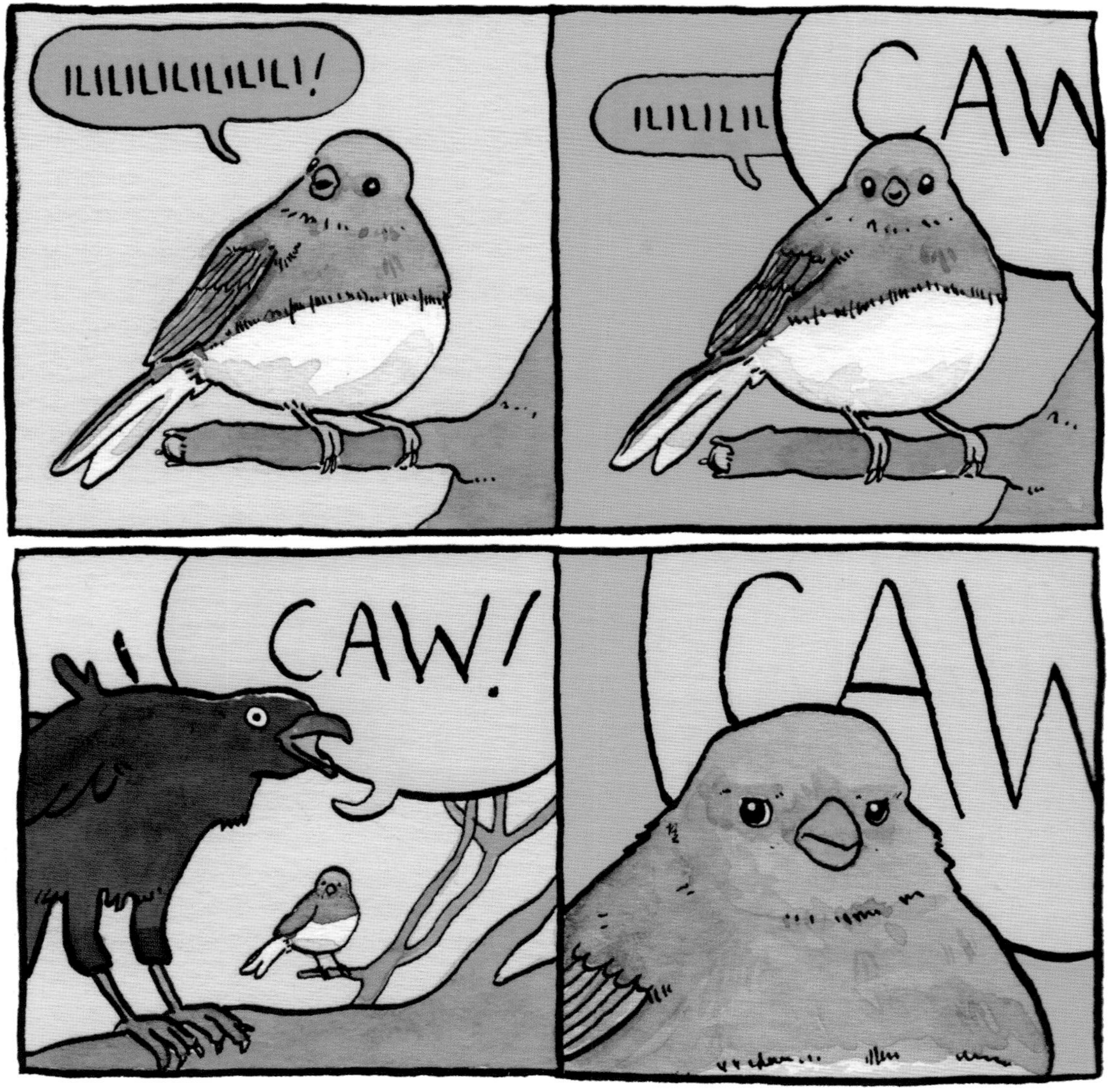
ILILILILILILILI!
ILILILIL
CAW
CAW!
CAW

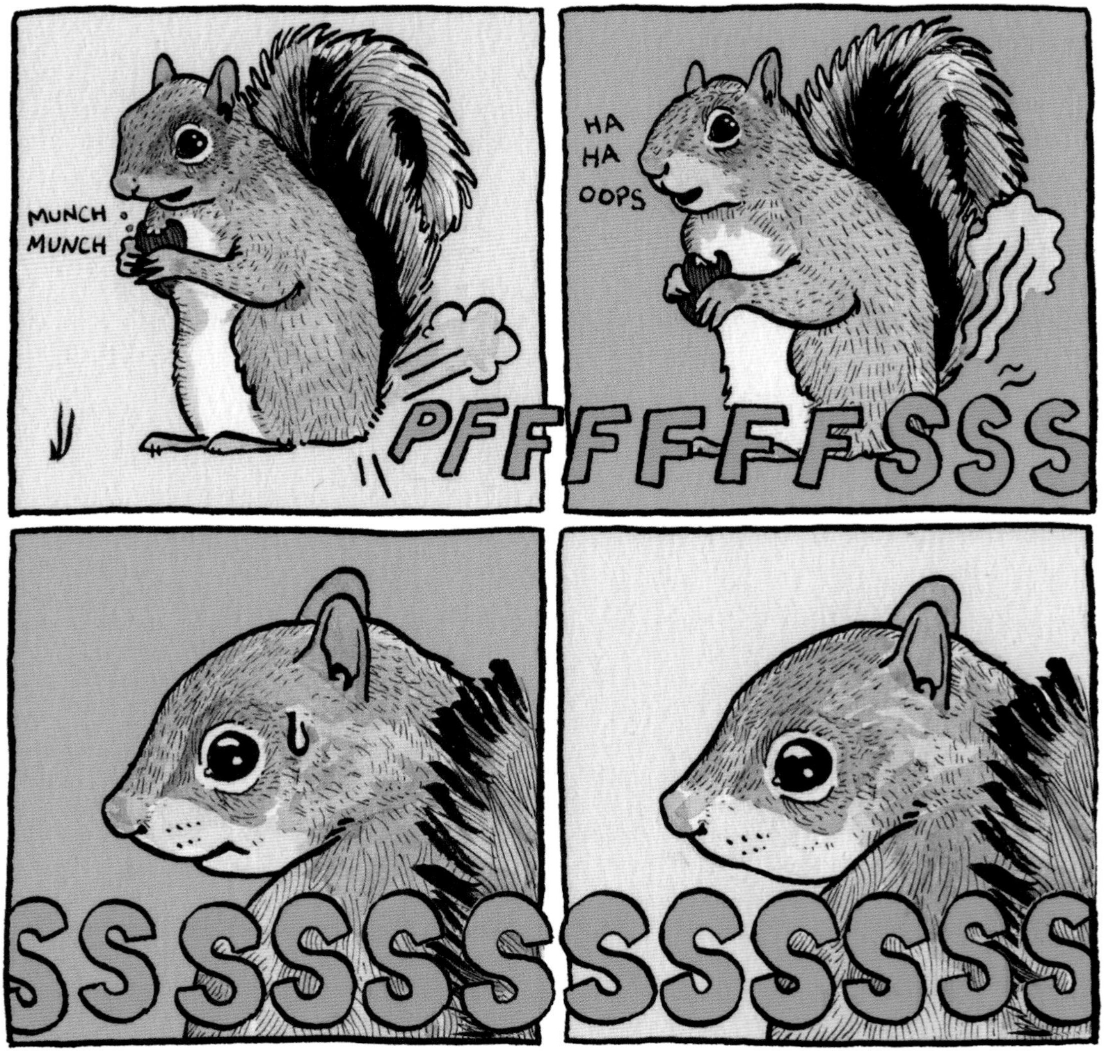
MUNCH
MUNCH
HA
HA
OOPS
PFFFFFFFSSS
SSSSSSSSSSSS

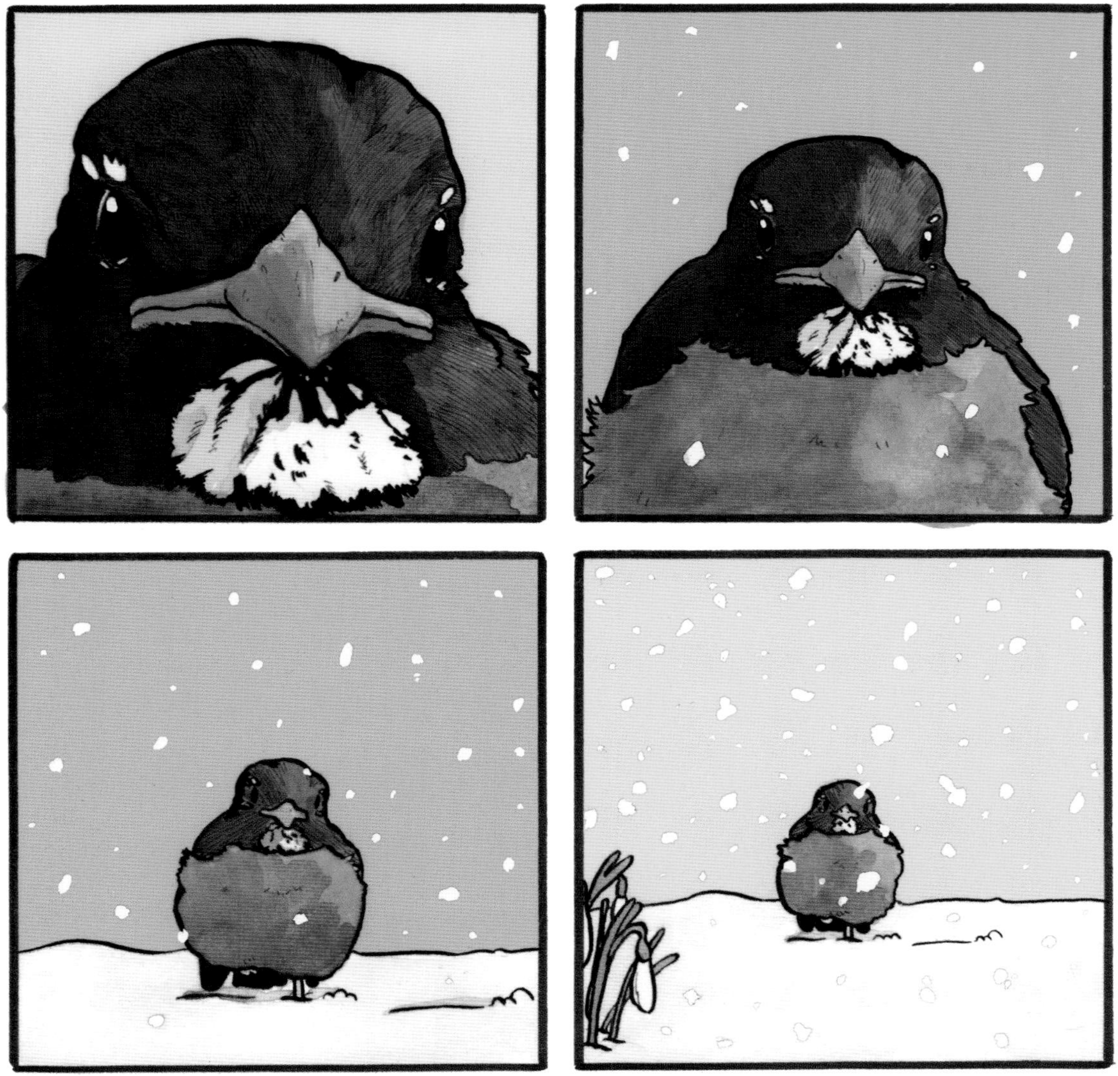

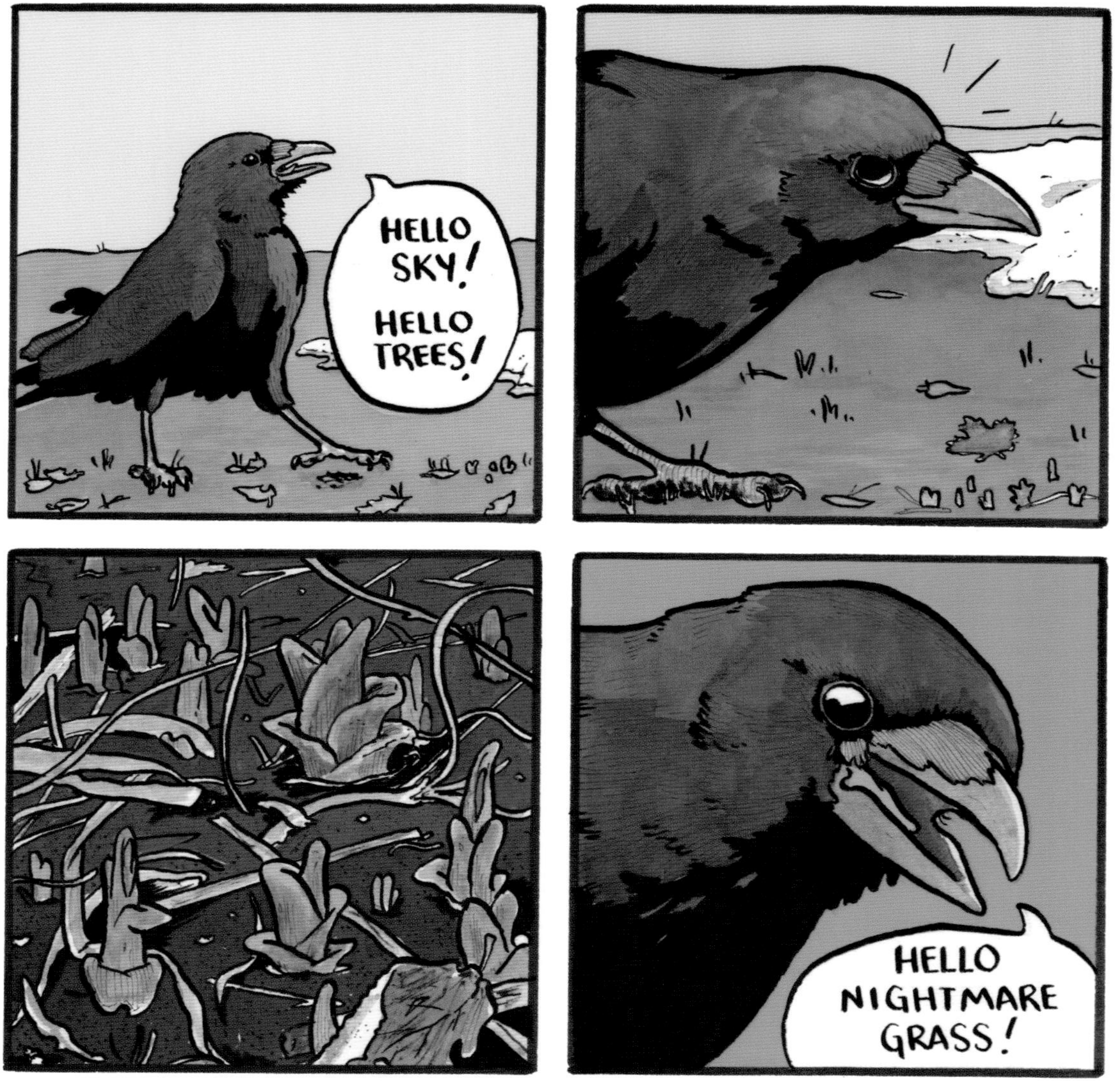
HELLO SKY!
HELLO TREES!
HELLO NIGHTMARE GRASS!

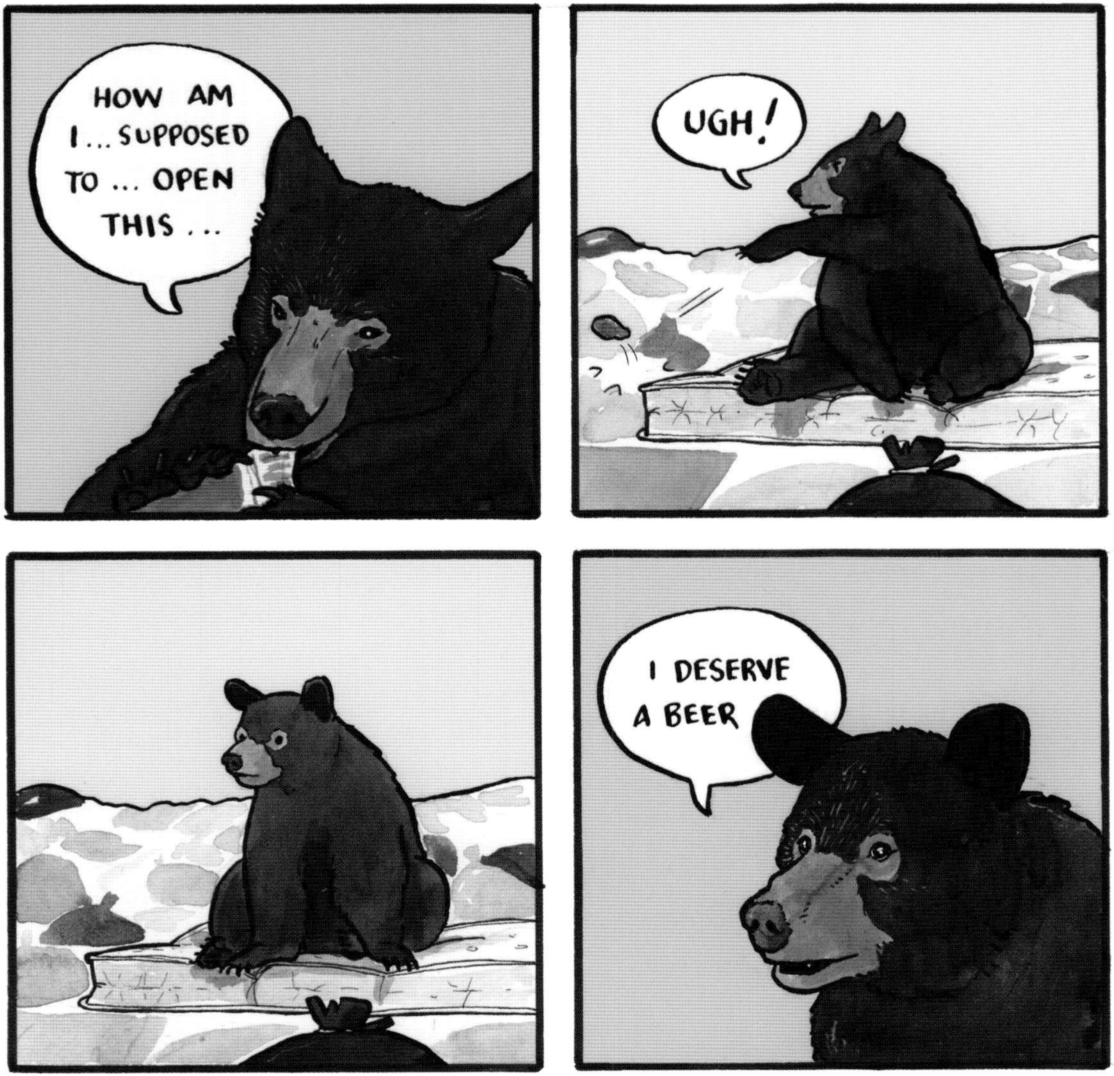
HOW AM I... SUPPOSED TO ... OPEN THIS ...
UGH!
I DESERVE A BEER

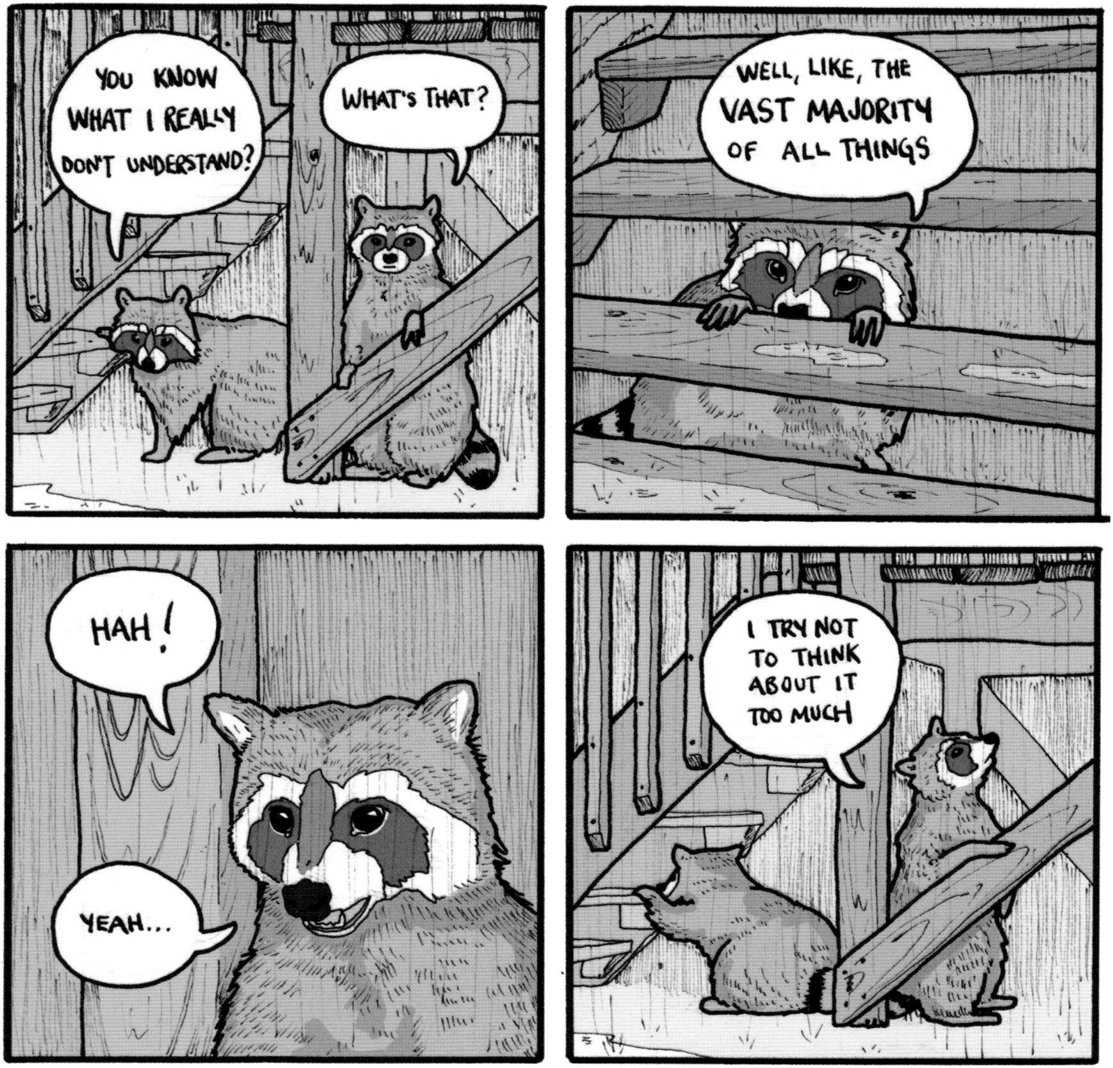
YOU KNOW WHAT I REALLY DON'T UNDERSTAND?
WHAT'S THAT?
WELL, LIKE, THE VAST MAJORITY OF ALL THINGS
HAH!
YEAH...
I TRY NOT TO THINK ABOUT IT TOO MUCH

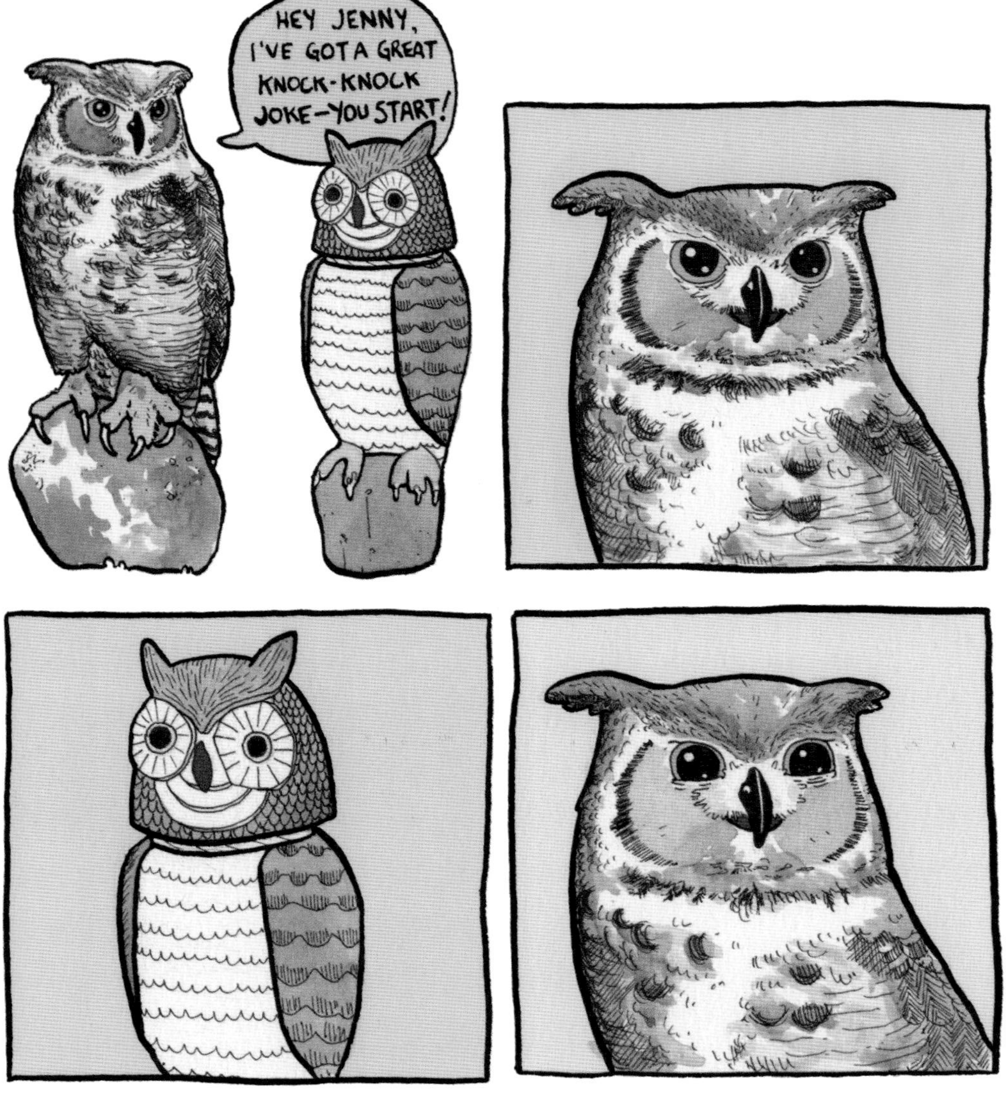
HEY JENNY, I'VE GOT A GREAT KNOCK-KNOCK JOKE—YOU START!

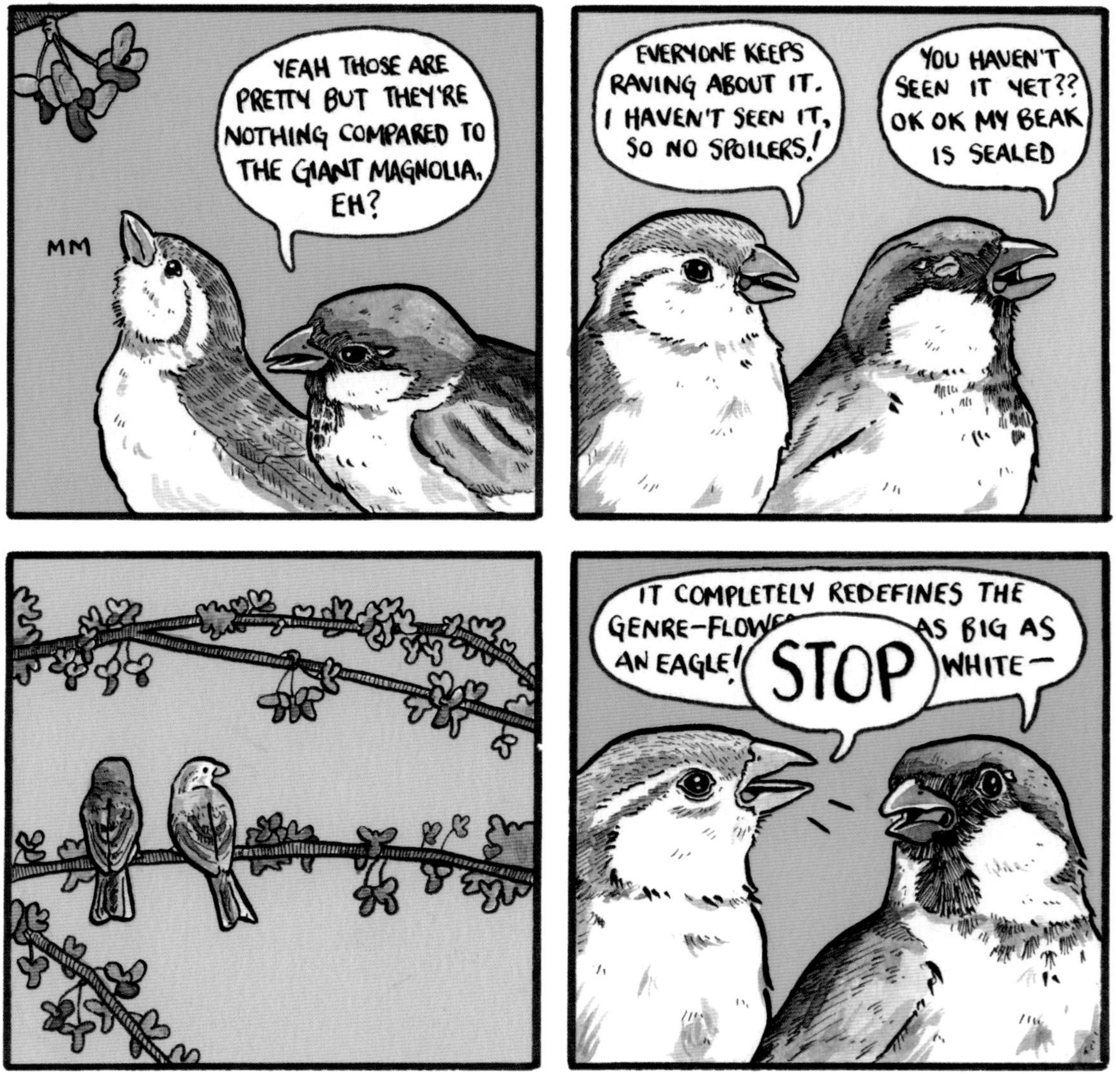
YEAH THOSE ARE PRETTY BUT THEY'RE NOTHING COMPARED TO THE GIANT MAGNOLIA, EH?
MM
EVERYONE KEEPS RAVING ABOUT IT. I HAVEN'T SEEN IT, SO NO SPOILERS!
YOU HAVEN'T SEEN IT YET?? OK OK MY BEAK IS SEALED
IT COMPLETELY REDEFINES THE GENRE-FLOW AS BIG AS AN EAGLE! WHITE-
STOP

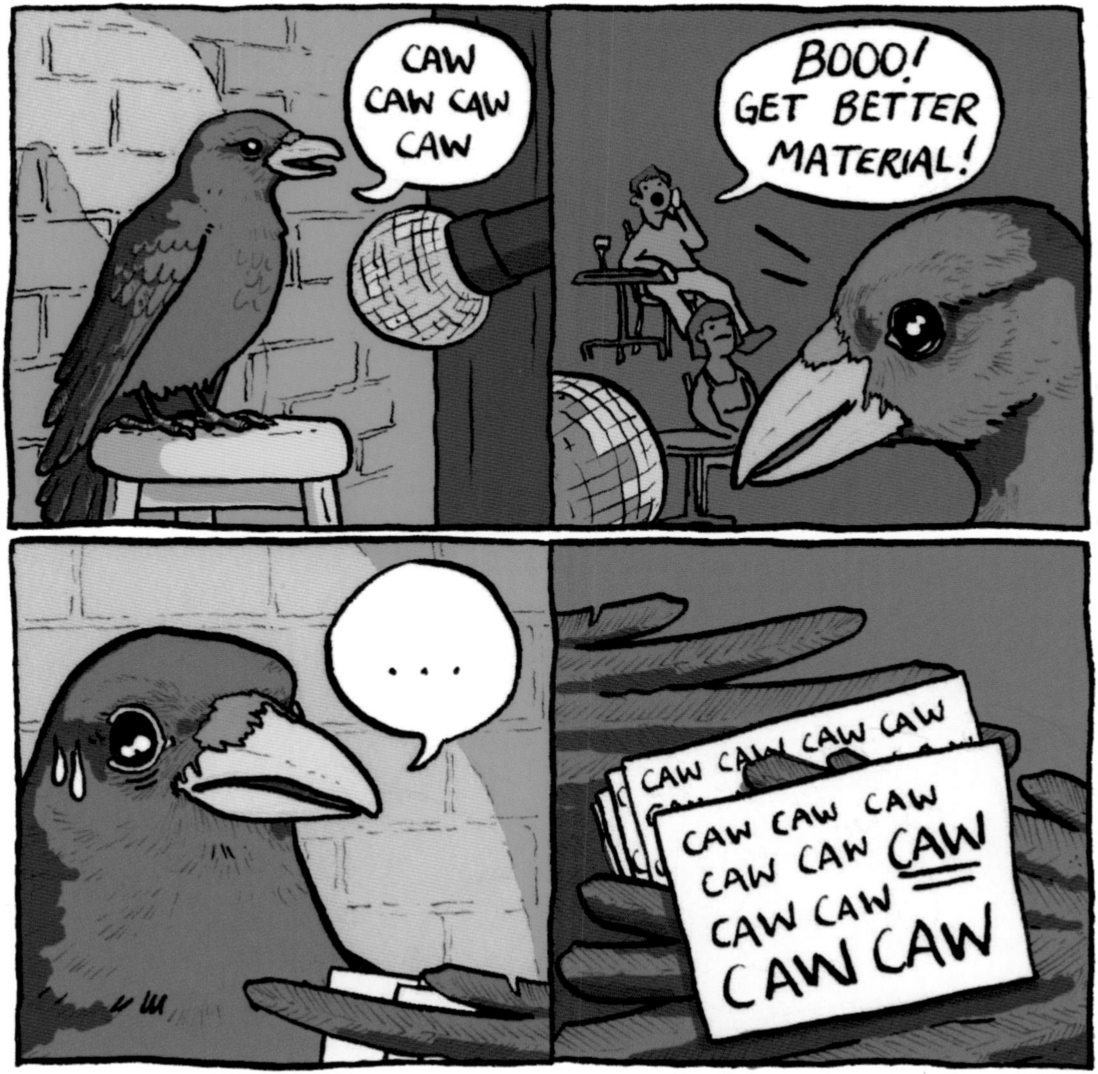
CAW CAW CAW CAW
BOOO! GET BETTER MATERIAL!
. . .
CAW CAW CAW
CAW CAW CAW
CAW CAW
CAW CAW

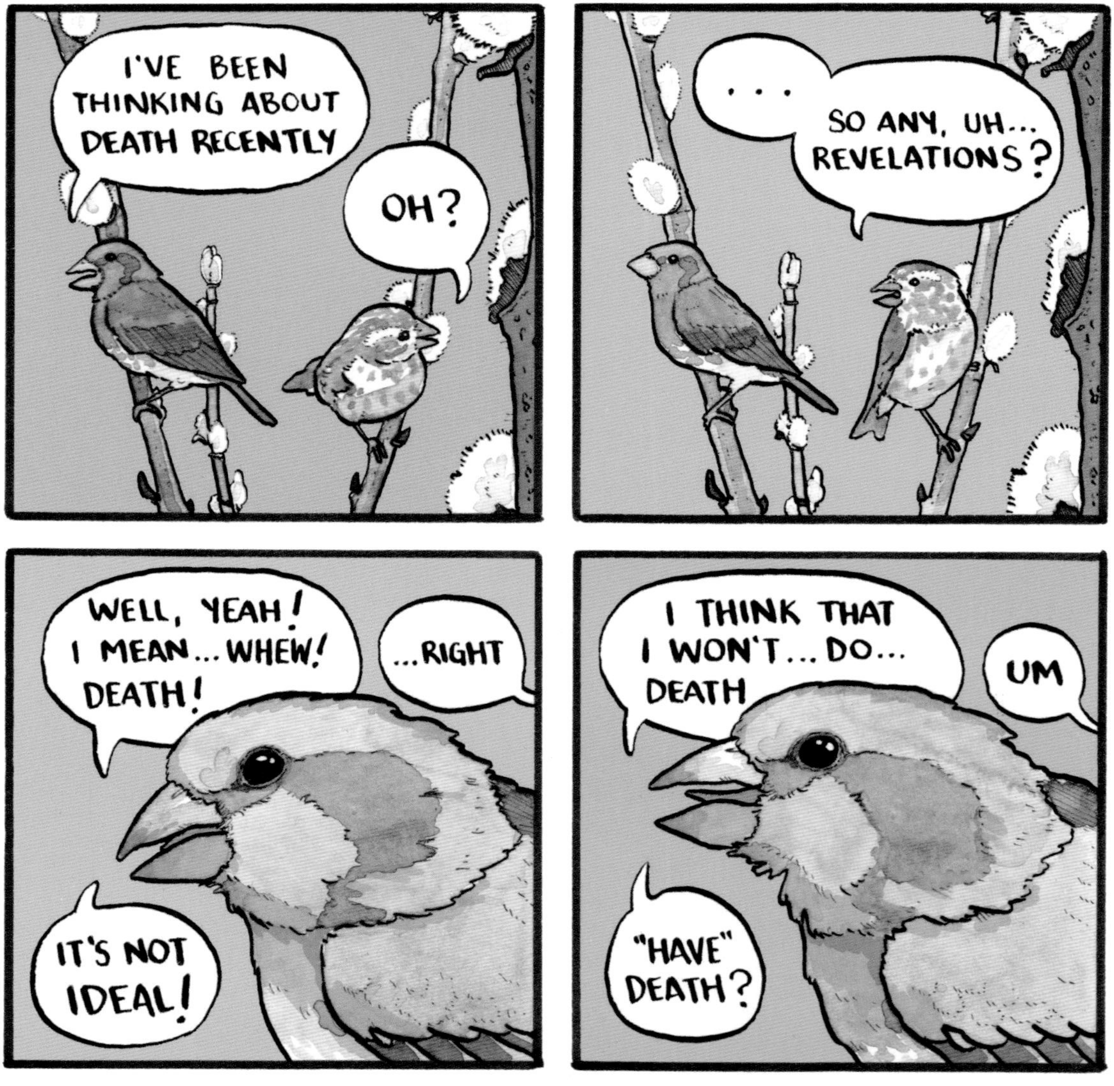
I'VE BEEN THINKING ABOUT DEATH RECENTLY
OH?
. . .
SO ANY, UH... REVELATIONS?
WELL, YEAH! I MEAN... WHEW! DEATH!
...RIGHT
IT'S NOT IDEAL!
I THINK THAT I WON'T... DO... DEATH
UM
"HAVE" DEATH?

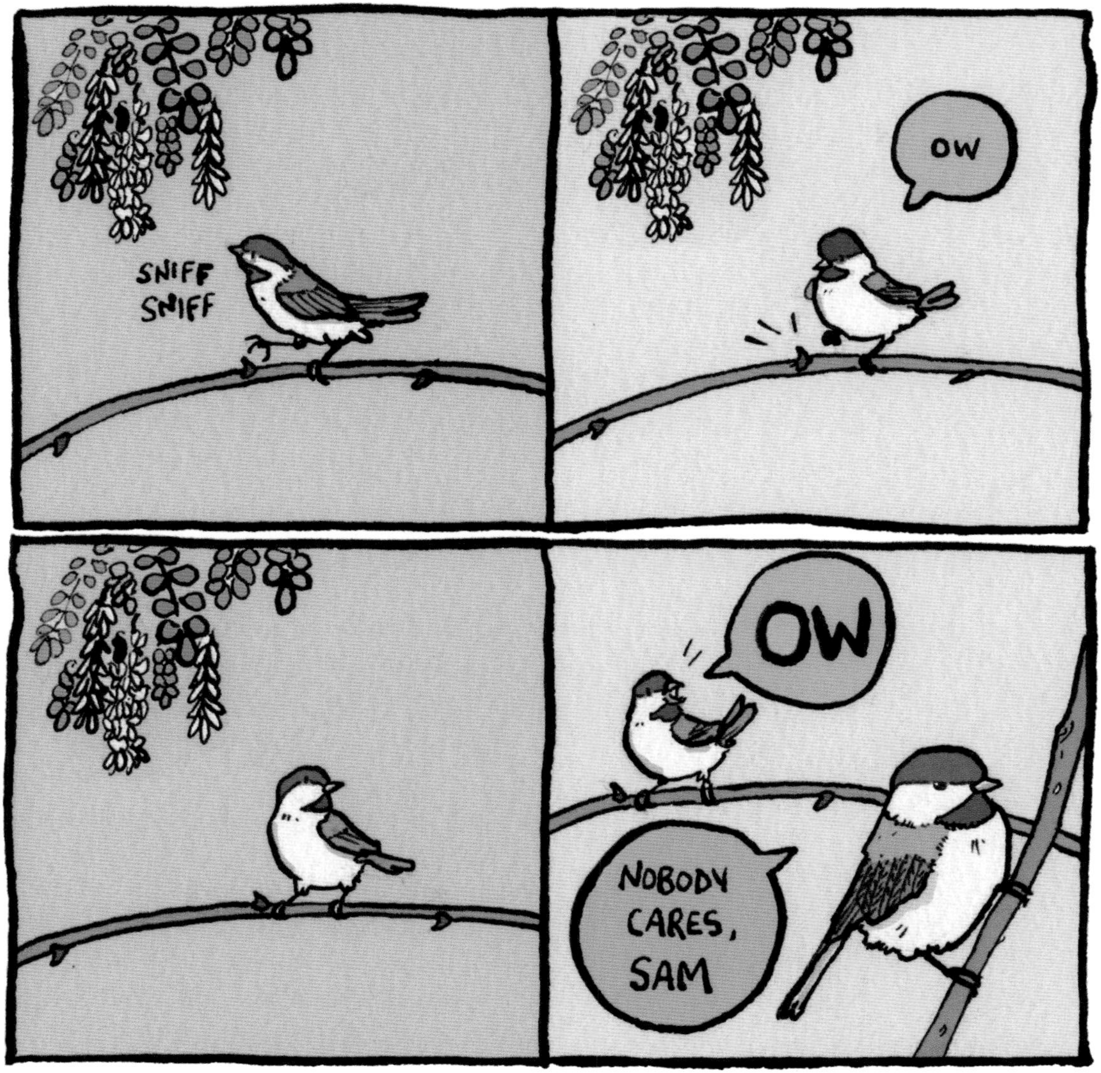
SNIFF
SNIFF
OW
OW
NOBODY CARES, SAM

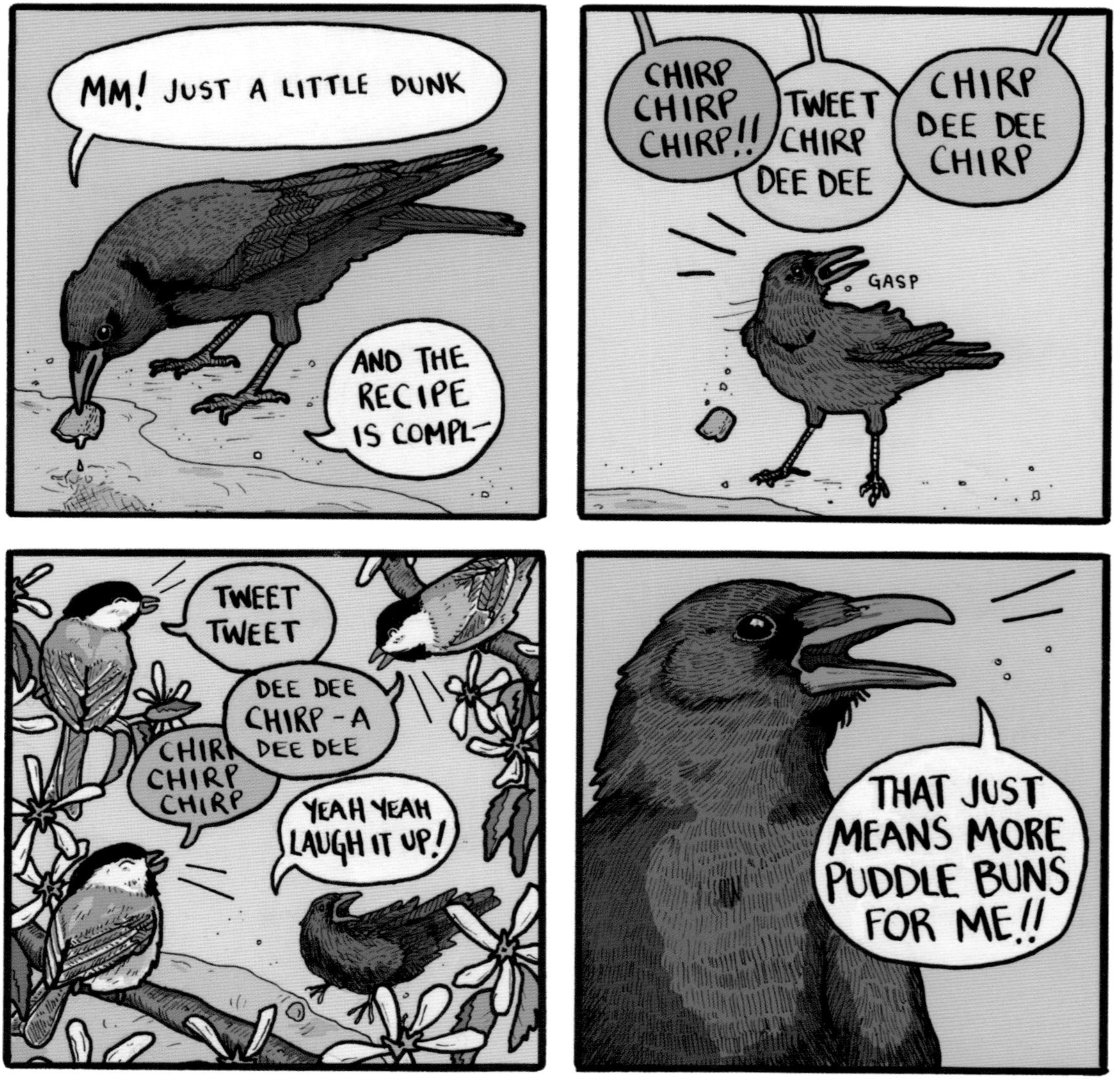
MM! JUST A LITTLE DUNK
AND THE RECIPE IS COMPL-
CHIRP CHIRP CHIRP!!
TWEET CHIRP DEE DEE
CHIRP DEE DEE CHIRP
GASP
TWEET TWEET
DEE DEE CHIRP-A DEE DEE
CHIRP CHIRP CHIRP
YEAH YEAH LAUGH IT UP!
THAT JUST MEANS MORE PUDDLE BUNS FOR ME!!

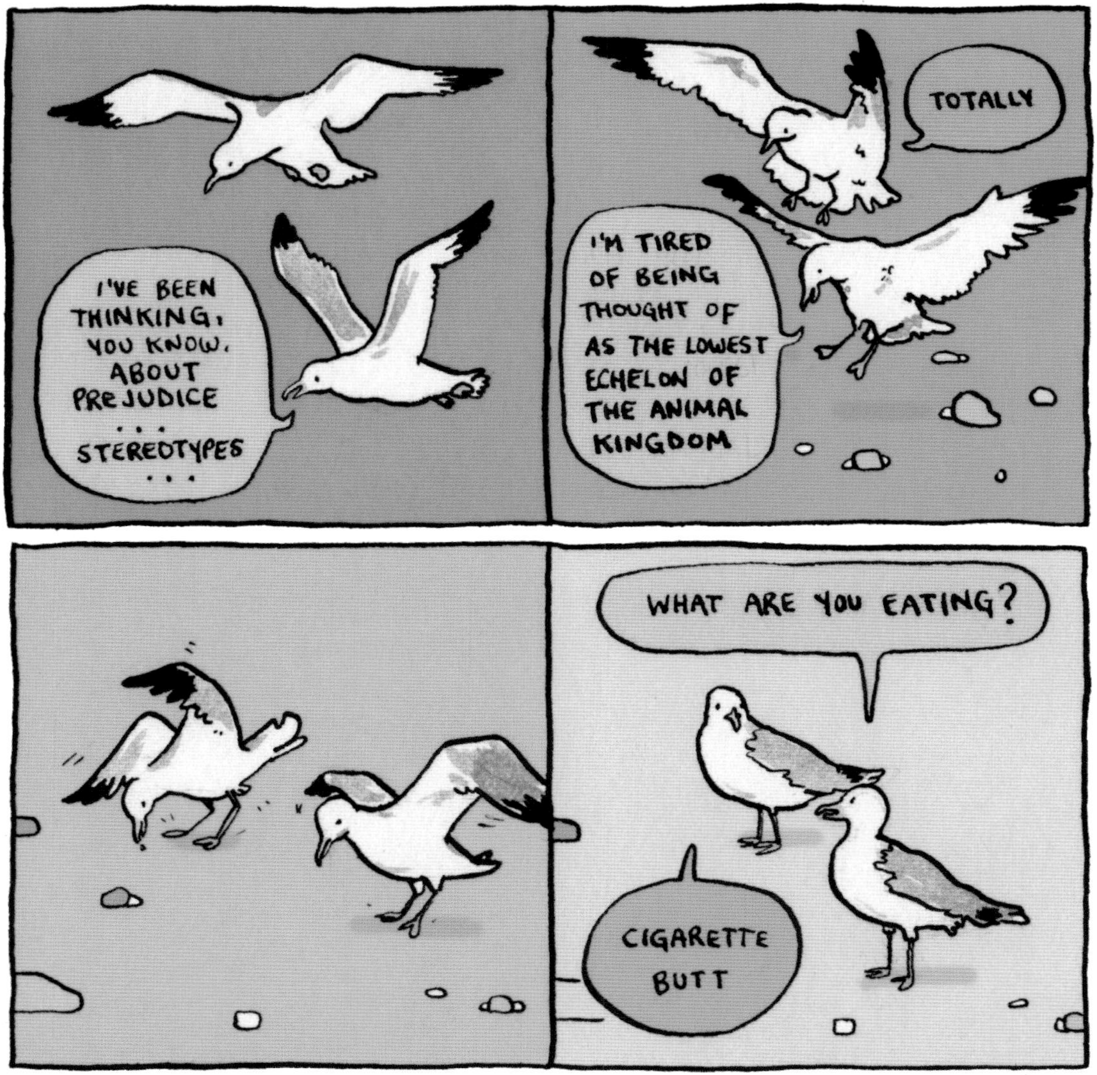
I'VE BEEN THINKING, YOU KNOW, ABOUT PREJUDICE . . . STEREOTYPES . . .
TOTALLY
I'M TIRED OF BEING THOUGHT OF AS THE LOWEST ECHELON OF THE ANIMAL KINGDOM
WHAT ARE YOU EATING?
CIGARETTE BUTT

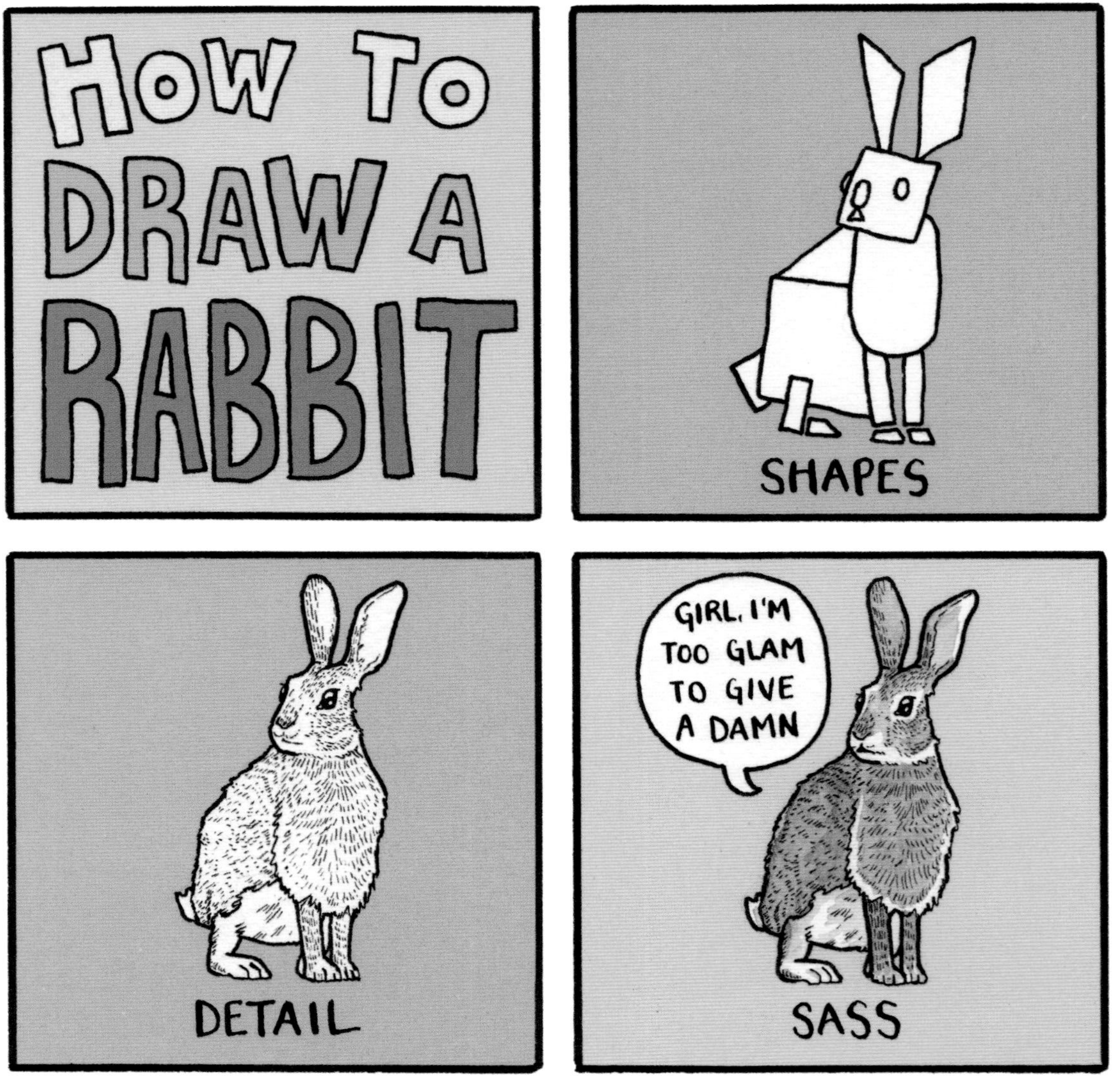
HOW TO DRAW A RABBIT
SHAPES
DETAIL
GIRL, I'M TOO GLAM TO GIVE A DAMN
SASS

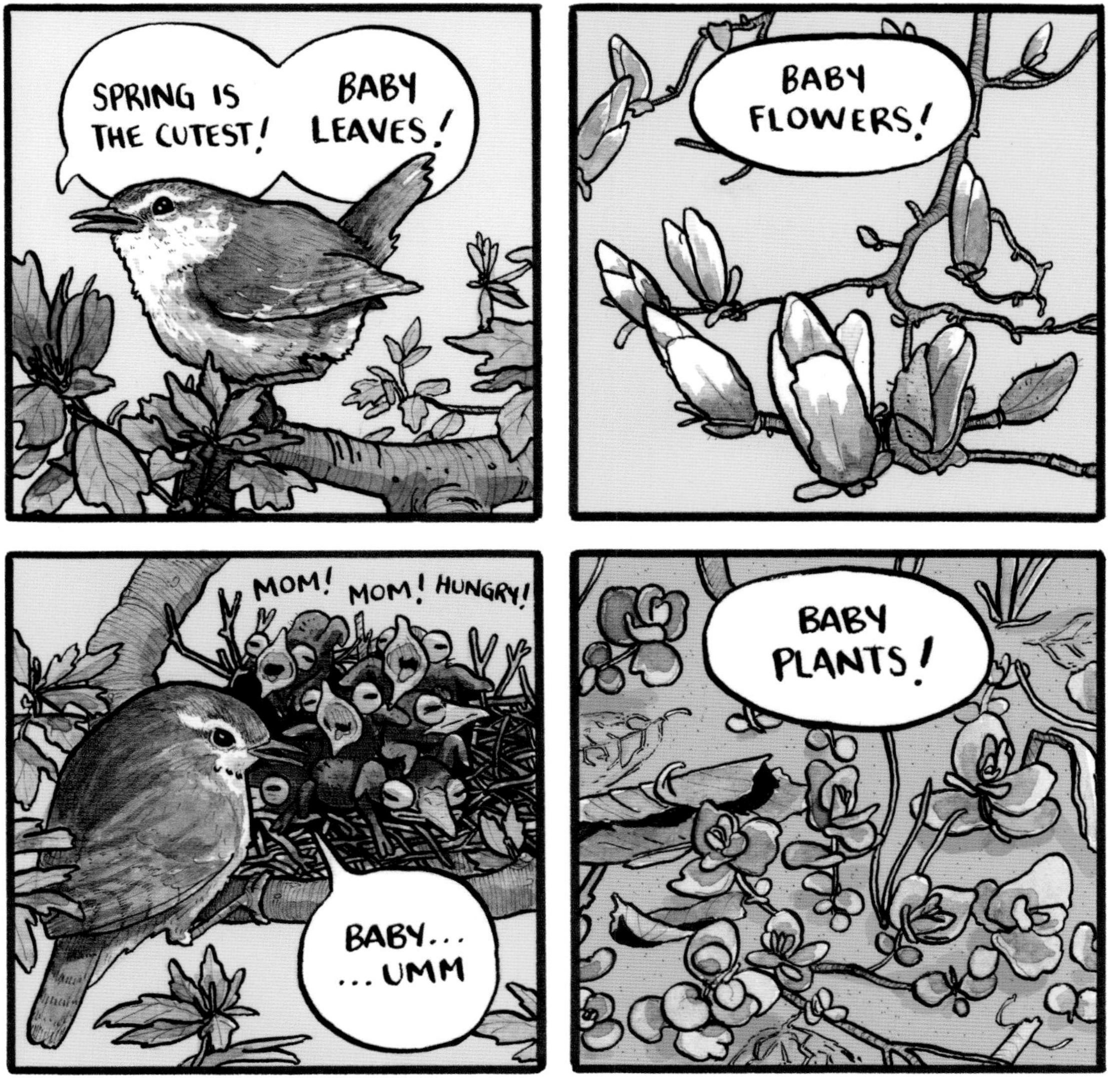
SPRING IS THE CUTEST!
BABY LEAVES!
BABY FLOWERS!
MOM! MOM! HUNGRY!
BABY... ...UMM
BABY PLANTS!

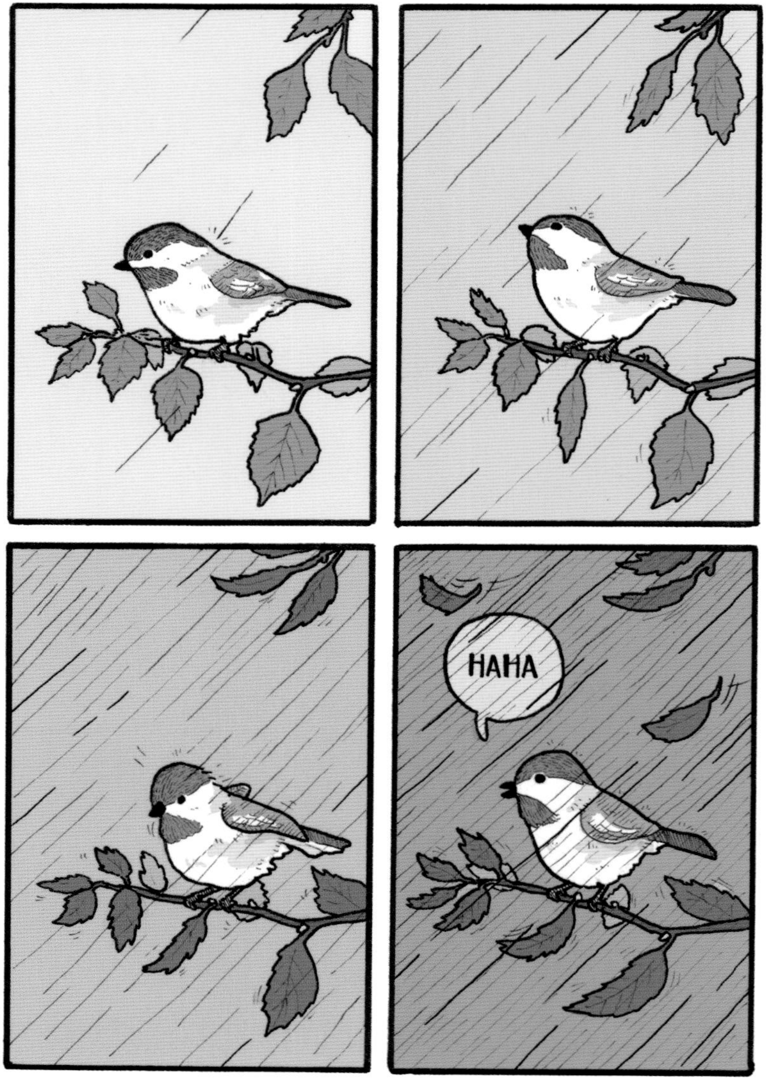
HAHA

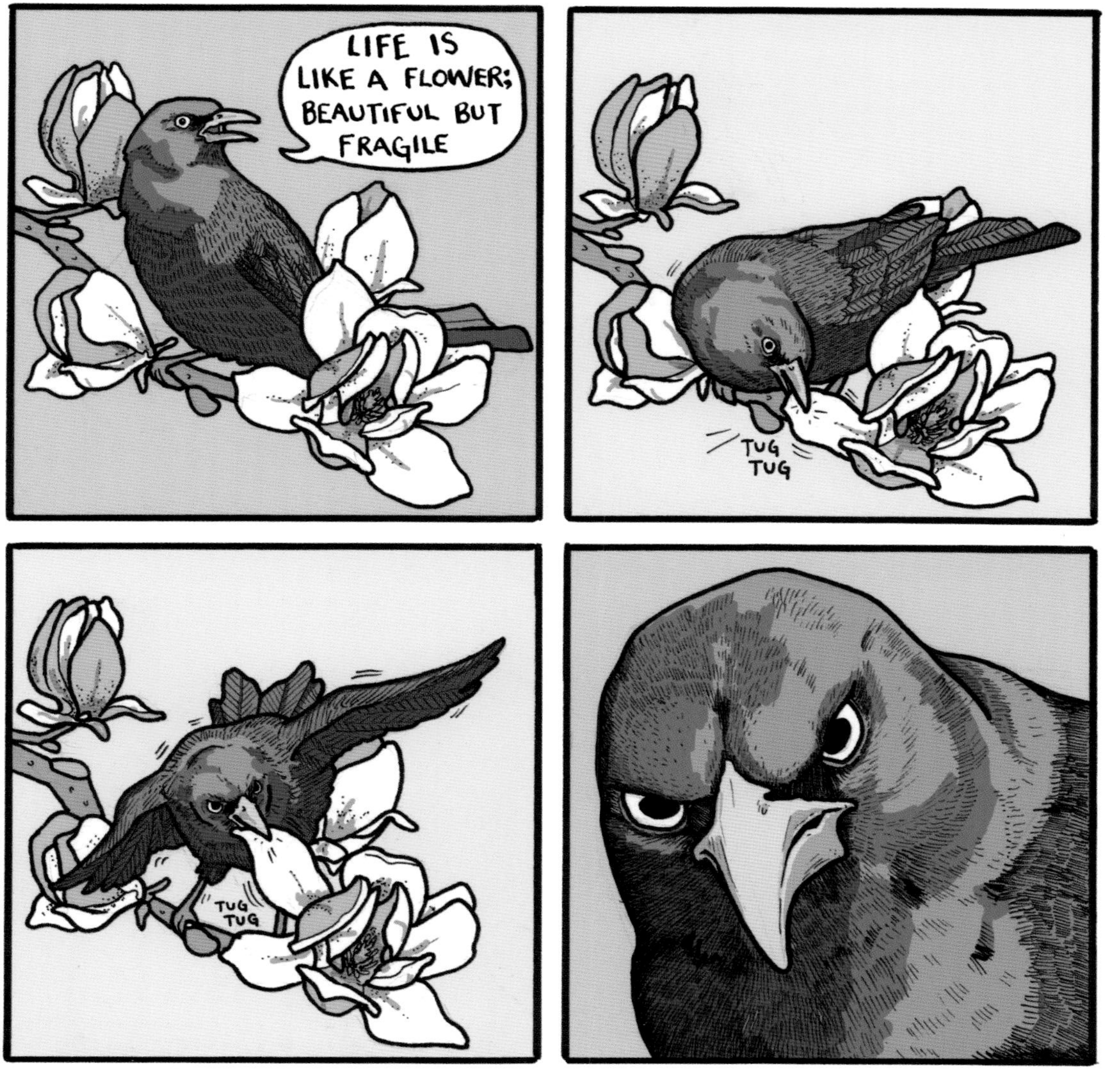
LIFE IS LIKE A FLOWER; BEAUTIFUL BUT FRAGILE
TUG TUG
TUG TUG

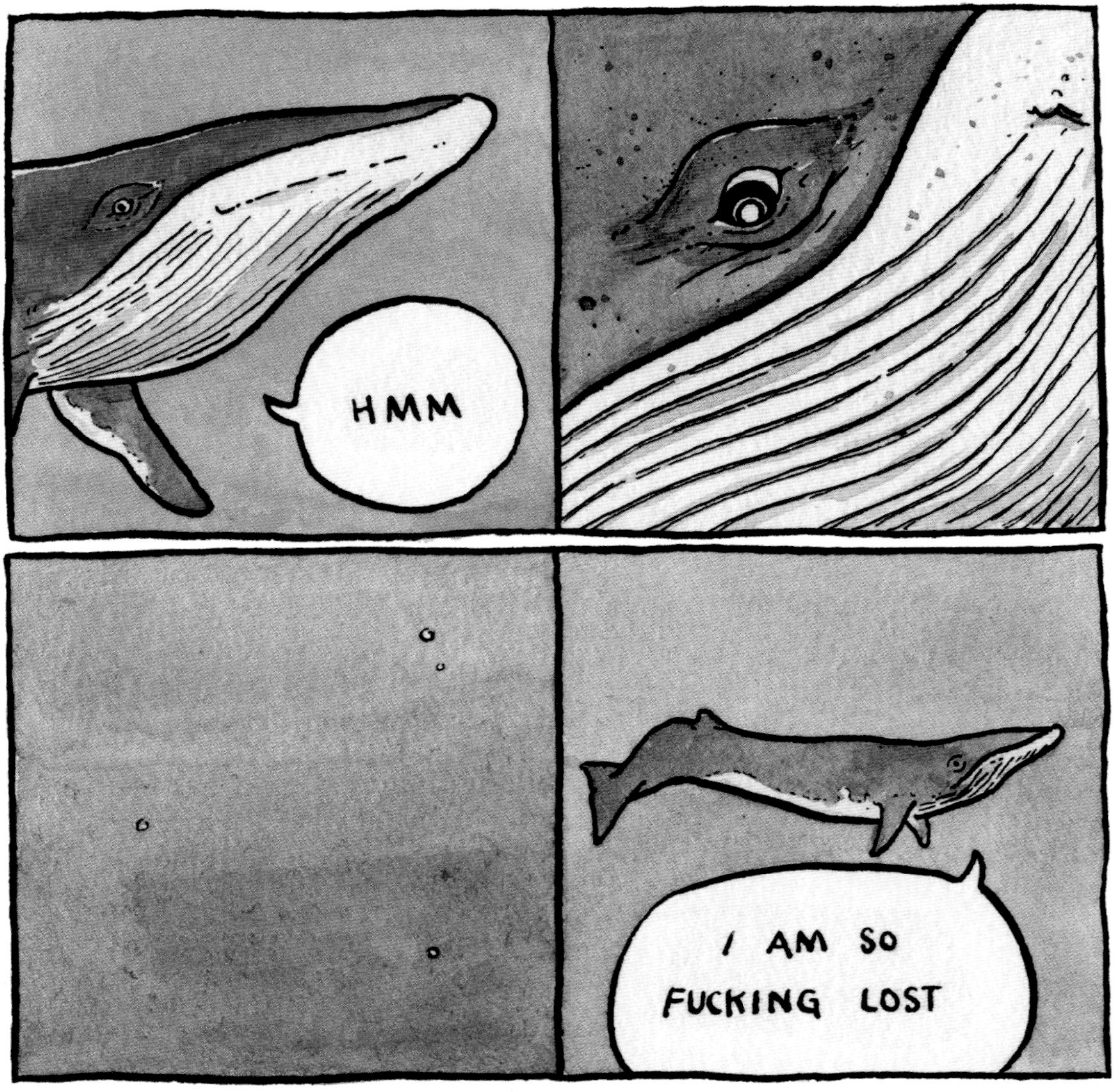
HMM
I AM SO FUCKING LOST

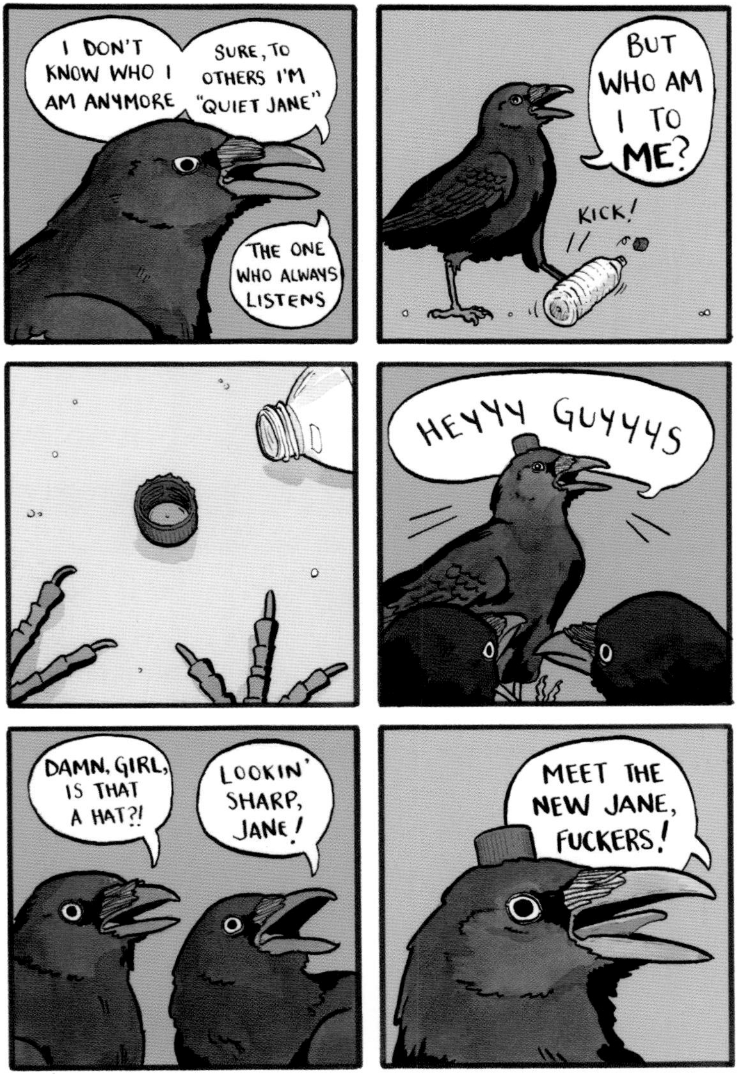
I DON'T KNOW WHO I AM ANYMORE
SURE, TO OTHERS I'M "QUIET JANE"
THE ONE WHO ALWAYS LISTENS
BUT WHO AM I TO ME?
KICK!
HEYYY GUYYYS
DAMN, GIRL, IS THAT A HAT?!
LOOKIN' SHARP, JANE!
MEET THE NEW JANE, FUCKERS!

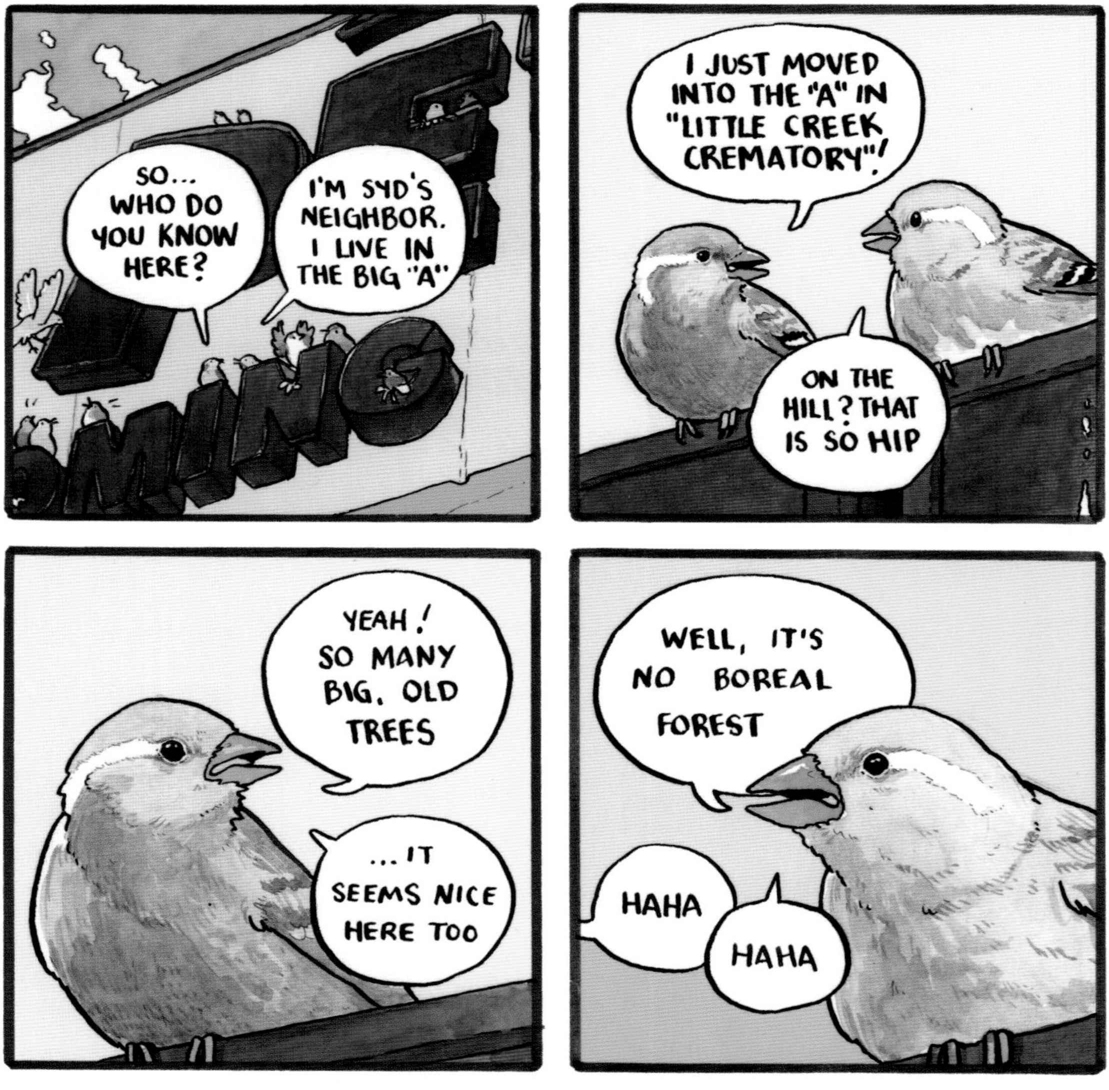
SO... WHO DO YOU KNOW HERE?
I'M SYD'S NEIGHBOR. I LIVE IN THE BIG "A"
I JUST MOVED INTO THE "A" IN "LITTLE CREEK CREMATORY"!
ON THE HILL? THAT IS SO HIP
YEAH! SO MANY BIG, OLD TREES
...IT SEEMS NICE HERE TOO
WELL, IT'S NO BOREAL FOREST
HAHA
HAHA

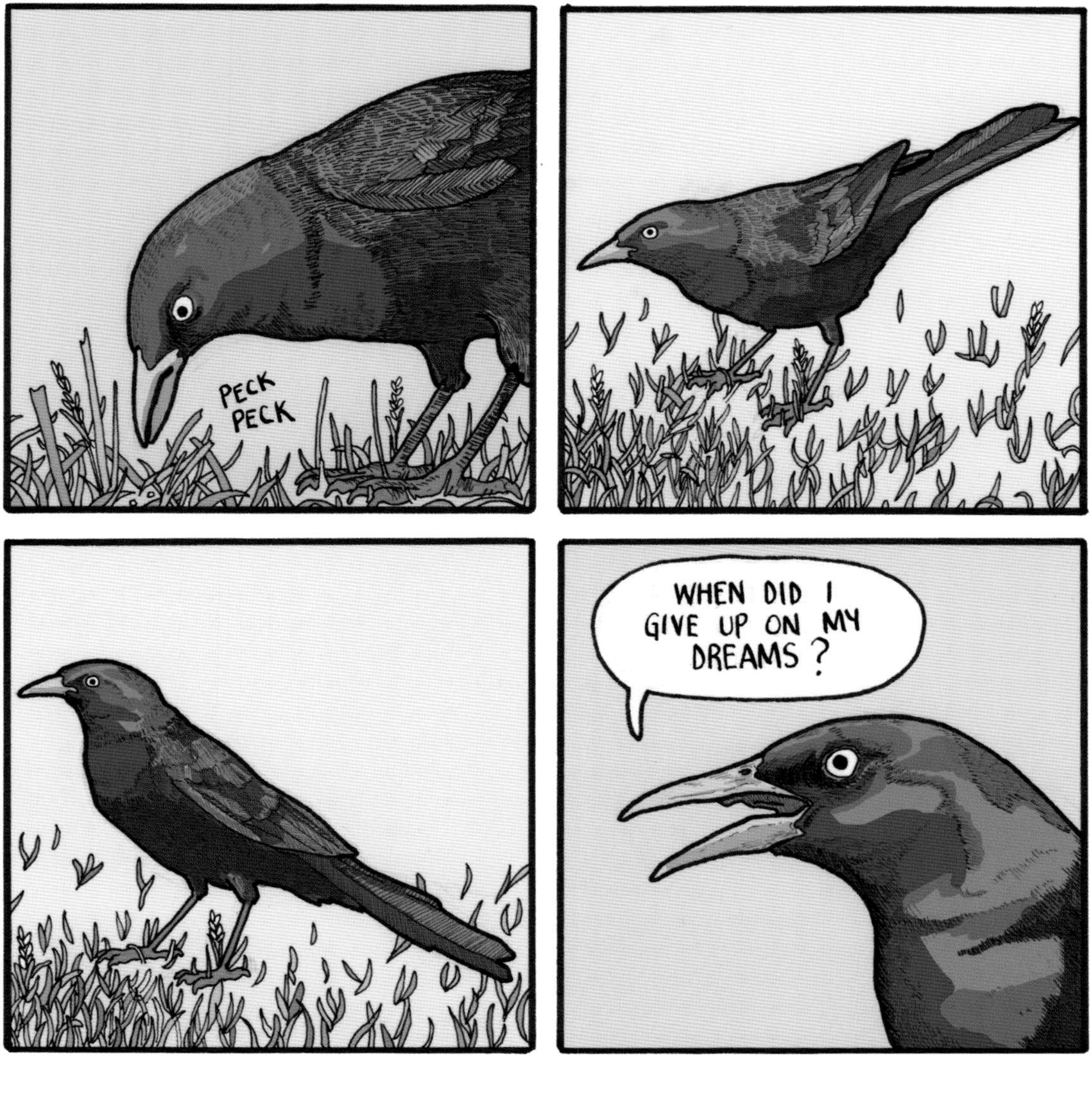
PECK
PECK
WHEN DID I GIVE UP ON MY DREAMS?

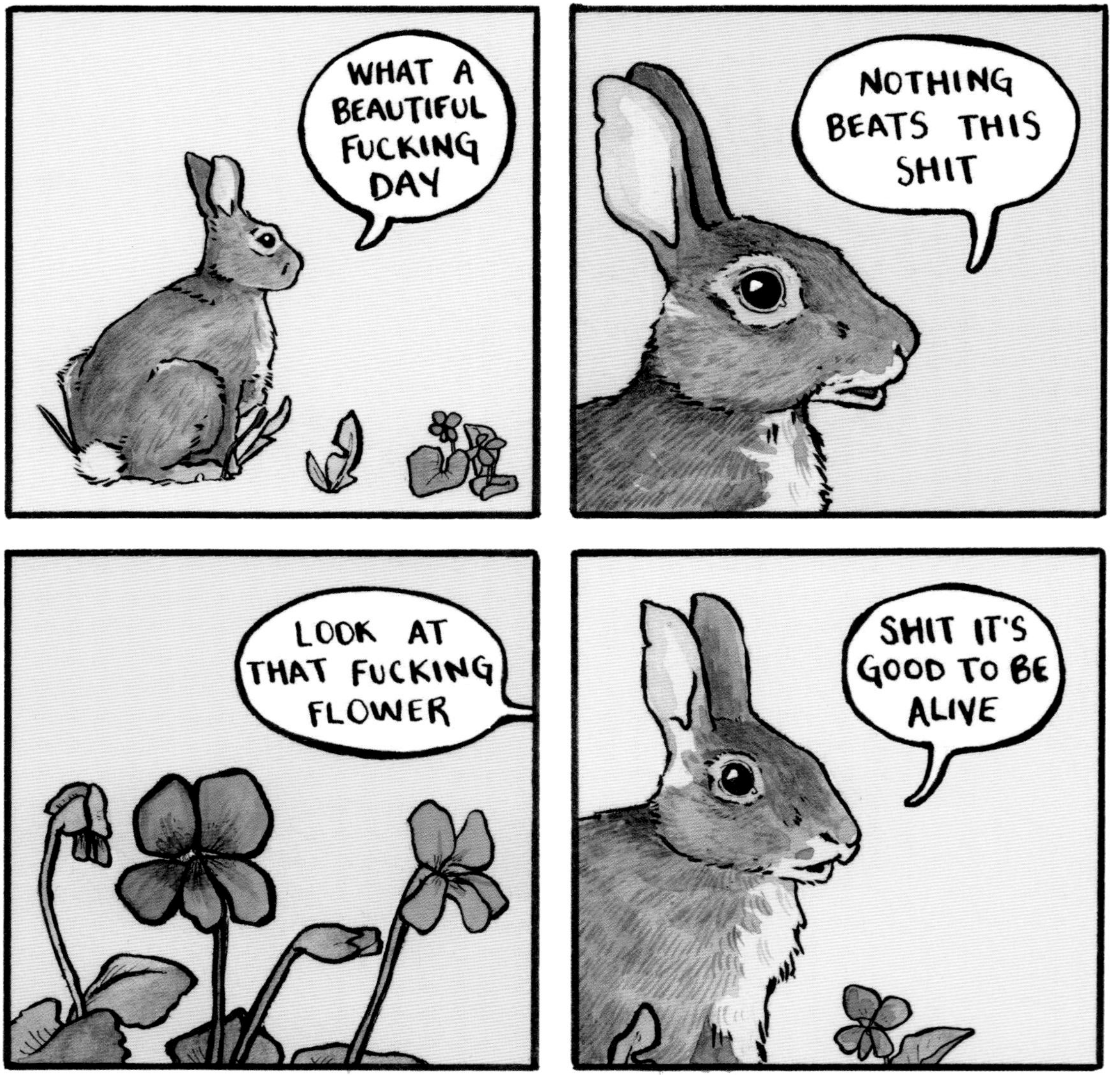
WHAT A BEAUTIFUL FUCKING DAY
NOTHING BEATS THIS SHIT
LOOK AT THAT FUCKING FLOWER
SHIT IT'S GOOD TO BE ALIVE

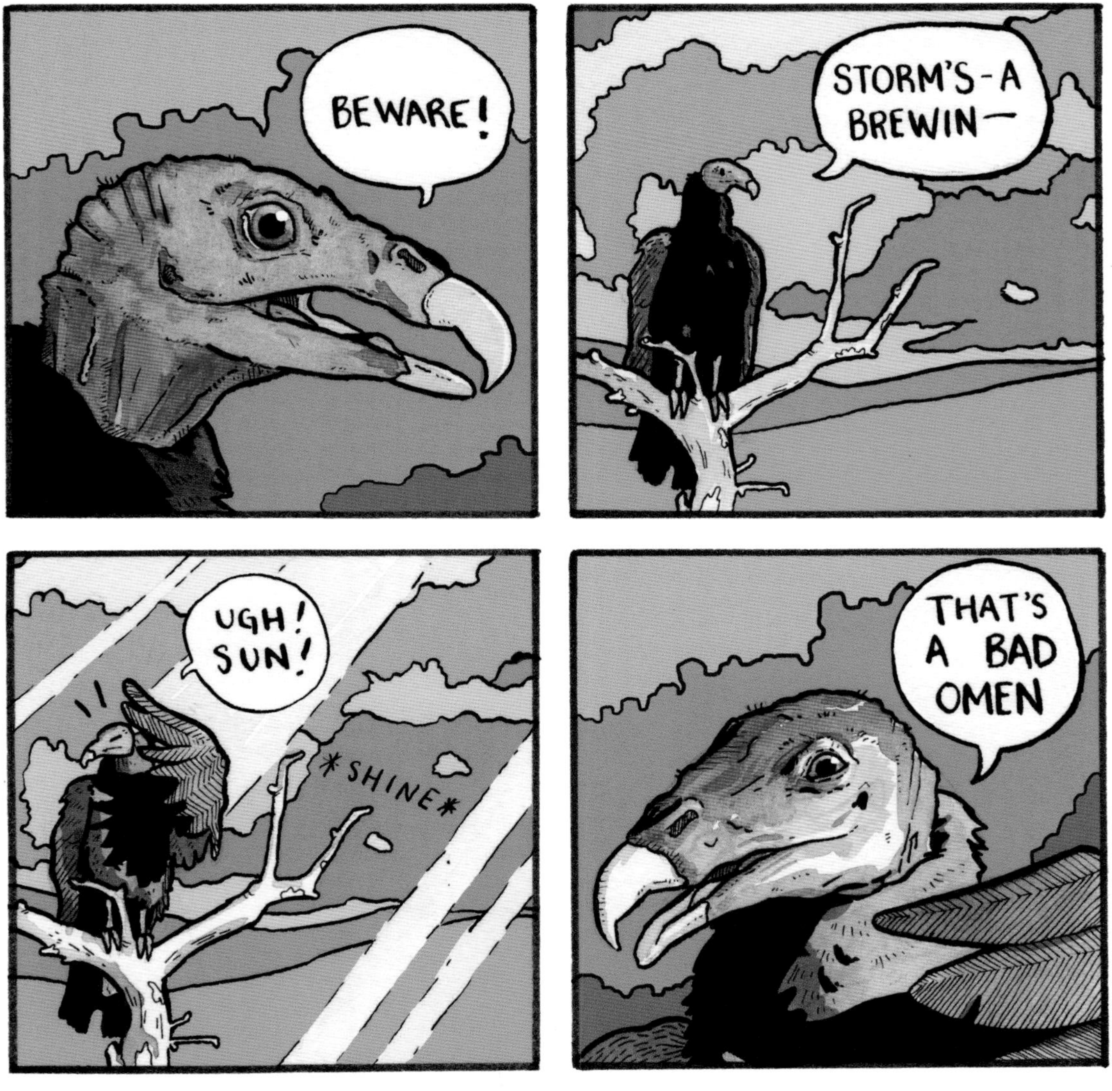
BEWARE!
STORM'S-A BREWIN—
UGH! SUN!
SHINE
THAT'S A BAD OMEN

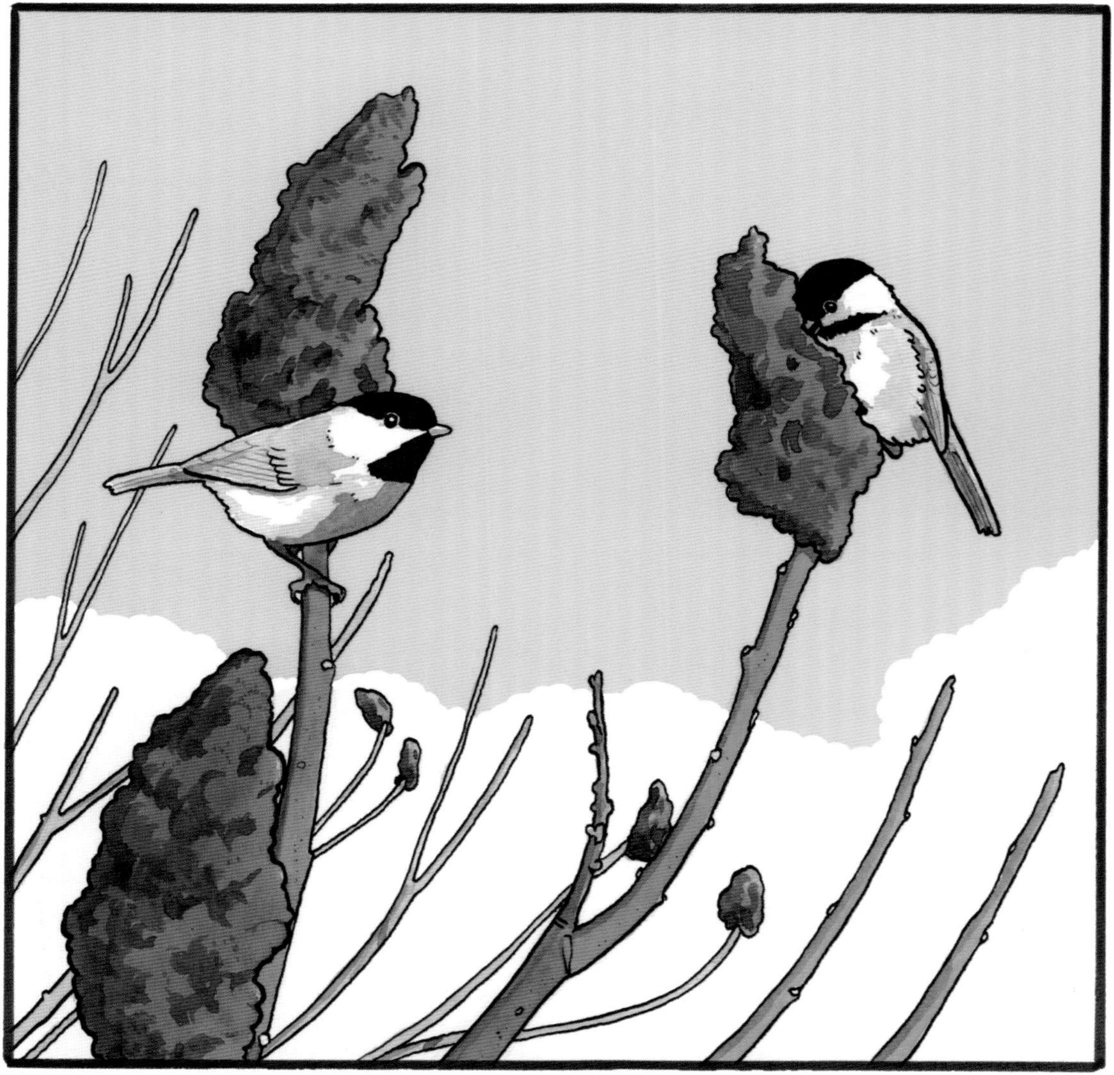

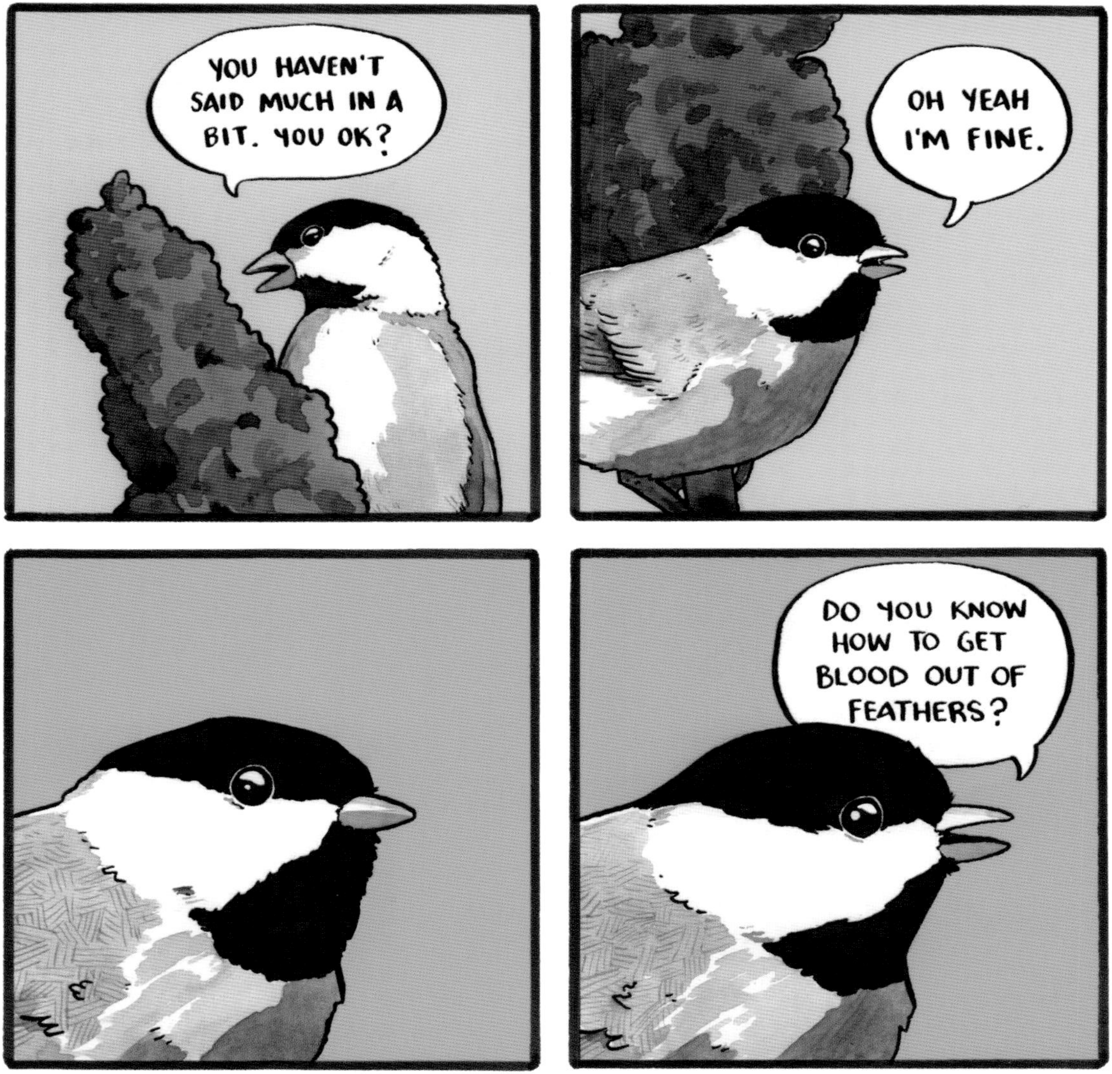
YOU HAVEN'T SAID MUCH IN A BIT. YOU OK?
OH YEAH I'M FINE.
DO YOU KNOW HOW TO GET BLOOD OUT OF FEATHERS?

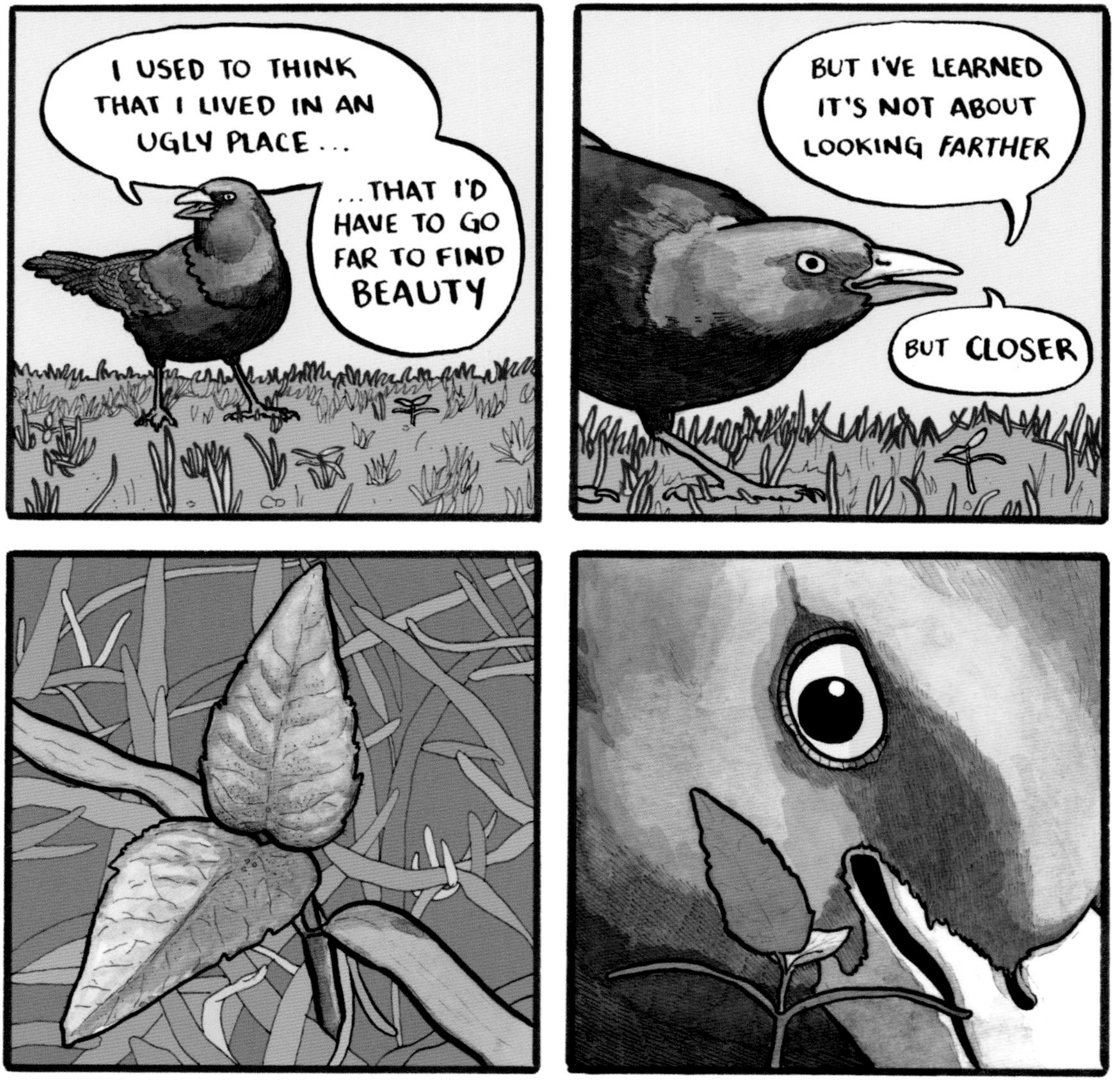
I USED TO THINK THAT I LIVED IN AN UGLY PLACE...
...THAT I'D HAVE TO GO FAR TO FIND BEAUTY
BUT I'VE LEARNED IT'S NOT ABOUT LOOKING FARTHER
BUT CLOSER

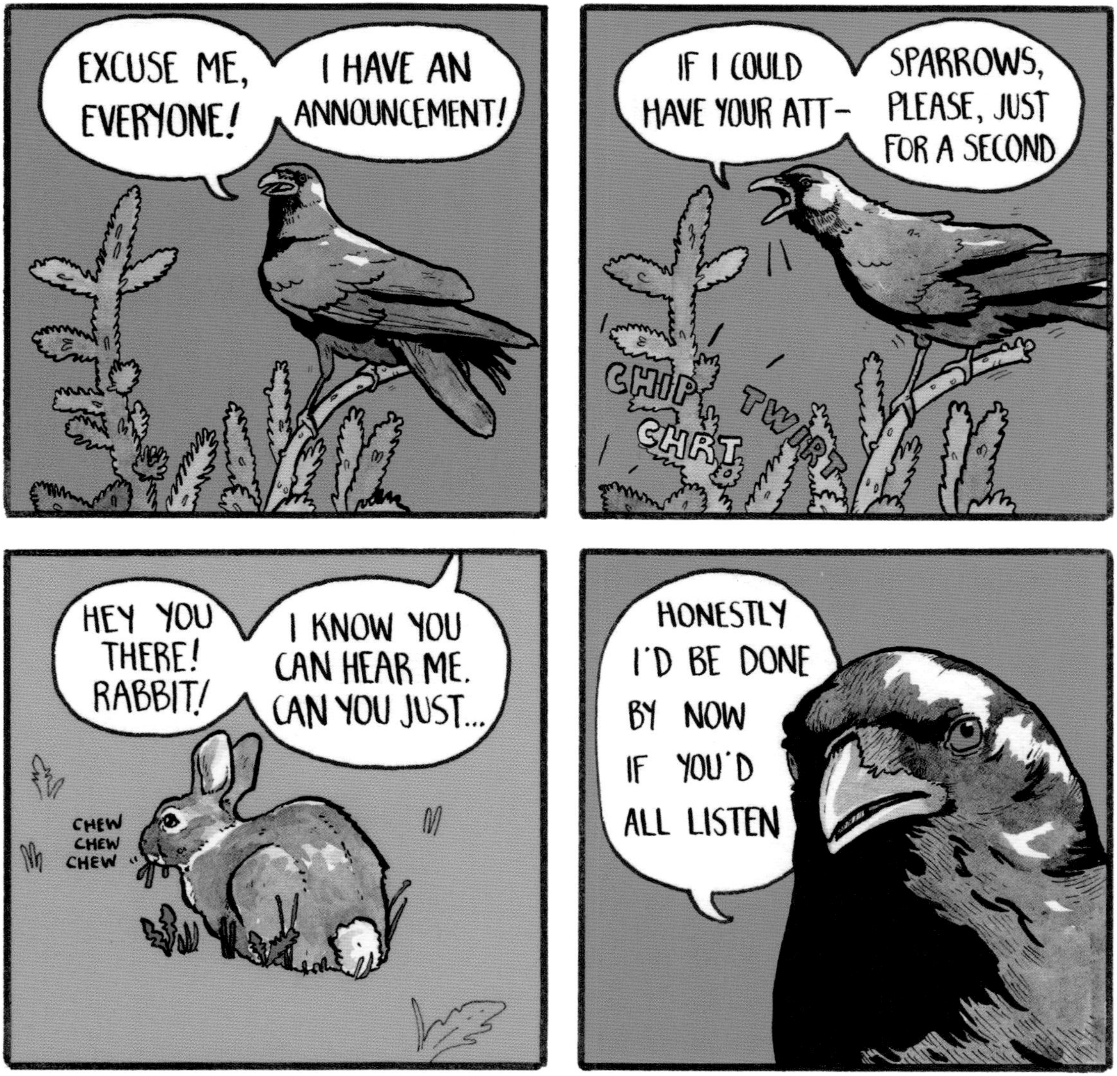
EXCUSE ME, EVERYONE!
I HAVE AN ANNOUNCEMENT!
IF I COULD HAVE YOUR ATT-
SPARROWS, PLEASE, JUST FOR A SECOND
CHIP
CHRT
TWIRT
HEY YOU THERE! RABBIT!
I KNOW YOU CAN HEAR ME. CAN YOU JUST...
CHEW CHEW CHEW
HONESTLY I'D BE DONE BY NOW IF YOU'D ALL LISTEN

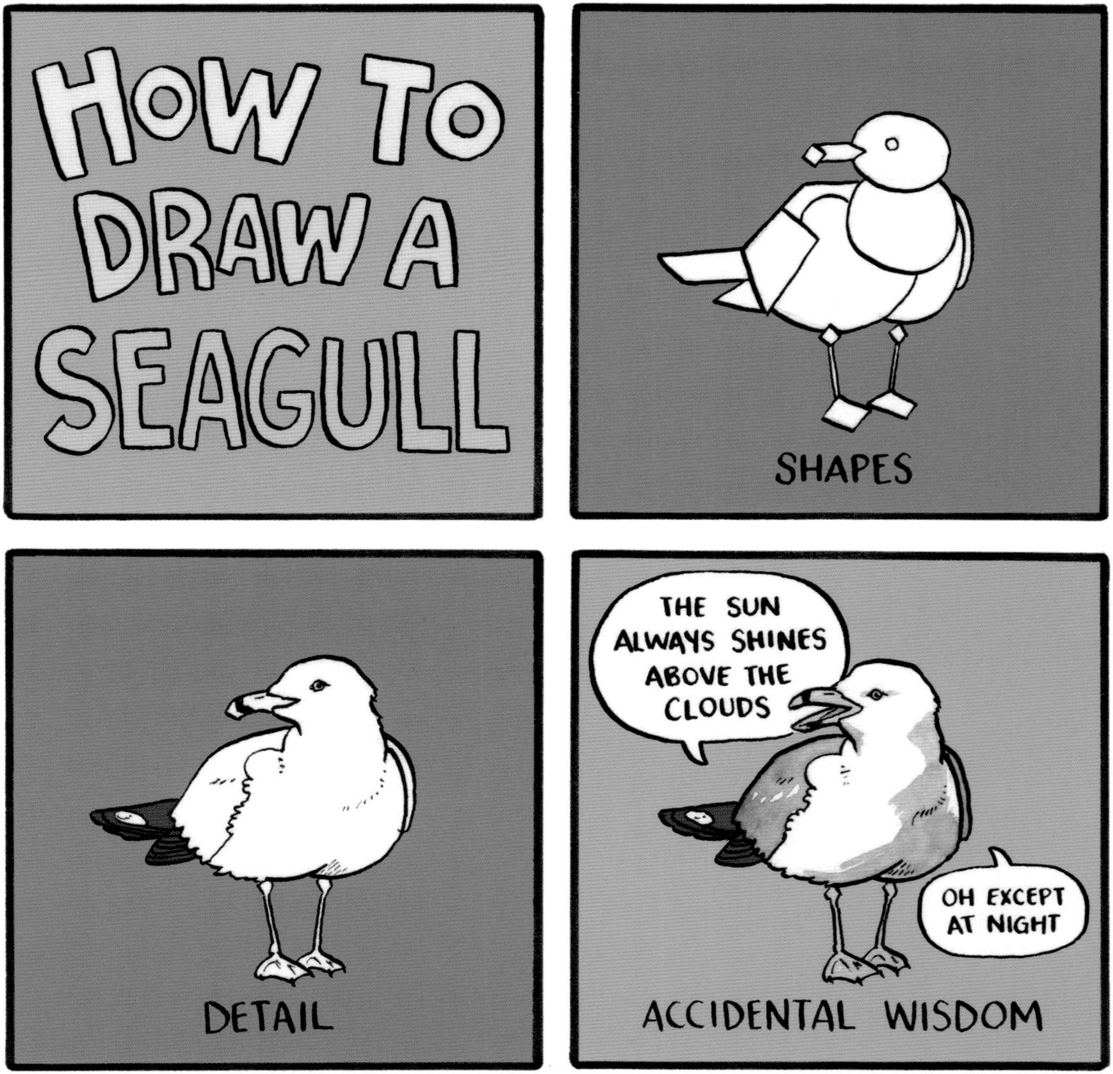
HOW TO DRAW A SEAGULL
SHAPES
DETAIL
THE SUN ALWAYS SHINES ABOVE THE CLOUDS
OH EXCEPT AT NIGHT
ACCIDENTAL WISDOM

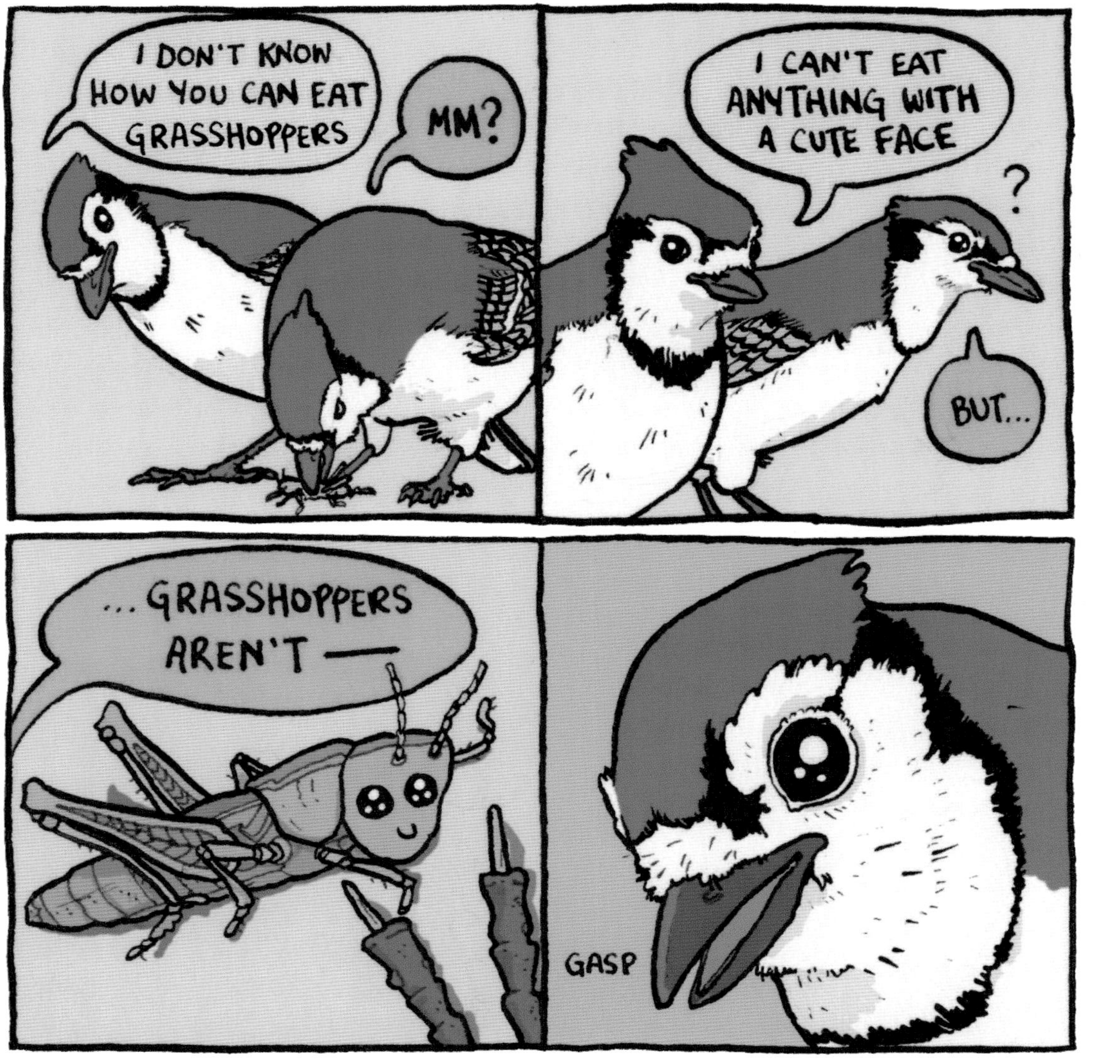
I DON'T KNOW HOW YOU CAN EAT GRASSHOPPERS
MM?
I CAN'T EAT ANYTHING WITH A CUTE FACE
?
BUT...
...GRASSHOPPERS AREN'T —
GASP

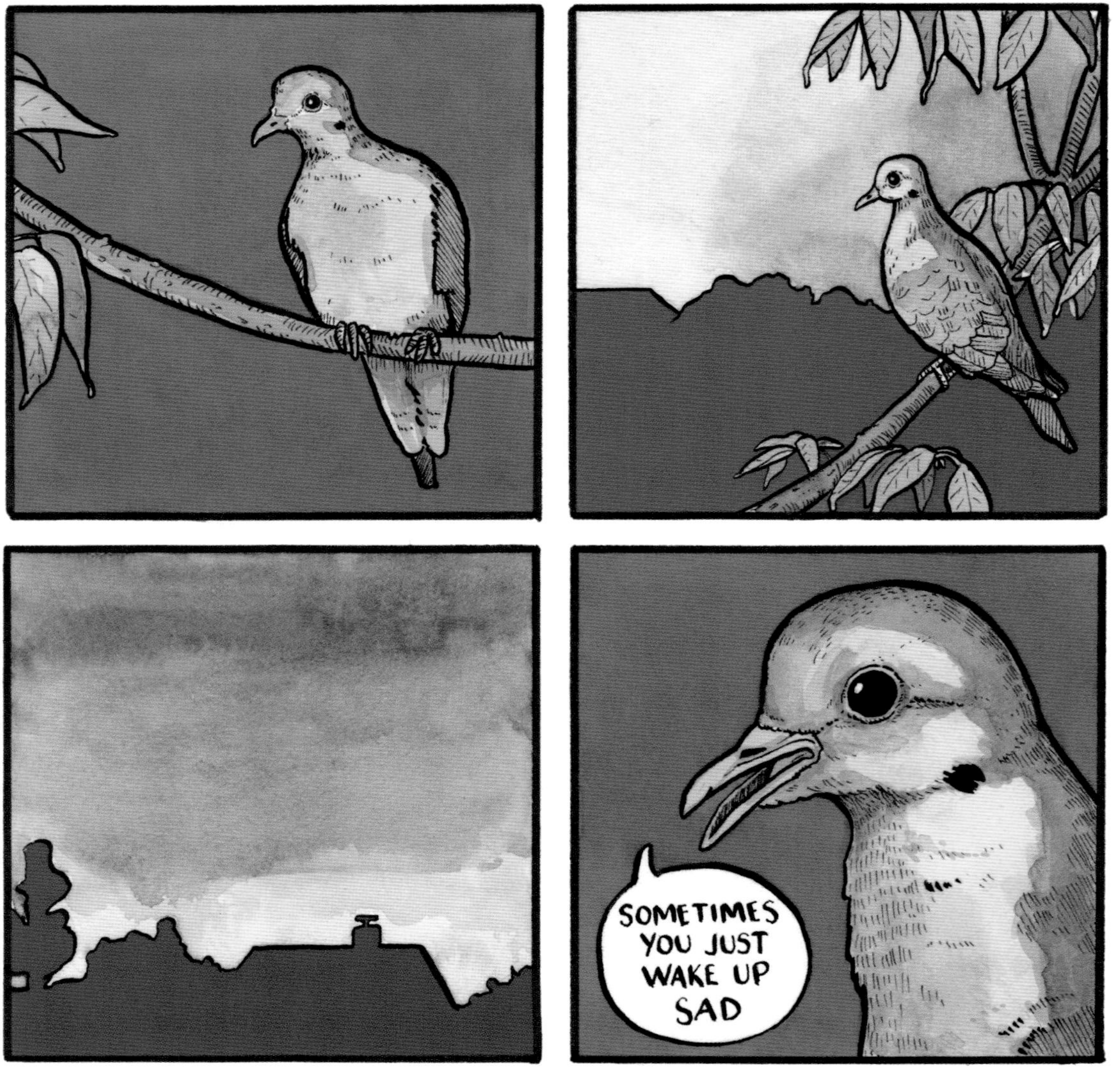
SOMETIMES YOU JUST WAKE UP SAD

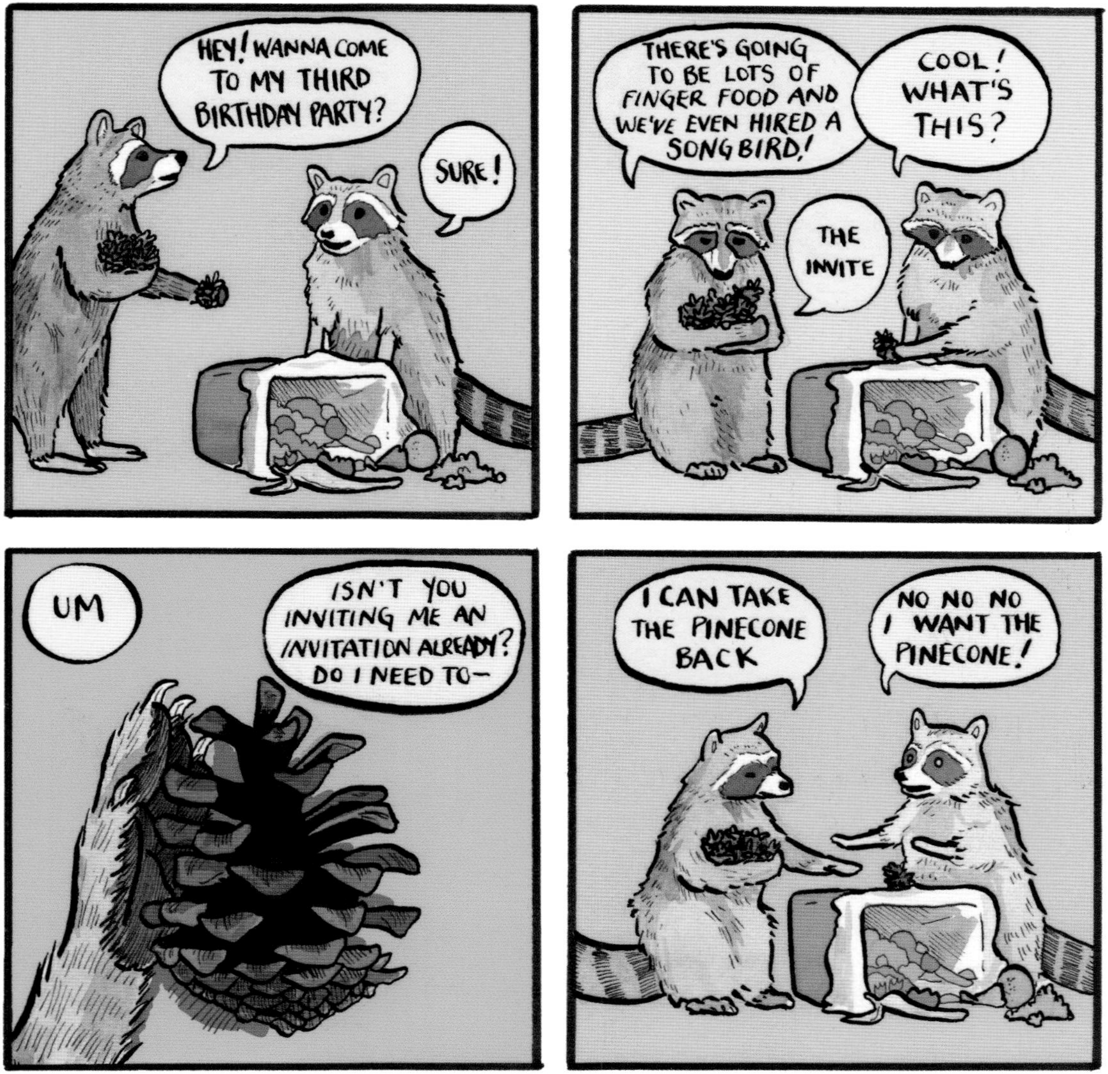
HEY! WANNA COME TO MY THIRD BIRTHDAY PARTY?
SURE!
THERE'S GOING TO BE LOTS OF FINGER FOOD AND WE'VE EVEN HIRED A SONGBIRD!
COOL! WHAT'S THIS?
THE INVITE
UM
ISN'T YOU INVITING ME AN INVITATION ALREADY? DO I NEED TO—
I CAN TAKE THE PINECONE BACK
NO NO NO I WANT THE PINECONE!

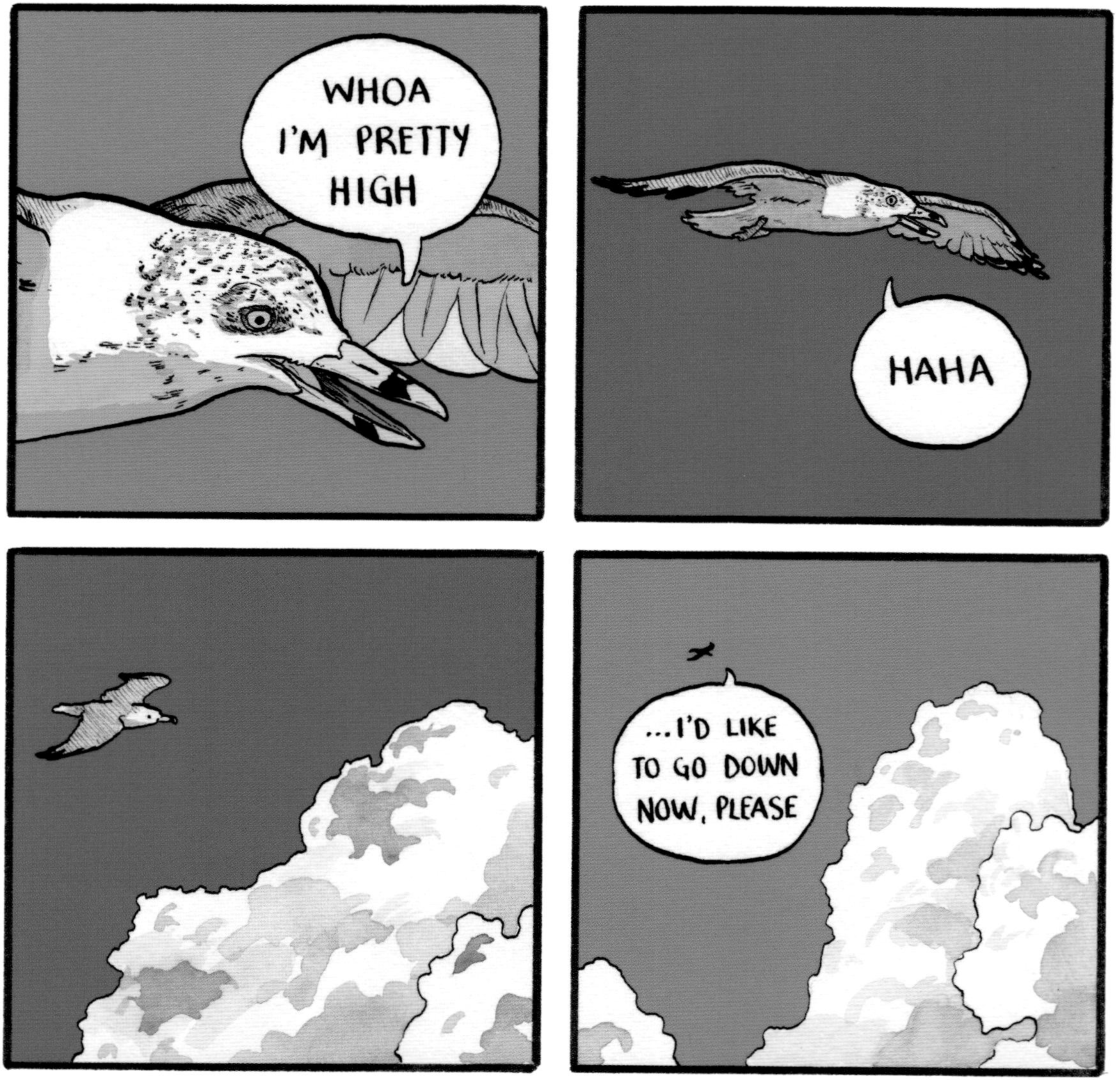
WHOA I'M PRETTY HIGH
HAHA
...I'D LIKE TO GO DOWN NOW, PLEASE

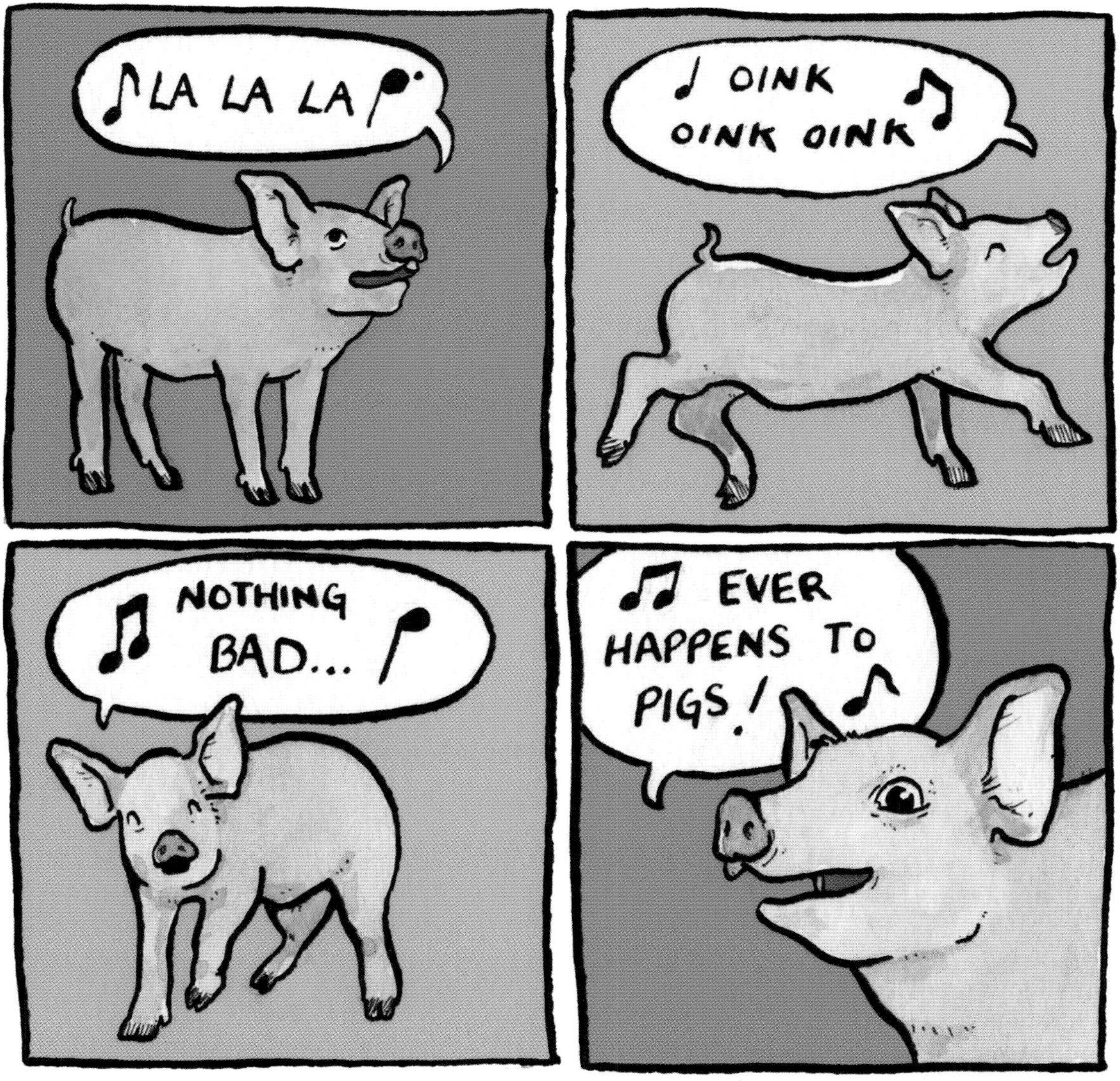
LA LA LA
OINK OINK OINK
NOTHING BAD...
EVER HAPPENS TO PIGS!

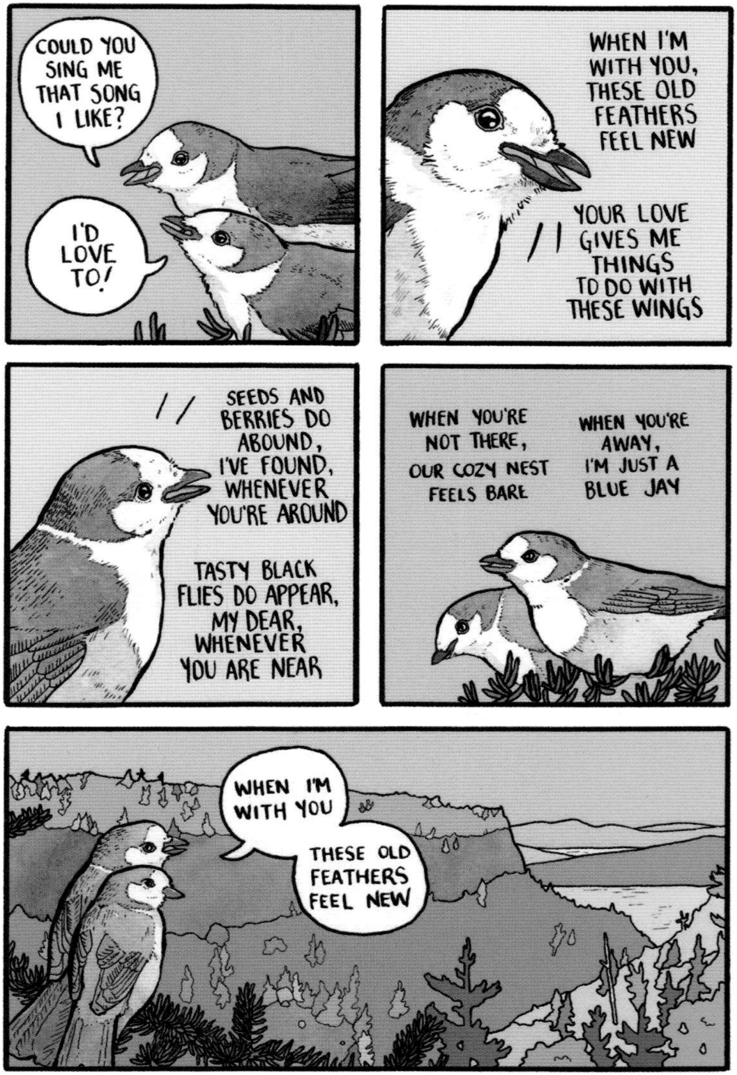
COULD YOU SING ME THAT SONG I LIKE?
I'D LOVE TO!
WHEN I'M WITH YOU, THESE OLD FEATHERS FEEL NEW
YOUR LOVE GIVES ME THINGS TO DO WITH THESE WINGS
SEEDS AND BERRIES DO ABOUND, I'VE FOUND, WHENEVER YOU'RE AROUND
TASTY BLACK FLIES DO APPEAR, MY DEAR, WHENEVER YOU ARE NEAR
WHEN YOU'RE NOT THERE, OUR COZY NEST FEELS BARE
WHEN YOU'RE AWAY, I'M JUST A BLUE JAY
WHEN I'M WITH YOU
THESE OLD FEATHERS FEEL NEW

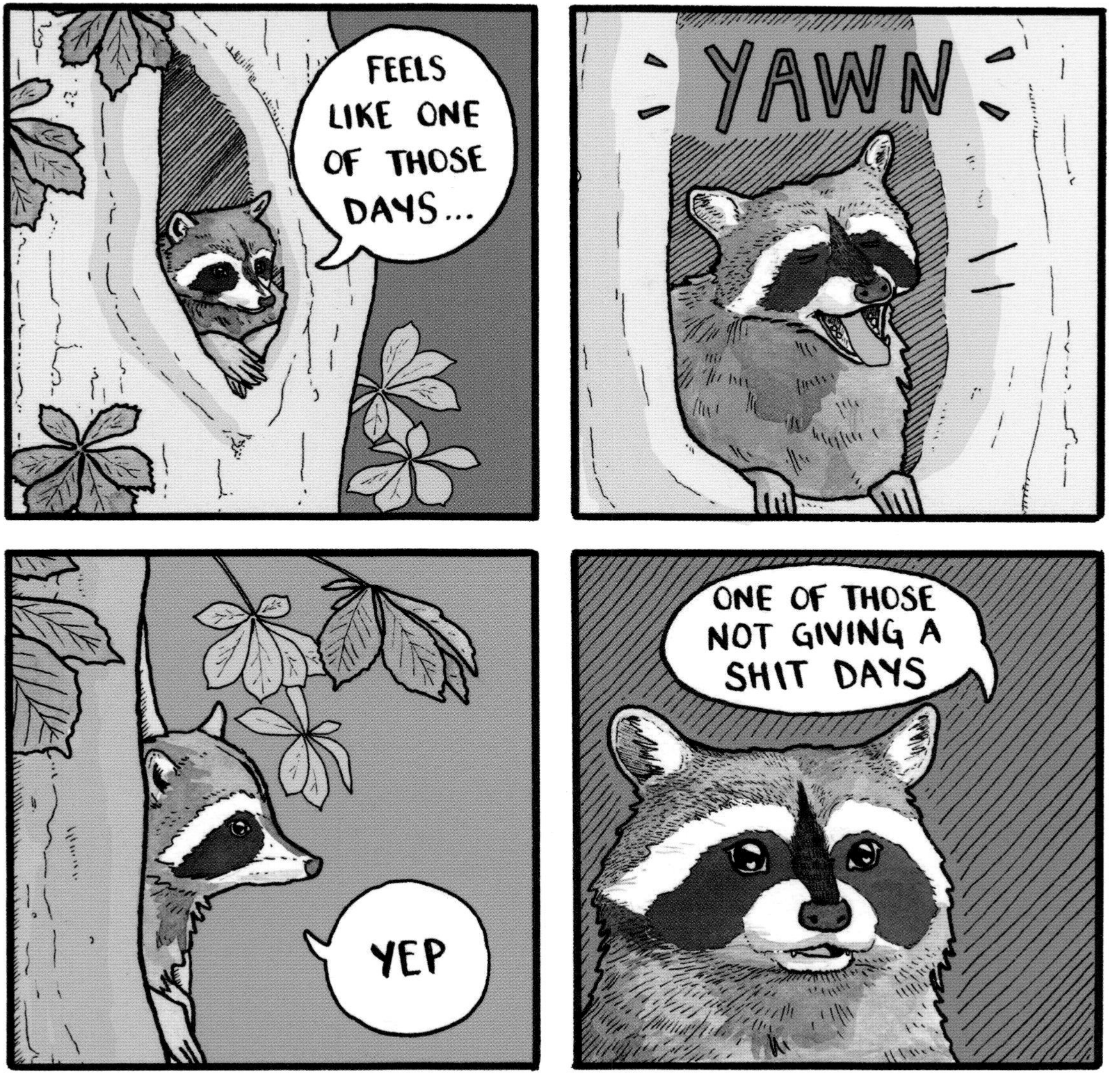
FEELS LIKE ONE OF THOSE DAYS...
YAWN
YEP
ONE OF THOSE NOT GIVING A SHIT DAYS

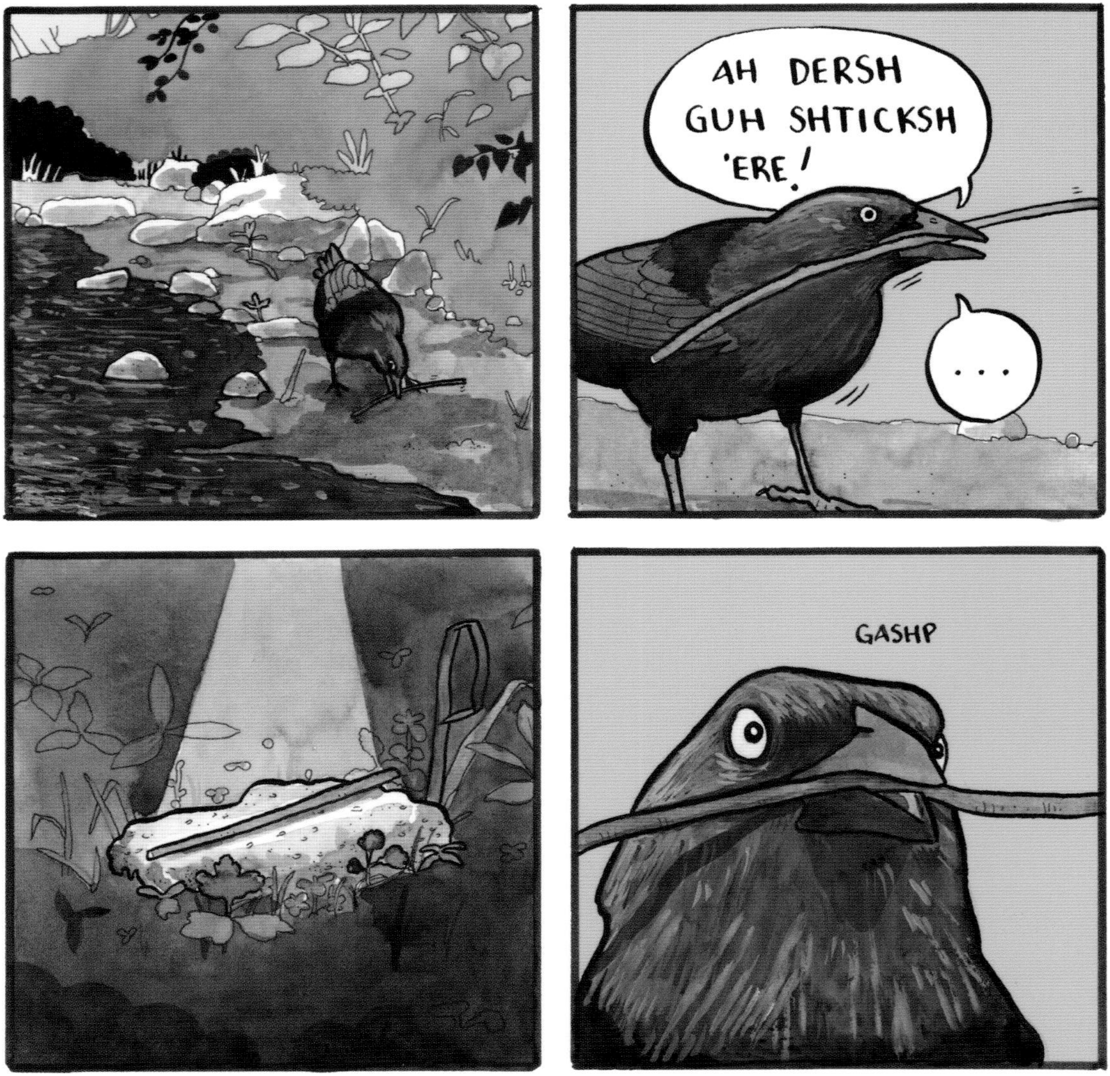
AH DERSH GUH SHTICKSH 'ERE!
...
GASHP

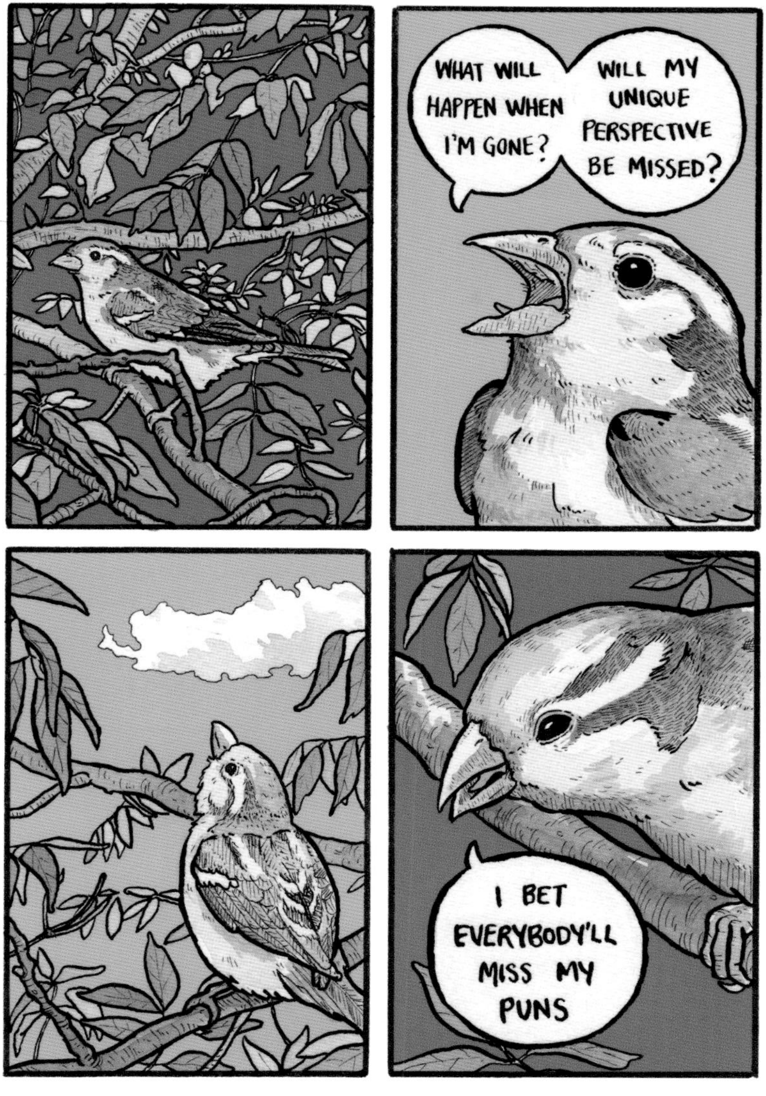
WHAT WILL HAPPEN WHEN I'M GONE?
WILL MY UNIQUE PERSPECTIVE BE MISSED?
I BET EVERYBODY'LL MISS MY PUNS

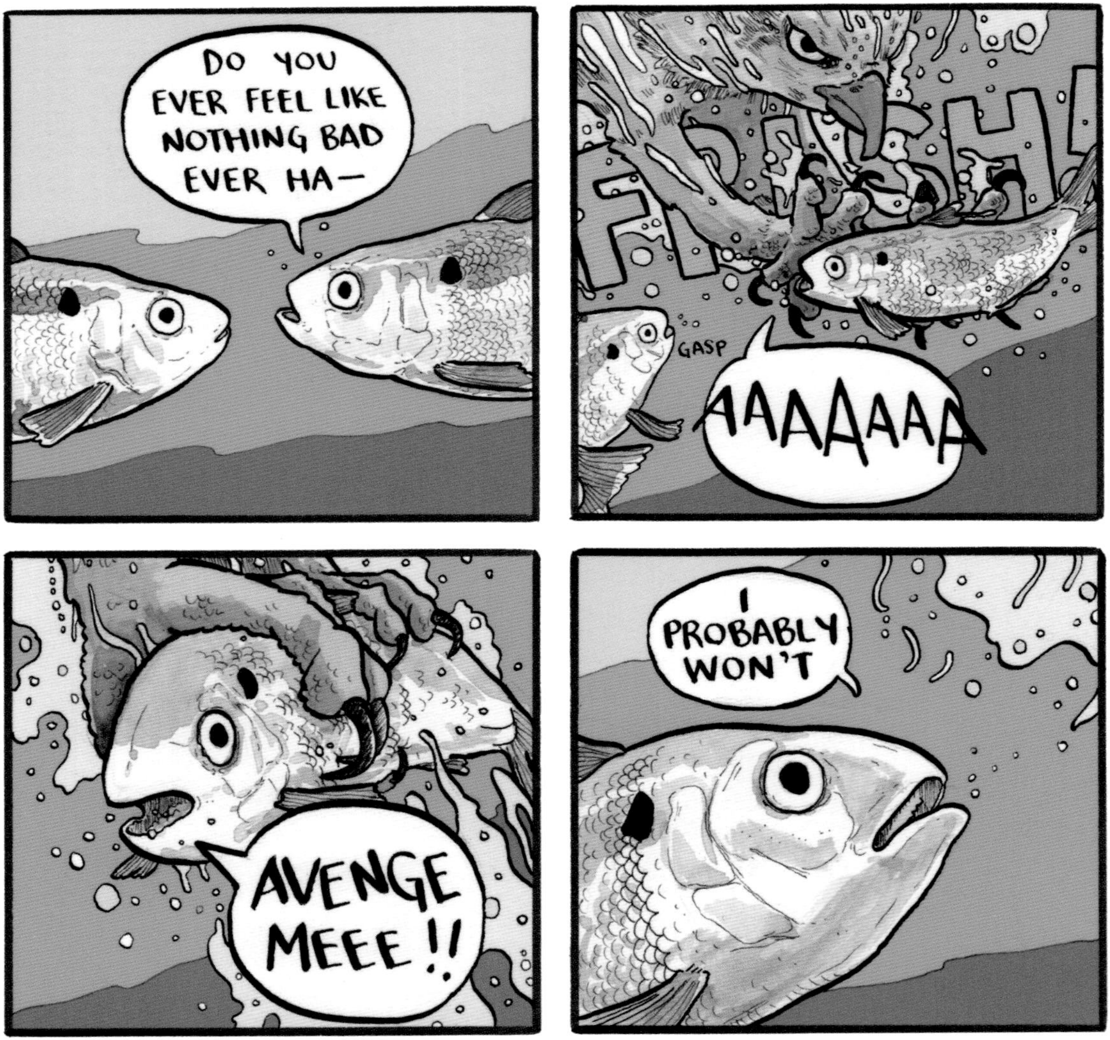
DO YOU EVER FEEL LIKE NOTHING BAD EVER HA—
GASP
AAAAAAA
AVENGE MEEE !!
I PROBABLY WON'T

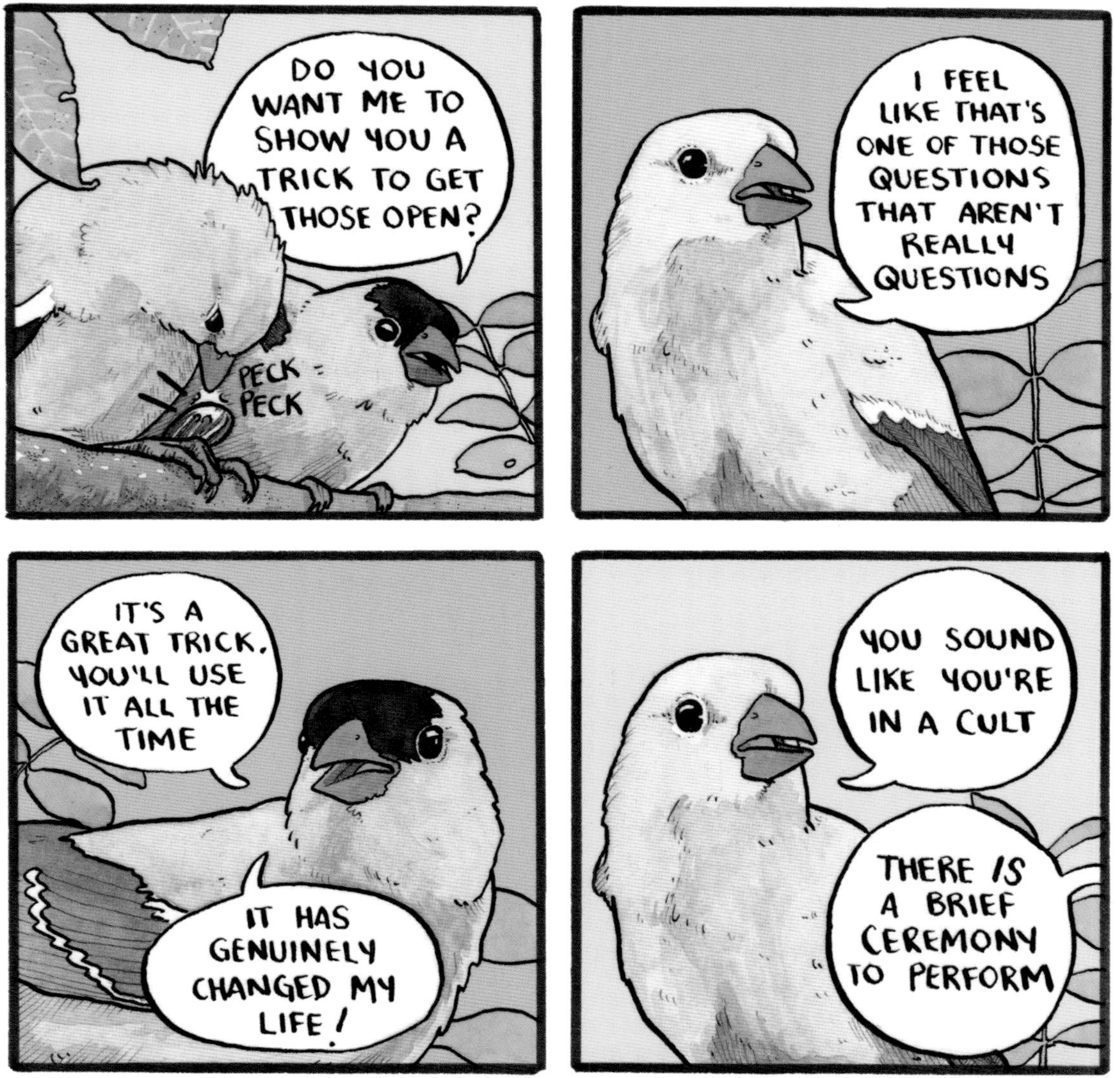
DO YOU WANT ME TO SHOW YOU A TRICK TO GET THOSE OPEN?
PECK PECK
I FEEL LIKE THAT'S ONE OF THOSE QUESTIONS THAT AREN'T REALLY QUESTIONS
IT'S A GREAT TRICK. YOU'LL USE IT ALL THE TIME
IT HAS GENUINELY CHANGED MY LIFE!
YOU SOUND LIKE YOU'RE IN A CULT
THERE *IS* A BRIEF CEREMONY TO PERFORM

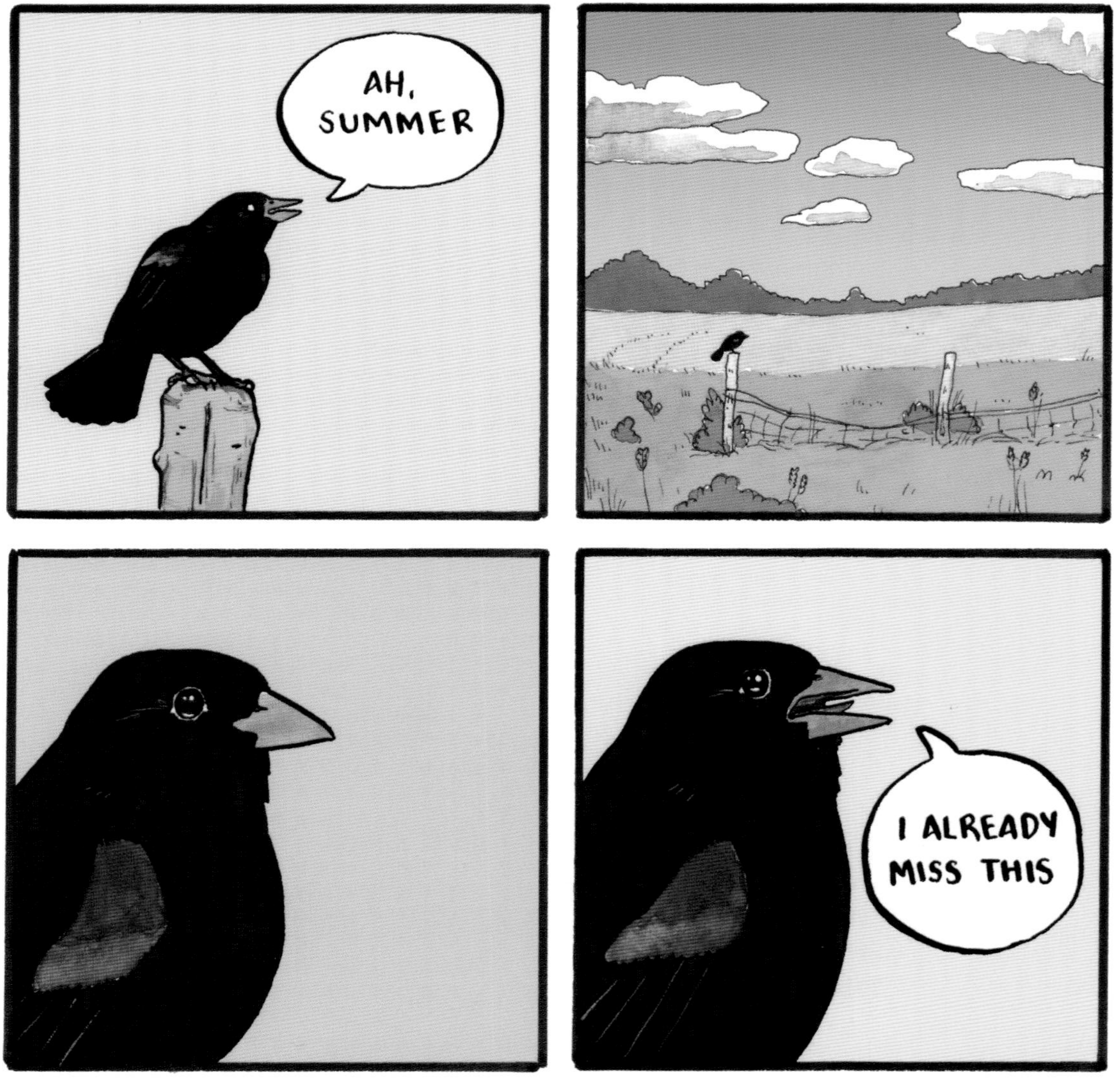
AH, SUMMER
I ALREADY MISS THIS

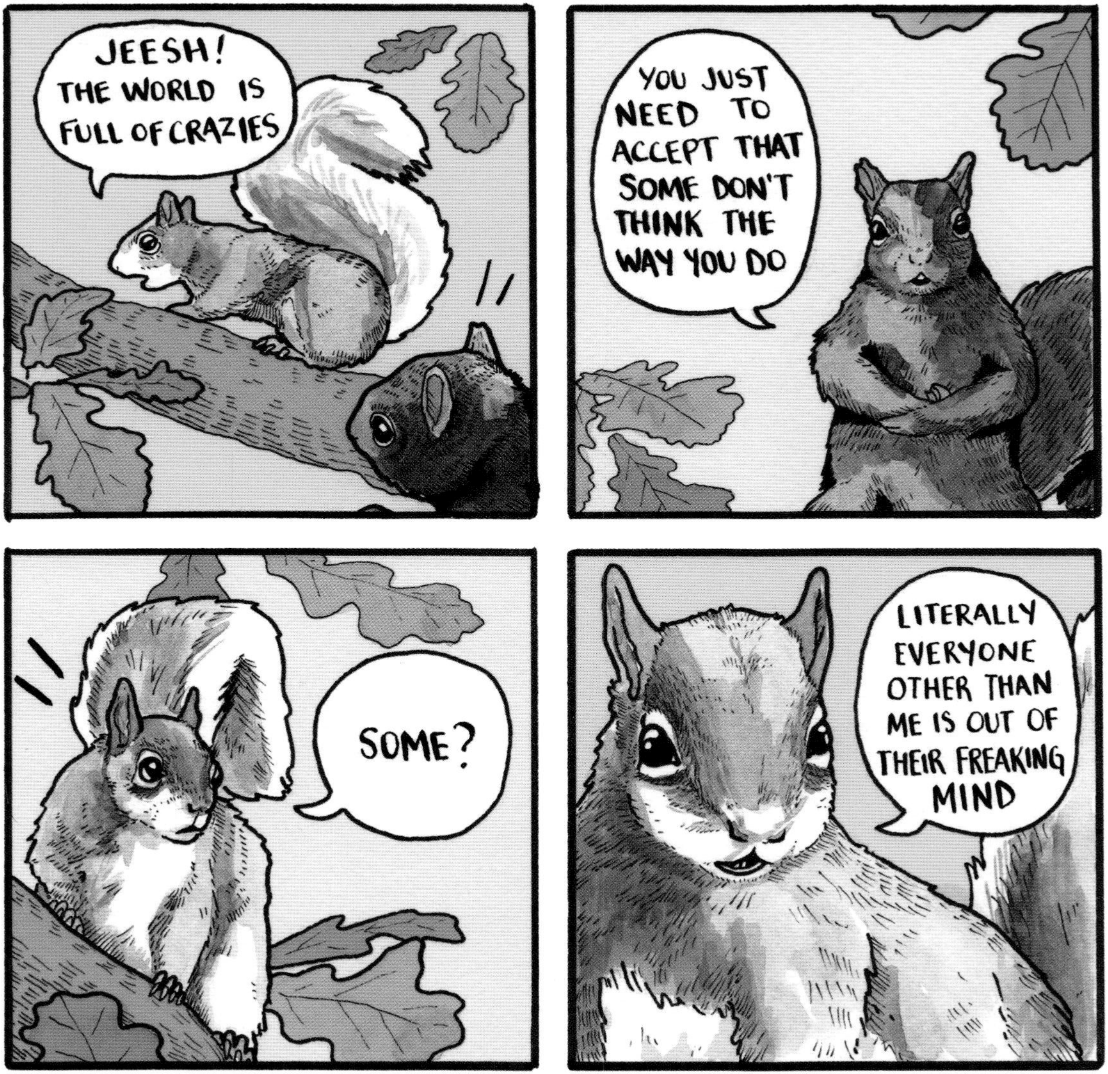
JEESH! THE WORLD IS FULL OF CRAZIES
YOU JUST NEED TO ACCEPT THAT SOME DON'T THINK THE WAY YOU DO
SOME?
LITERALLY EVERYONE OTHER THAN ME IS OUT OF THEIR FREAKING MIND

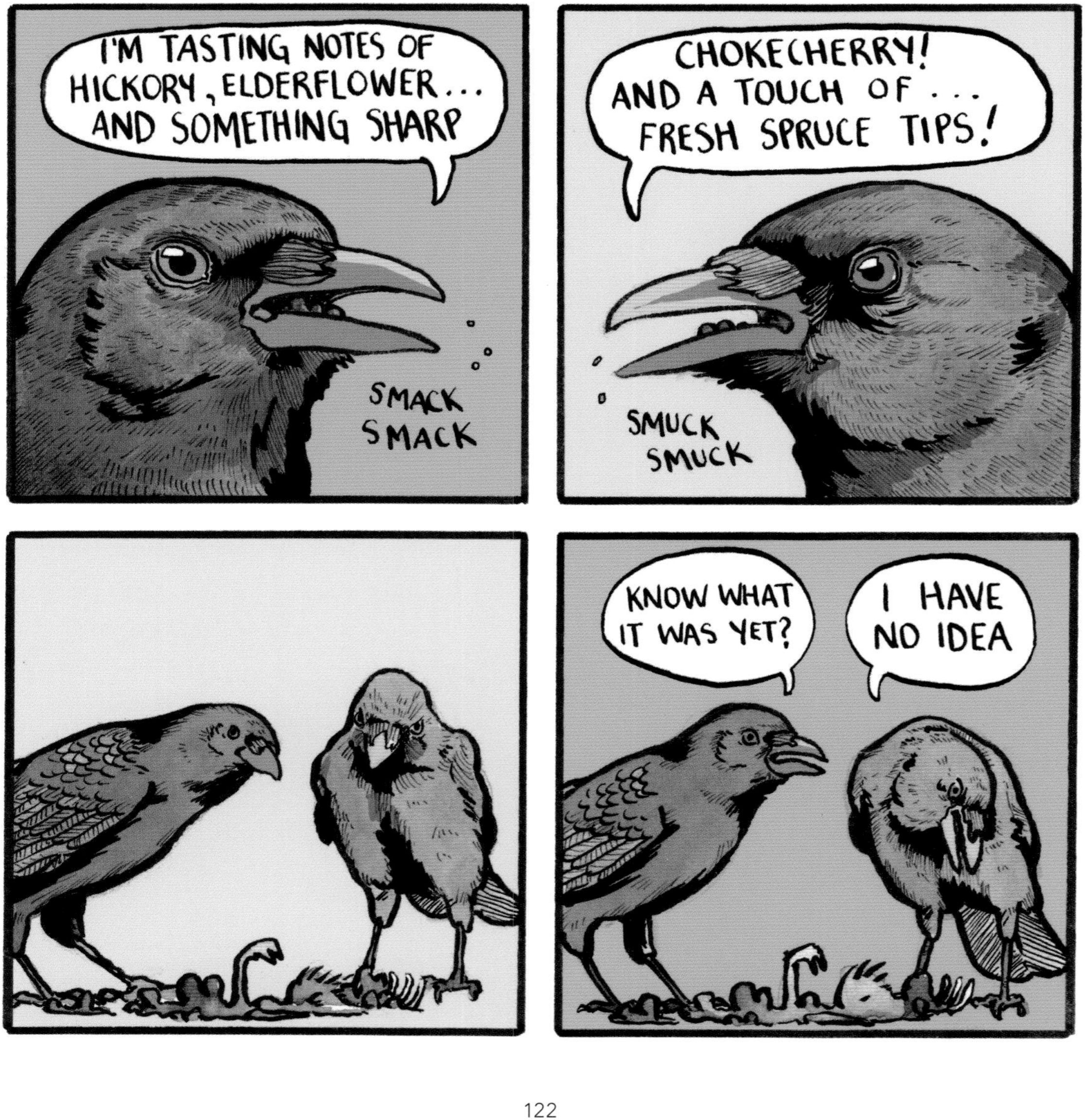
I'M TASTING NOTES OF HICKORY, ELDERFLOWER... AND SOMETHING SHARP
SMACK SMACK
CHOKECHERRY! AND A TOUCH OF ... FRESH SPRUCE TIPS!
SMUCK SMUCK
KNOW WHAT IT WAS YET?
I HAVE NO IDEA

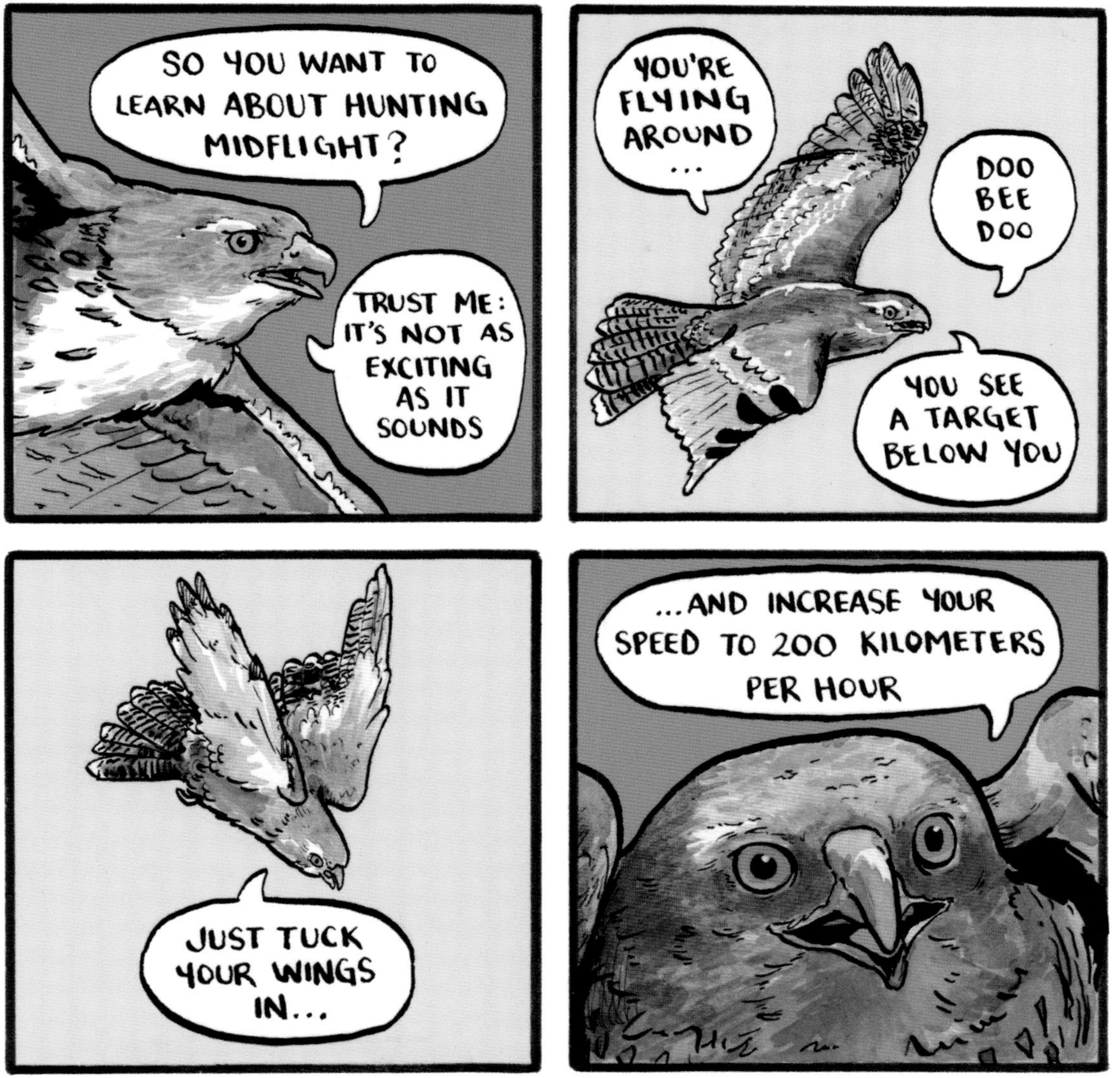
SO YOU WANT TO LEARN ABOUT HUNTING MIDFLIGHT?
TRUST ME: IT'S NOT AS EXCITING AS IT SOUNDS
YOU'RE FLYING AROUND ...
DOO BEE DOO
YOU SEE A TARGET BELOW YOU
JUST TUCK YOUR WINGS IN...
...AND INCREASE YOUR SPEED TO 200 KILOMETERS PER HOUR

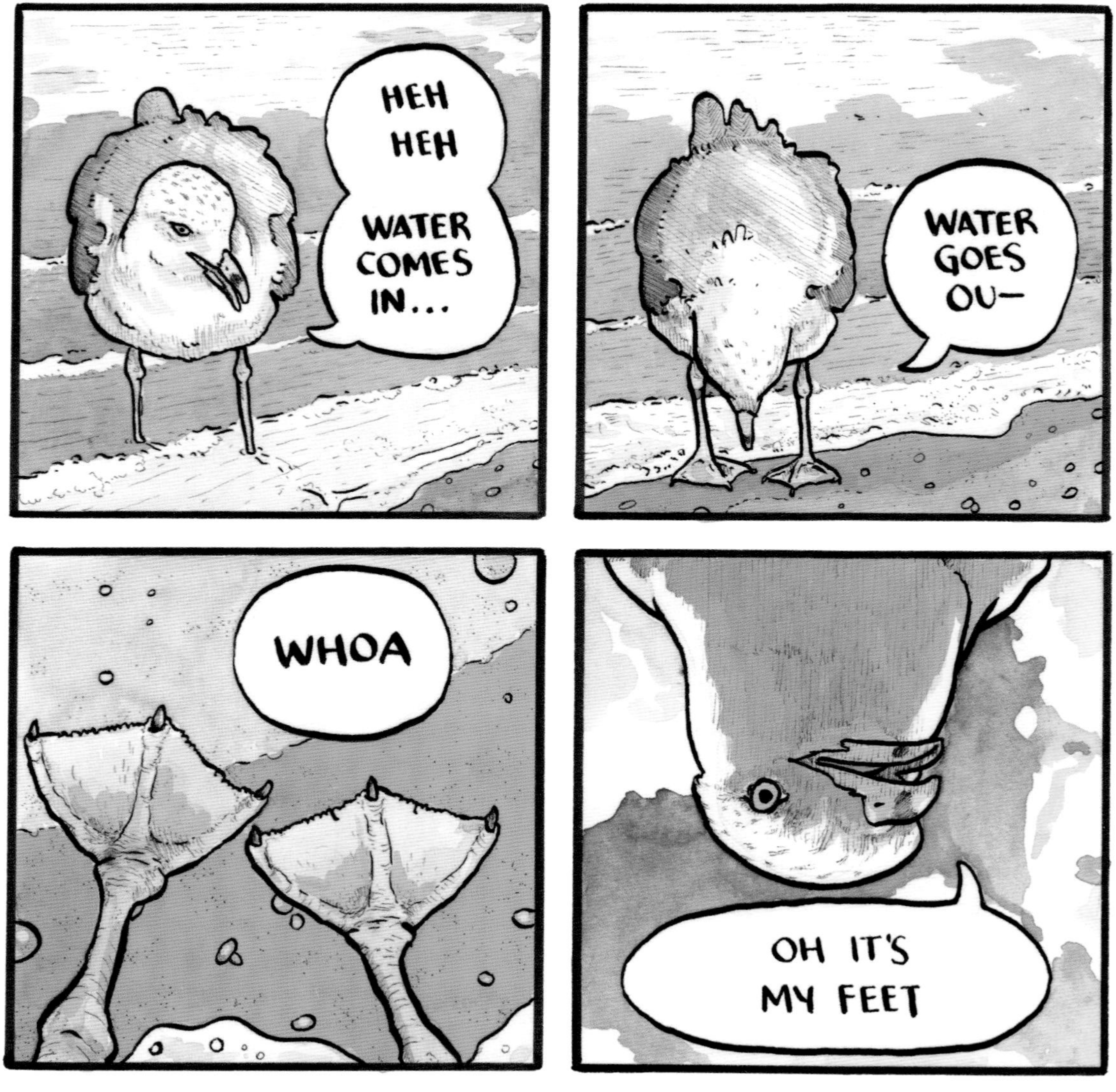
HEH HEH
WATER COMES IN...
WATER GOES OU–
WHOA
OH IT'S MY FEET

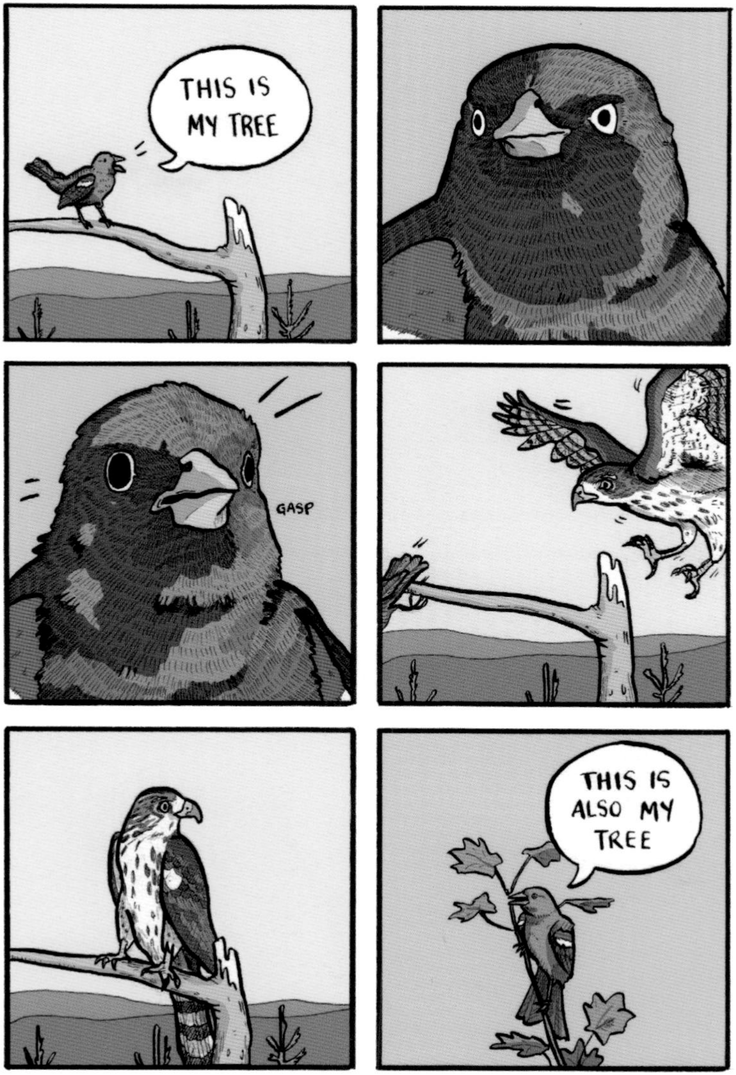
THIS IS MY TREE
GASP
THIS IS ALSO MY TREE

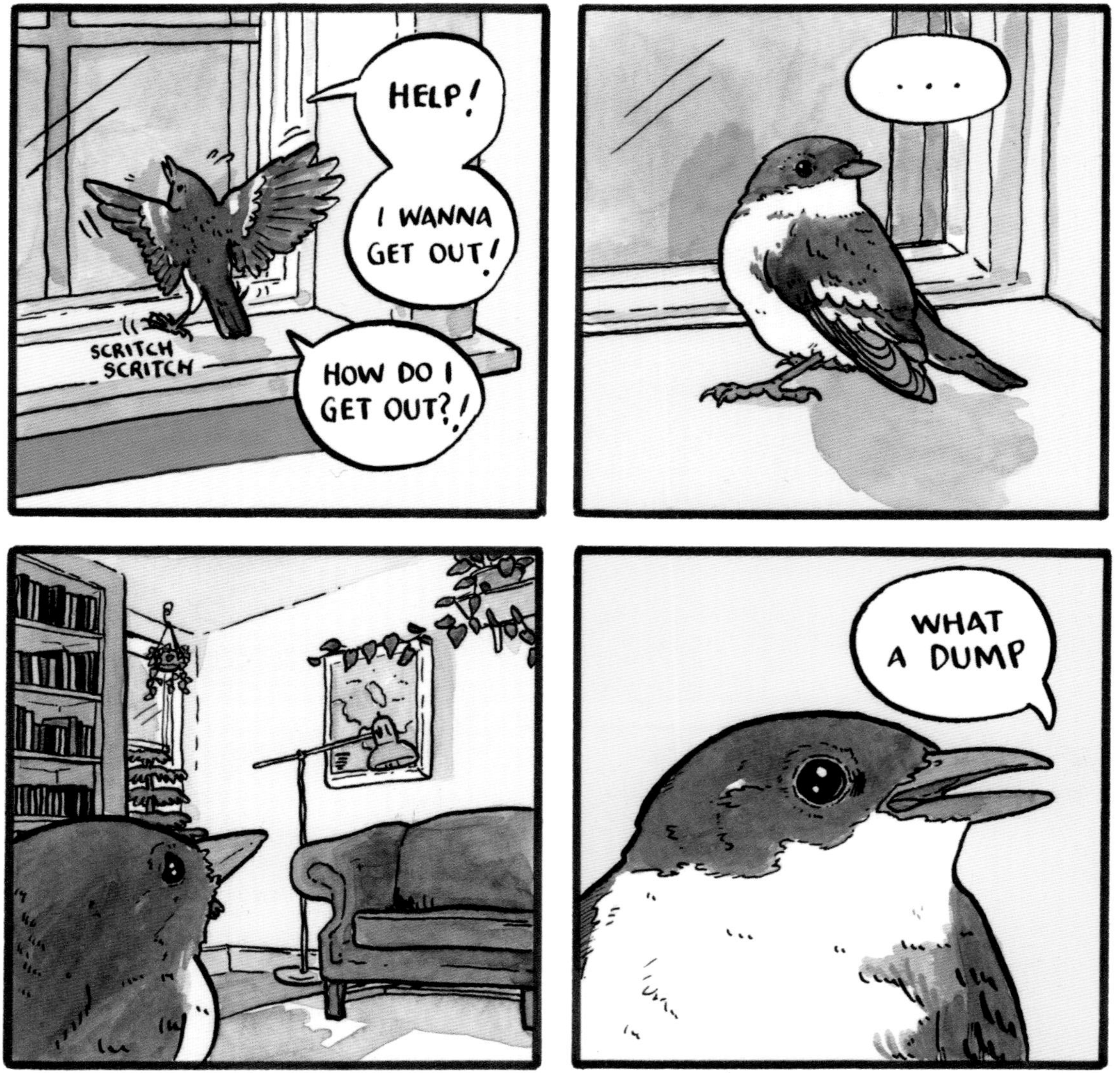
HELP!
I WANNA GET OUT!
SCRITCH SCRITCH
HOW DO I GET OUT?!
. . .
WHAT A DUMP

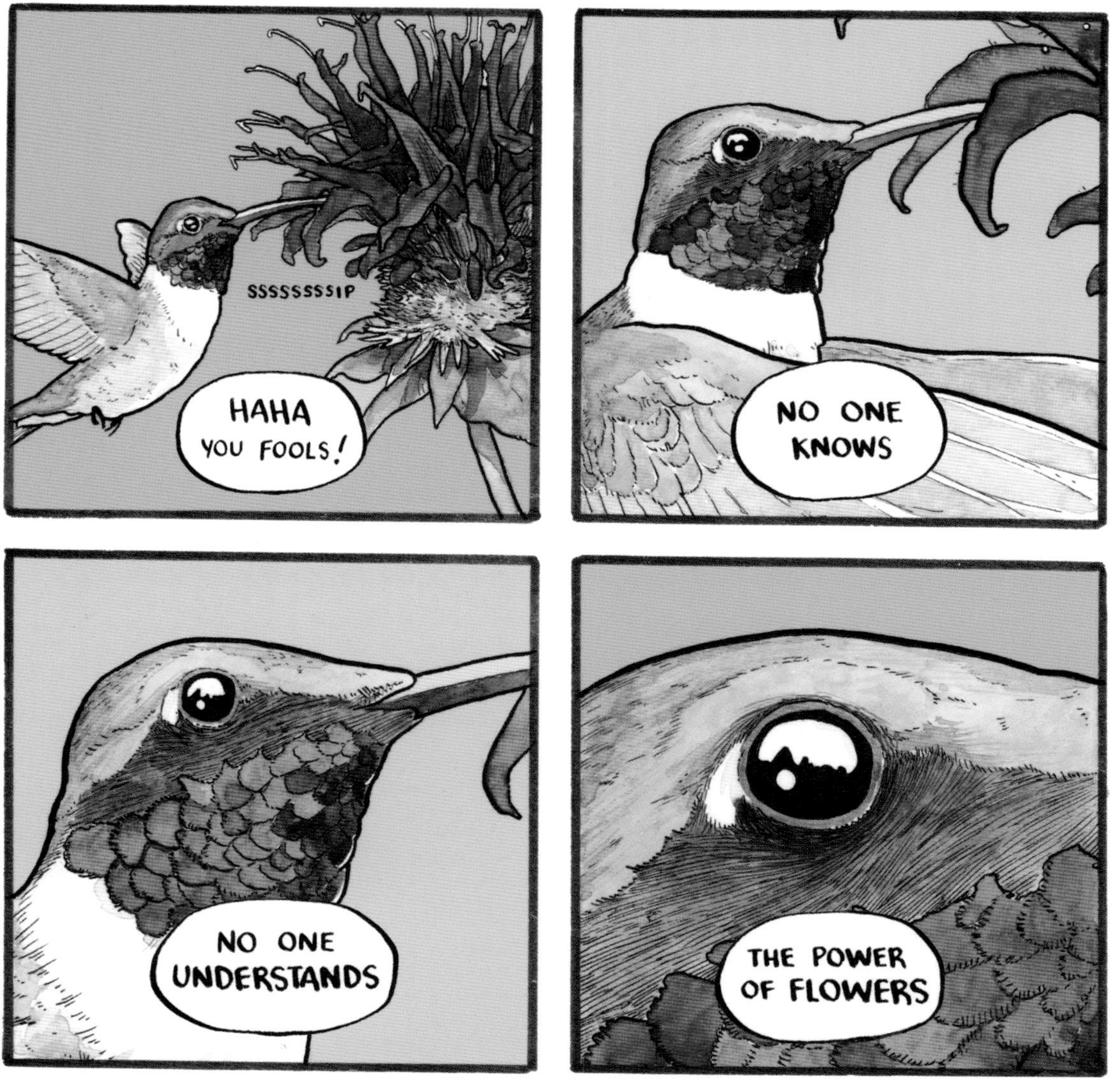
SSSSSSSSIP
HAHA YOU FOOLS!
NO ONE KNOWS
NO ONE UNDERSTANDS
THE POWER OF FLOWERS

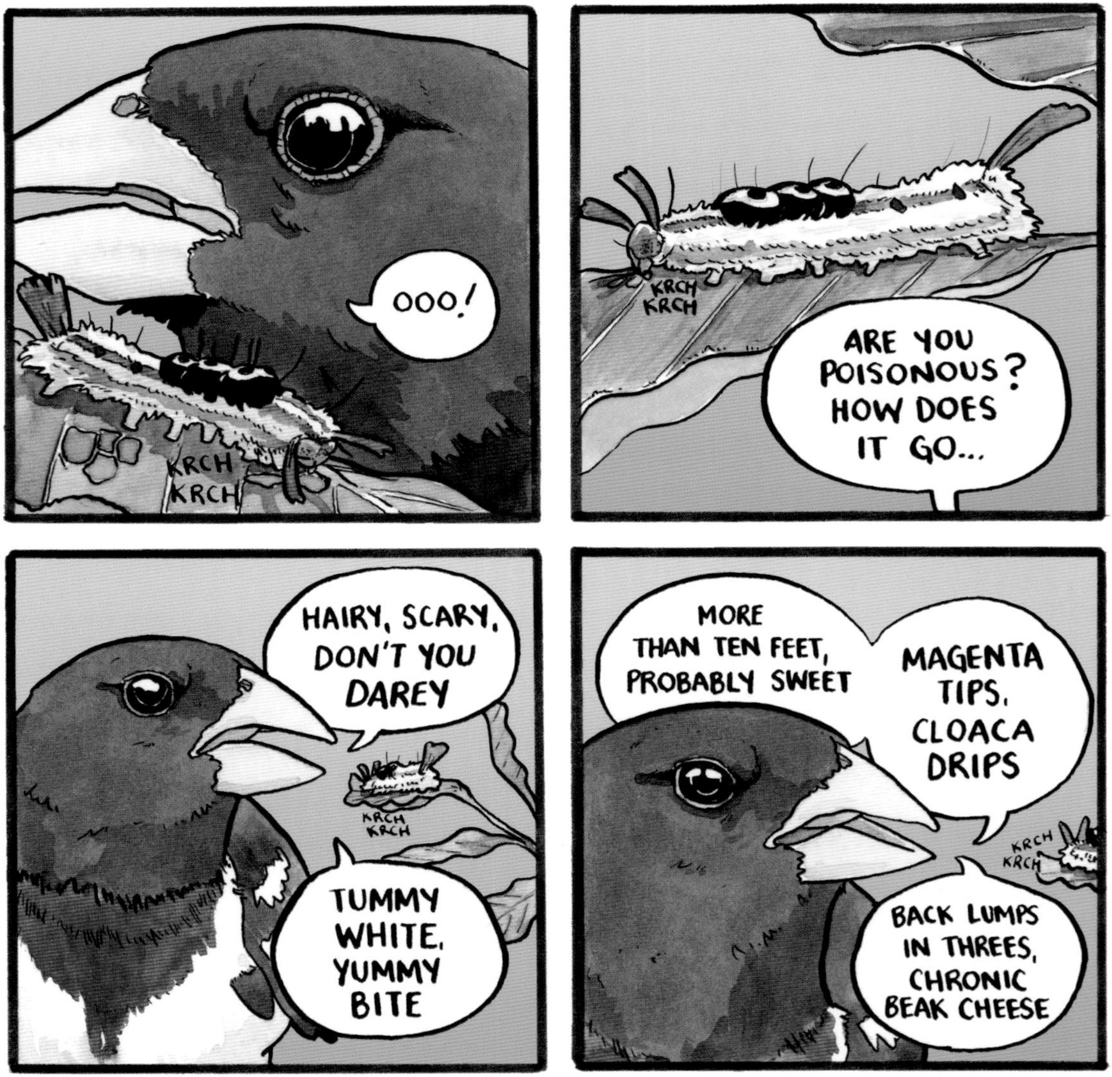
OOO!
KRCH KRCH
KRCH KRCH
ARE YOU POISONOUS? HOW DOES IT GO...
HAIRY, SCARY, DON'T YOU DAREY
KRCH KRCH
TUMMY WHITE, YUMMY BITE
MORE THAN TEN FEET, PROBABLY SWEET
MAGENTA TIPS, CLOACA DRIPS
KRCH KRCH
BACK LUMPS IN THREES, CHRONIC BEAK CHEESE

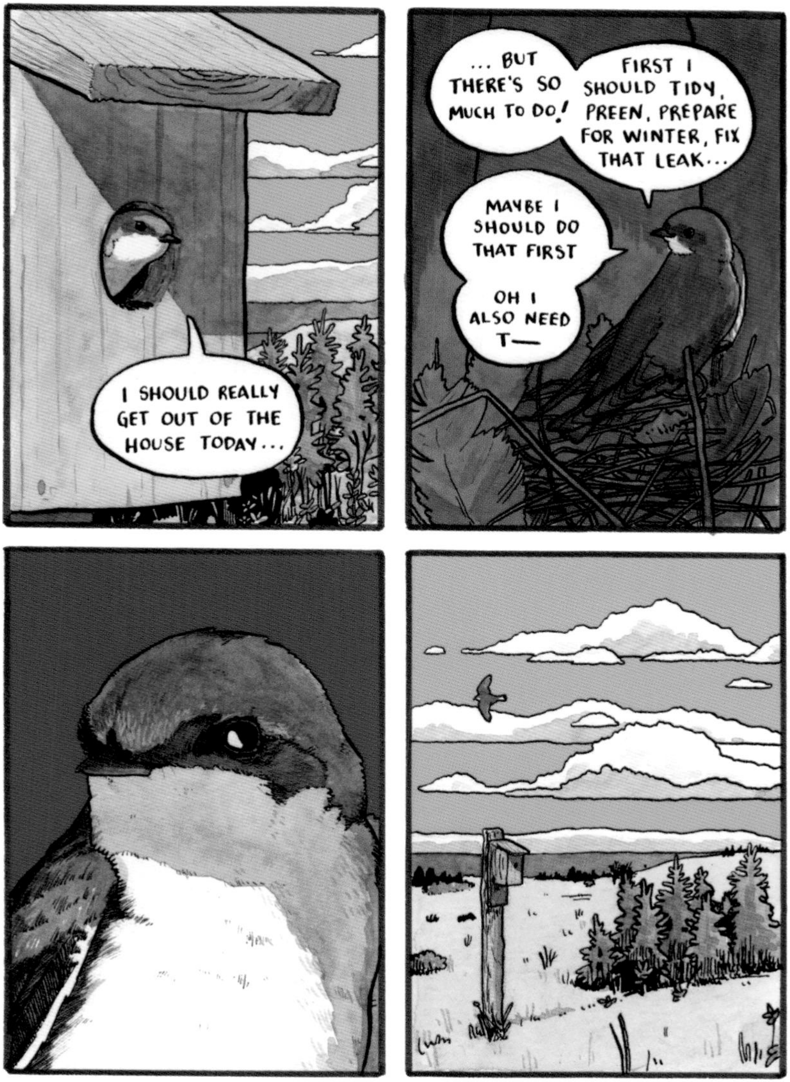
I SHOULD REALLY GET OUT OF THE HOUSE TODAY...
... BUT THERE'S SO MUCH TO DO!
FIRST I SHOULD TIDY, PREEN, PREPARE FOR WINTER, FIX THAT LEAK...
MAYBE I SHOULD DO THAT FIRST
OH I ALSO NEED T—

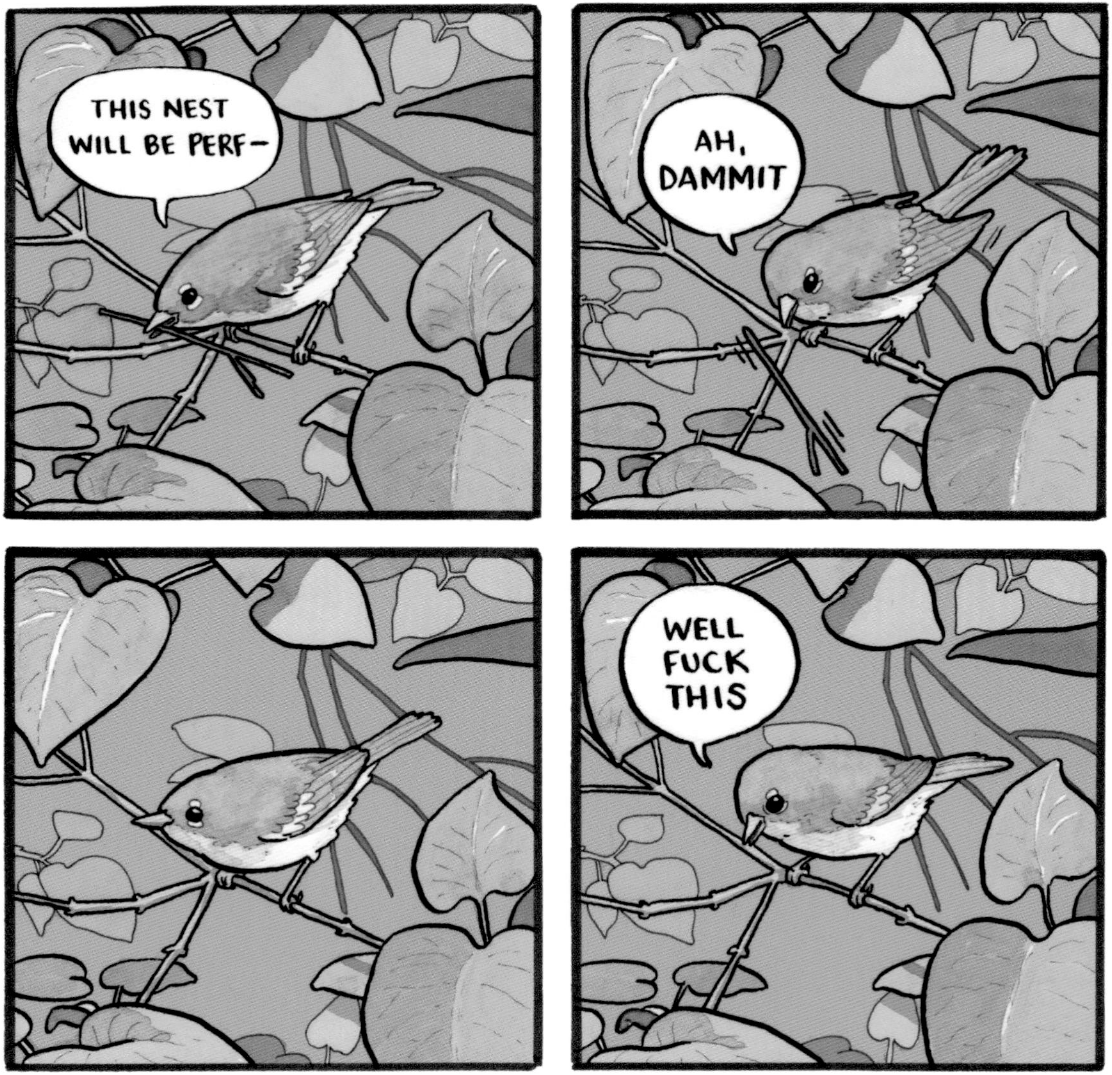
THIS NEST WILL BE PERF—
AH, DAMMIT
WELL FUCK THIS

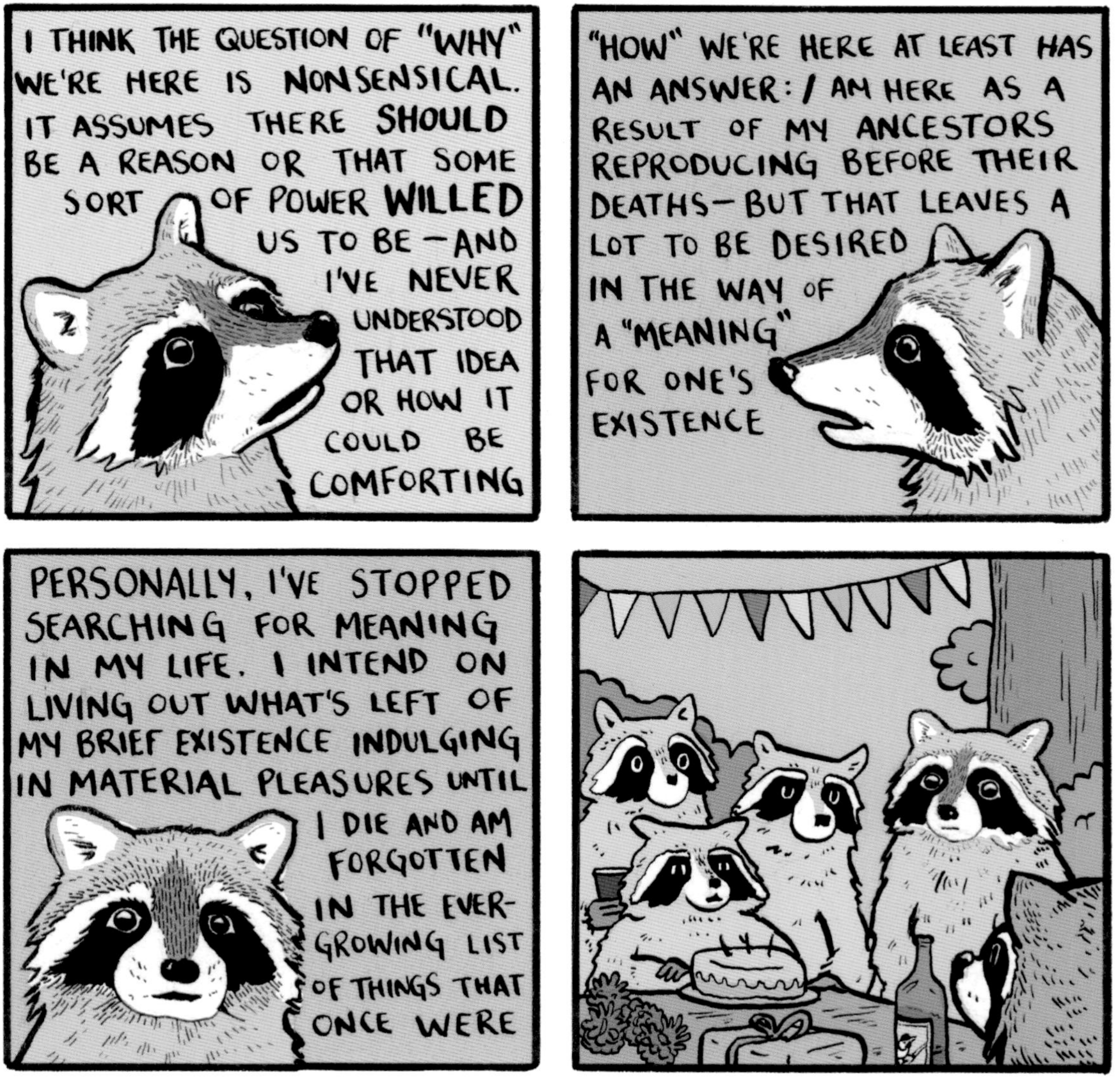
I THINK THE QUESTION OF "WHY" WE'RE HERE IS NONSENSICAL. IT ASSUMES THERE SHOULD BE A REASON OR THAT SOME SORT OF POWER WILLED US TO BE—AND I'VE NEVER UNDERSTOOD THAT IDEA OR HOW IT COULD BE COMFORTING
"HOW" WE'RE HERE AT LEAST HAS AN ANSWER: I AM HERE AS A RESULT OF MY ANCESTORS REPRODUCING BEFORE THEIR DEATHS—BUT THAT LEAVES A LOT TO BE DESIRED IN THE WAY OF A "MEANING" FOR ONE'S EXISTENCE
PERSONALLY, I'VE STOPPED SEARCHING FOR MEANING IN MY LIFE. I INTEND ON LIVING OUT WHAT'S LEFT OF MY BRIEF EXISTENCE INDULGING IN MATERIAL PLEASURES UNTIL I DIE AND AM FORGOTTEN IN THE EVER-GROWING LIST OF THINGS THAT ONCE WERE

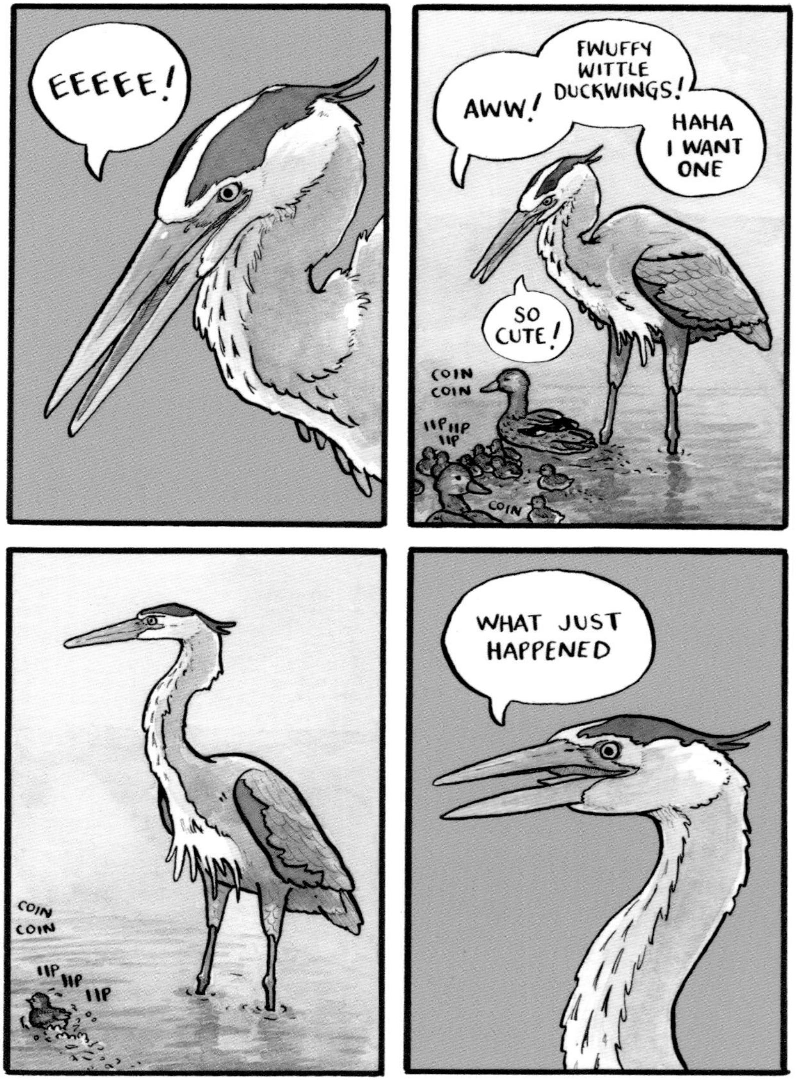
EEEEE!
AWW!
FWUFFY WITTLE DUCKWINGS!
HAHA I WANT ONE
SO CUTE!
COIN COIN
IIP IIP IIP
COIN
COIN COIN
IIP IIP IIP
WHAT JUST HAPPENED

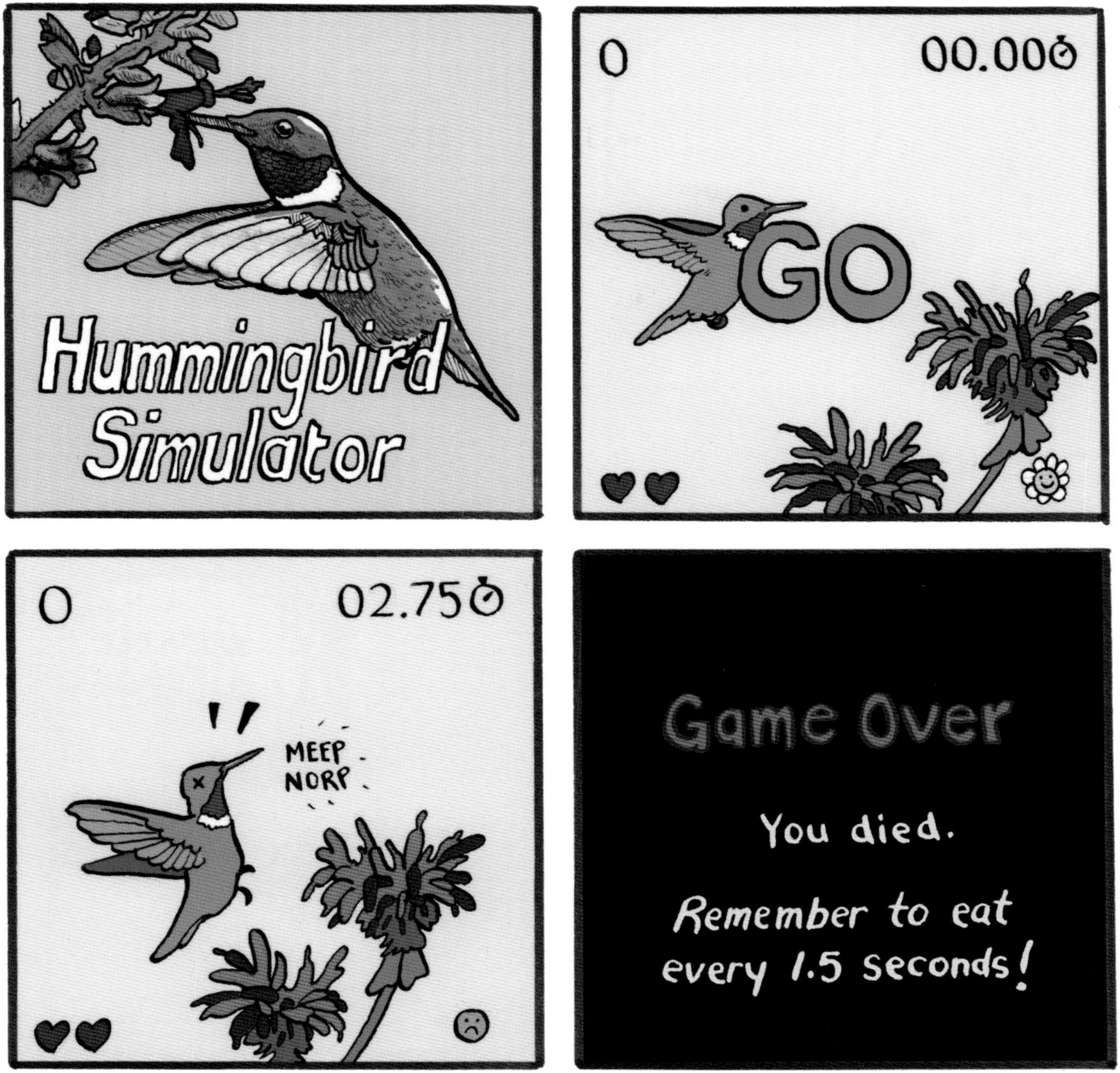
Hummingbird Simulator
0
00.00
GO
0
02.75
MEEP NORP
Game Over
You died.
Remember to eat every 1.5 seconds!

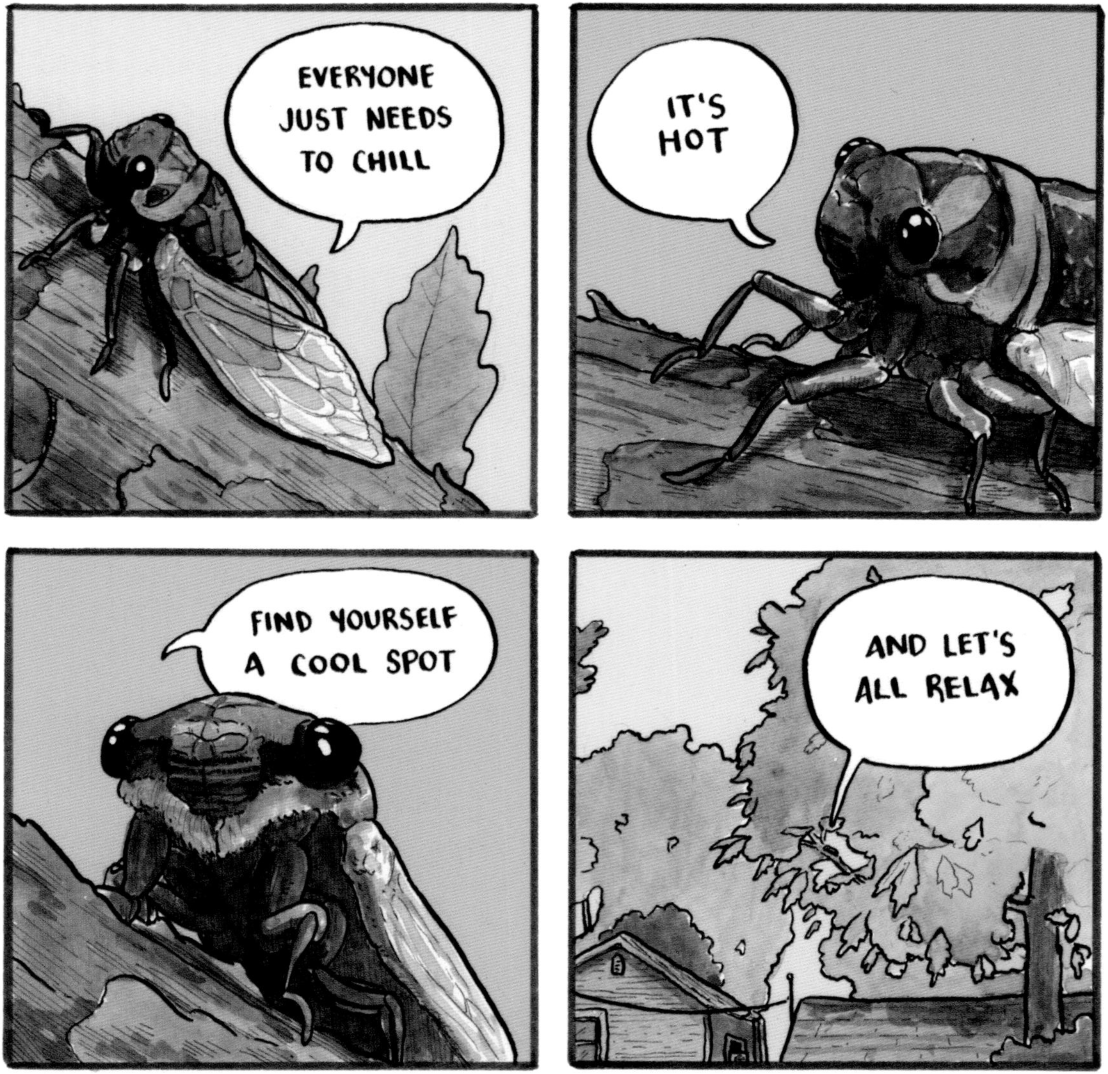
EVERYONE JUST NEEDS TO CHILL
IT'S HOT
FIND YOURSELF A COOL SPOT
AND LET'S ALL RELAX

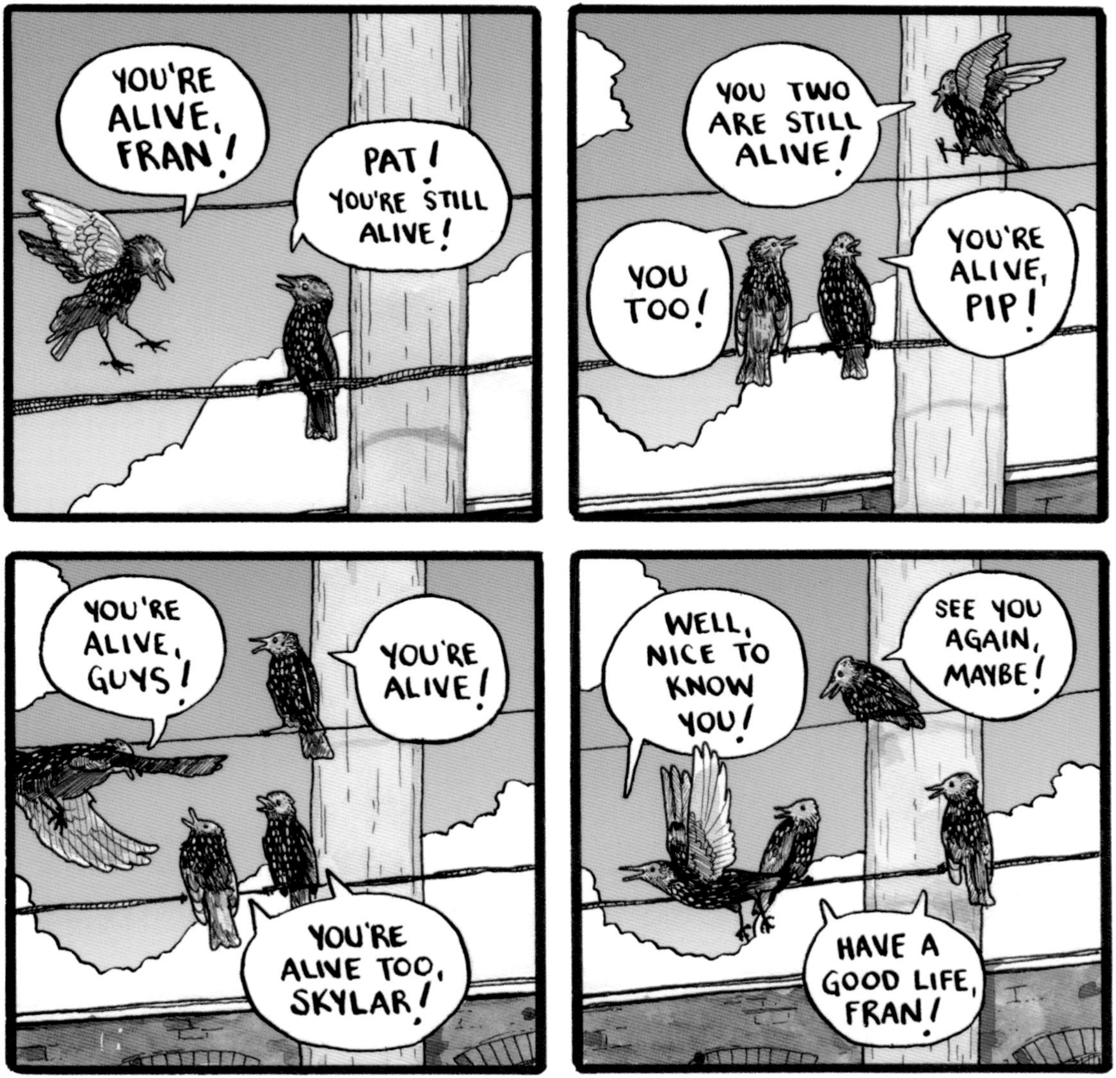
YOU'RE ALIVE, FRAN!
PAT! YOU'RE STILL ALIVE!
YOU TWO ARE STILL ALIVE!
YOU TOO!
YOU'RE ALIVE, PIP!
YOU'RE ALIVE, GUYS!
YOU'RE ALIVE!
YOU'RE ALIVE TOO, SKYLAR!
WELL, NICE TO KNOW YOU!
SEE YOU AGAIN, MAYBE!
HAVE A GOOD LIFE, FRAN!

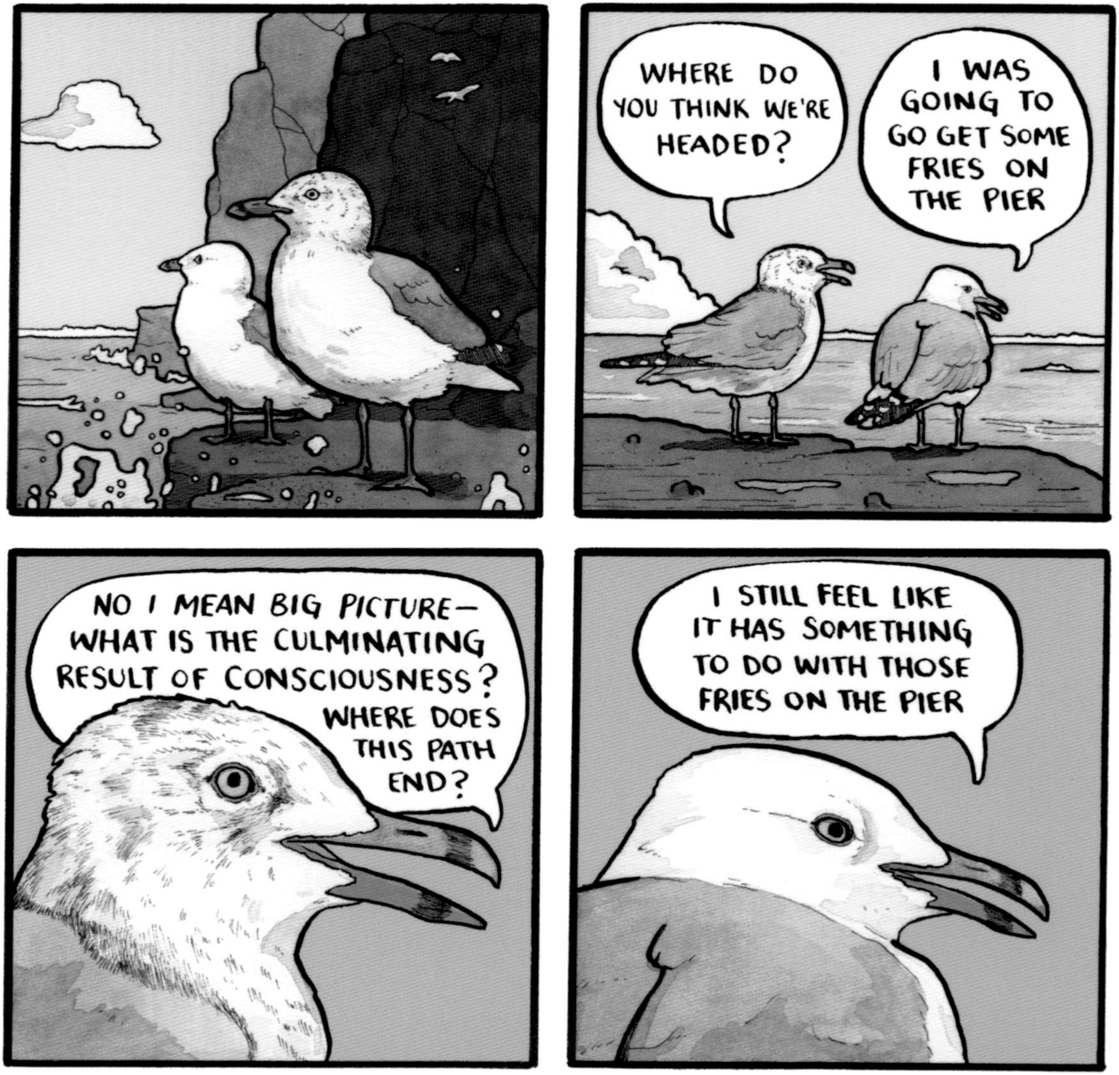
WHERE DO YOU THINK WE'RE HEADED?
I WAS GOING TO GO GET SOME FRIES ON THE PIER
NO I MEAN BIG PICTURE— WHAT IS THE CULMINATING RESULT OF CONSCIOUSNESS? WHERE DOES THIS PATH END?
I STILL FEEL LIKE IT HAS SOMETHING TO DO WITH THOSE FRIES ON THE PIER

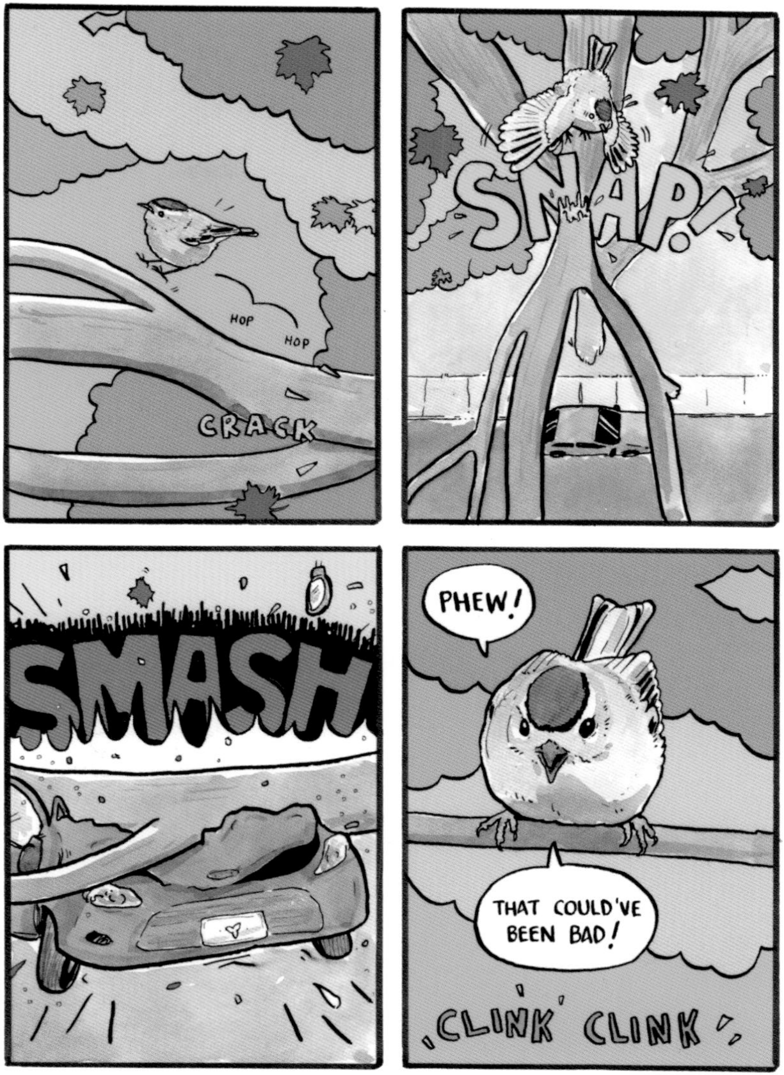
HOP
HOP
CRACK
SNAP!
SMASH
PHEW!
THAT COULD'VE BEEN BAD!
CLINK CLINK

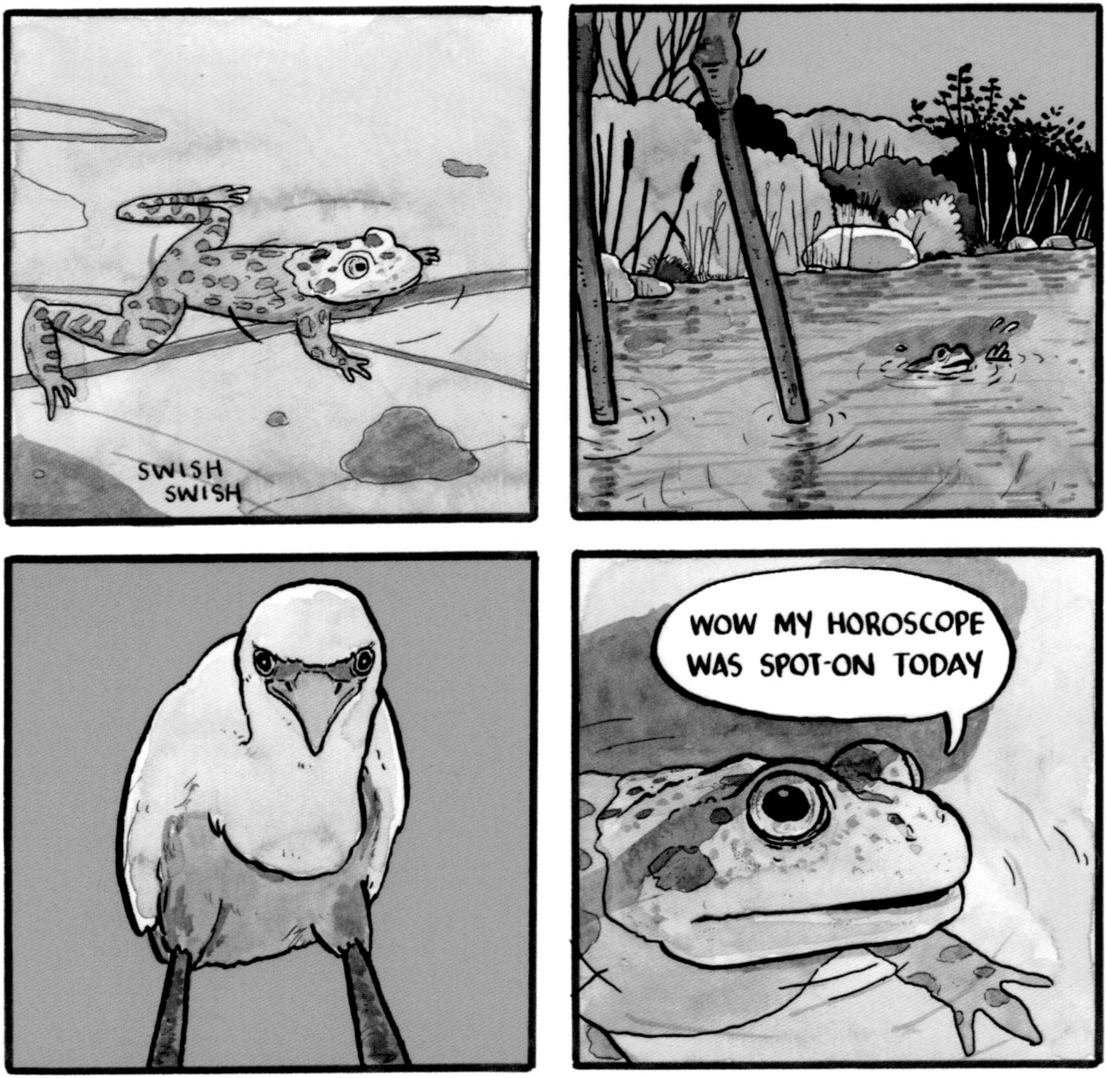
SWISH
SWISH
WOW MY HOROSCOPE WAS SPOT-ON TODAY

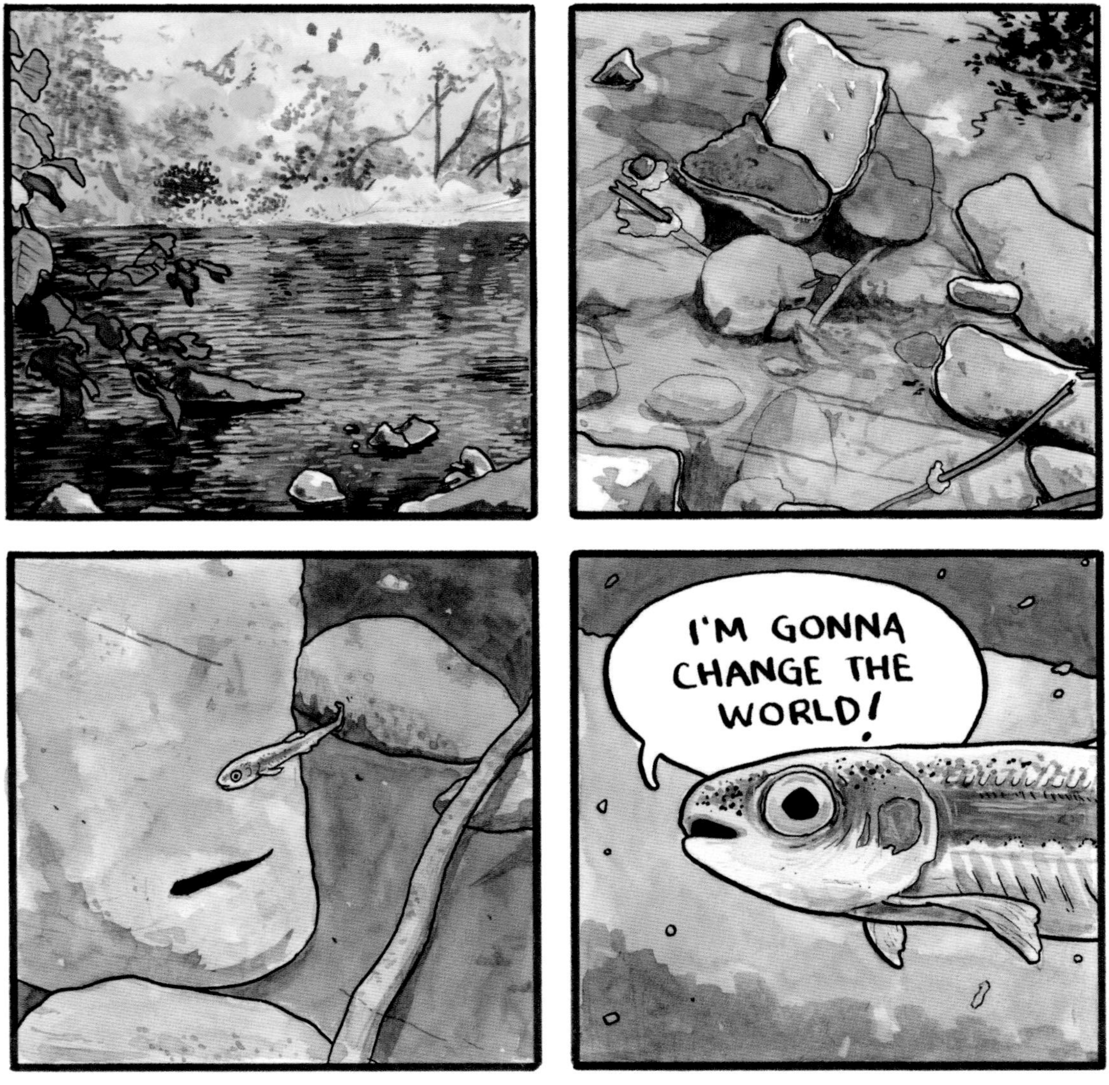
I'M GONNA CHANGE THE WORLD!

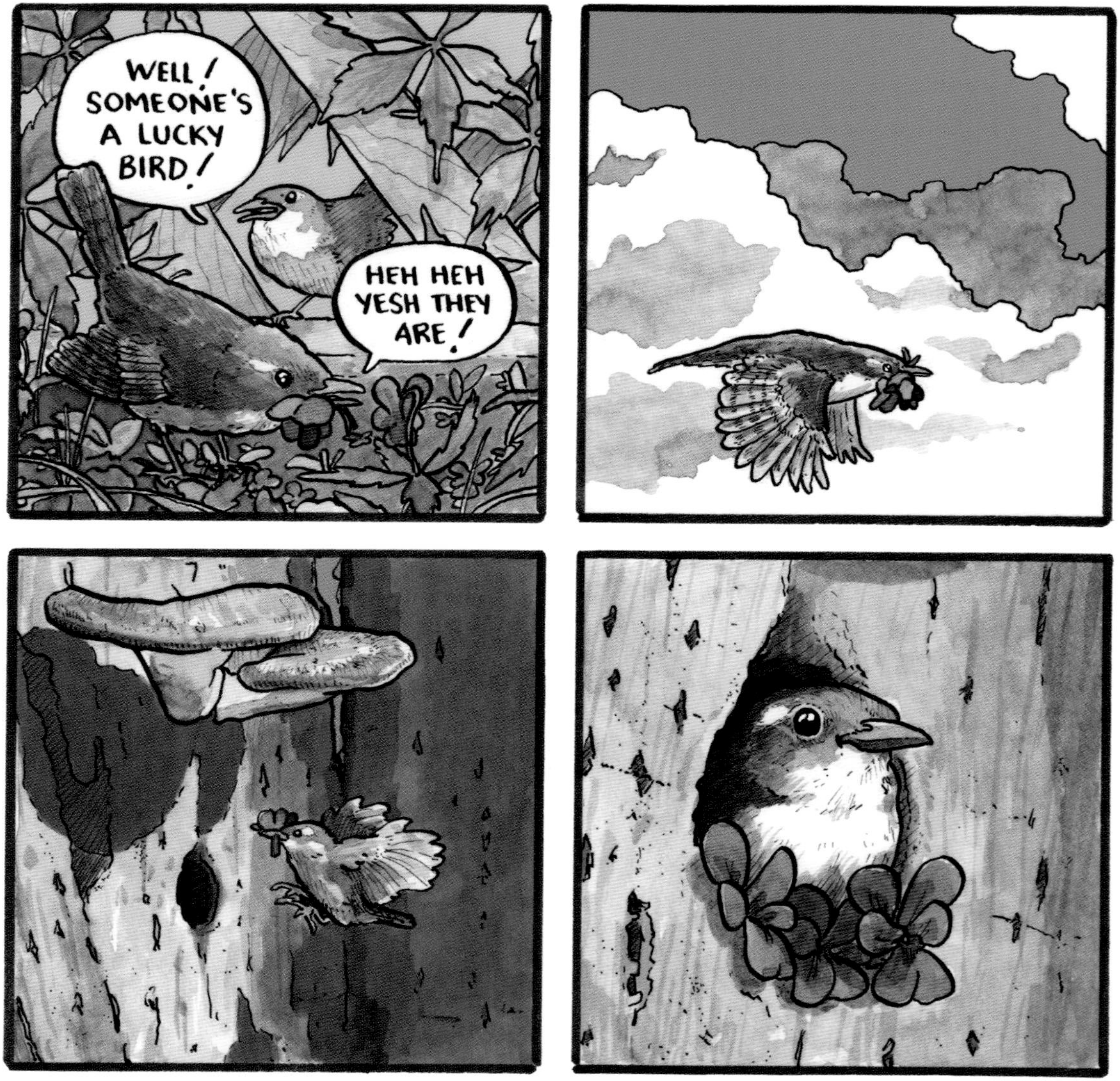
WELL! SOMEONE'S A LUCKY BIRD!
HEH HEH YESH THEY ARE!

FALSE KNEES

Andrews McMeel Publishing
a division of Andrews McMeel Universal
1130 Walnut Street, Kansas City, Missouri 64106

www.andrewsmcmeel.com

22 23 24 25 26 TEN 10 9 8 7 6 5

ISBN: 978-1-4494-9972-3

Library of Congress Control Number: 2019935691

Editor: Melissa R. Zahorsky
Art Director/Designer: Diane Marsh
Production Editor: Elizabeth A. Garcia
Production Manager: Tamara Haus

GOCOMICS.
www.gocomics.com

ATTENTION: SCHOOLS AND BUSINESSES
Andrews McMeel books are available at quantity discounts with bulk purchase for educational, business, or sales promotional use. For information, please e-mail the Andrews McMeel Publishing Special Sales Department: specialsales@amuniversal.com.